Fodor's

U.S. & BRITISH
VIRGIN ISLANDS

T0049120

Welcome to the U.S. & British Virgin Islands

This chain of over 120 islands—some inhabited, most not—share beautiful scenery and beaches, excellent opportunities for water sports, and great places to stay. The biggest resorts are in the U.S. Virgin Islands, but bring your passport and you can also escape to the British Virgin Islands for an even slower pace and more relaxed feel. Whichever one you choose, plan to recline with a Painkiller dark-rum cocktail in hand. As you plan your upcoming travels to the Virgin Islands, please confirm that places are still open and let us know when we need to make updates by writing to us at editors@fodors.com.

TOP REASONS TO GO

★ **Beaches:** Almost every island here has a great beach of white or golden sand.

★ **Sailing:** This archipelago is one of the world's top sailing destinations.

★ **Resorts:** You'll find everything from luxurious beachfront hideaways to simple inns.

★ **Shopping:** Bargains abound, especially in the U.S. Virgin Islands.

★ **Island culture:** Each island has its own traditions and unique identity.

★ **Food:** From local favorites to gourmet dining rooms, you'll eat very well.

Contents

Fodor's Features

MAPS

Chapter 1

EXPERIENCE THE U.S. AND BRITISH VIRGIN ISLANDS

15 ULTIMATE EXPERIENCES

The U.S. and British Virgin Islands offer terrific experiences that should be on every traveler's list. Here are Fodor's top picks for a memorable trip.

1 Sail in the British Virgin Islands

The best way to experience this compact archipelago is by boat. Charter a sail or powerboat in Tortola for a multiday adventure that includes stops at the beach bars of Jost Van Dyke, The Baths in Virgin Gorda, and reef-protected Anegada. *(Ch. 6–8)*

2 Hike Reef Bay Trail

Three-mile Reef Bay Trail is the jewel of St. John's Virgin Islands National Park, weaving through rain forests with ancient petroglyphs carved into stone. *(Ch. 4)*

3 Snorkel at Trunk Bay

Spot vibrant coral reefs and fish along the snorkeling trail of St. John's Trunk Bay, which is fringed by one of the most spectacular beaches in the Caribbean. *(Ch. 4)*

4 Sip a Painkiller

Try the potent mix of rum, pineapple, cream of coconut, and orange juice where it originated, the bar-lined island of Jost Van Dyke in the British Virgin Islands. *(Ch. 8)*

5 Explore The Baths

The Baths of Virgin Gorda is the perfect beach for people who don't like the beach. You can sit on the sand if you'd like, but the real attractions are the caves created by the giant boulders on shore. *(Ch. 7)*

6 Hit the Beach

While there's a beautiful beach on every island, Magens Bay in St. Thomas is one of the best. It's the rare Caribbean beach with an admission fee, but it's well worth it. *(Ch. 3)*

7 Hunt for Treasure

The sea caves of Norman Island are said to be hiding spots for buccaneer booty and even inspired Robert Louis Stevenson's *Treasure Island*. Snorkeling is a top activity. *(Ch. 8)*

8 Ride to Paradise Point

Take a cable car ride from the heart of Charlotte Amalie, St. Thomas, to the heights of Paradise Point for a memorable view of the harbor. Salute the sunset with a Bushwacker, invented here. *(Ch. 3)*

9 Roam the Gardens

Get lost in the greenery of the St. George Village Botanical Garden, St. Croix, where over 1,500 native and exotic species flourish. *(Ch. 5)*

10 Shop in Charlotte Amalie

St. Thomas's capital retains some of its original Danish street layout, creating a souklike warren of streets and alleys full of duty-free shops in the heart of downtown. *(Ch. 3)*

11 Relax at the Resort

Between island-hopping, don't forget to reserve time to lounge by the pool, especially if you're at a luxurious resort like Virgin Gorda's Rosewood Little Dix Bay. *(Ch. 7)*

12 Learn at Annaberg Plantation

Reflect on St. John's history at the 18th-century sugar mill ruins in Virgin Islands National Park. From the striking windmill you'll get spectacular ocean views. *(Ch. 4)*

13 Dive Among Shipwrecks

Anegada's reefs are full of dive sites, including shipwrecks dating back centuries and the awe-inspiring 1,200-foot plunge of the North Drop. *(Ch. 8)*

14 Day-Trip to Buck Island

A quick boat ride from Christiansted harbor in St. Croix, Buck Island is home to a great beach, hiking, and an underwater over-the-reef snorkeling trail. *(Ch. 5)*

15 Step Back in Time

The brilliant yellow walls of St. Croix's Fort Christiansvaern herald the fascinating history of Danish rule over the U.S. Virgin Islands, which lasted from 1733 to 1917. *(Ch. 5)*

WHAT'S WHERE

1 St. Thomas. The familiar and the foreign mingle perfectly here. Resorts run the gamut from plain and simple to luxurious, and the vibe is lively. Go for duty-free shopping, sights, and water sports.

2 St. John. The least developed of the USVI, two-thirds of the island is a U.S. national park. With its excellent snorkeling, good restaurants, and comfortable villas and resorts, many find this the perfect island.

3 St. Croix. The largest of the U.S. Virgin Islands is 40 miles (64 km) south of St. Thomas. Choose St. Croix if you enjoy history, quality restaurants, decent shopping, and nice beaches.

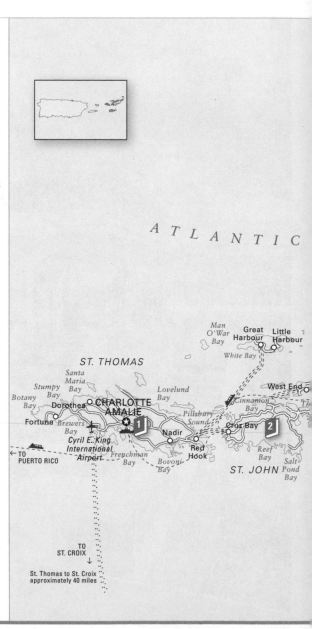

A T L A N T I C

Man O'War Bay
Great Harbour
Little Harbour
White Bay

ST. THOMAS

Santa Maria Bay
Stumpy Bay
Botany Bay
Dorothea
Fortuna
Brewers Bay
Loveland Bay
West End
Cinnamon Bay

CHARLOTTE AMALIE **1**

Pillsbury Sound
Cruz Bay **2**

Nadir
Cyril E. King International Airport
Frenchman Bay
Red Hook
Reef Bay
Salt Pond Bay

← TO PUERTO RICO
Bovoni Bay

ST. JOHN

TO ST. CROIX
↓
St. Thomas to St. Croix approximately 40 miles

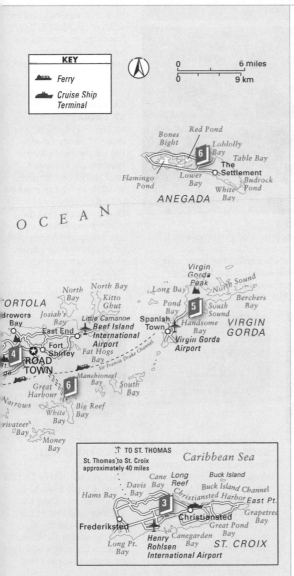

4 Tortola. A day might not be enough to tour this island because you're meant to relax while you're here. Go to Tortola if you want to do some shopping and enjoy a larger choice of restaurants than you can find on the other British Virgins.

5 Virgin Gorda. Progressing from laid-back to more laid-back, mountainous and arid Virgin Gorda offers beautiful beaches but a more relaxed scene, with far fewer restaurants and shopping opportunities than Tortola.

6 Other British Virgin Islands. There are about 50 islands in the British Virgin chain, many of them completely uninhabited, but several have a single hotel or at least a beach that is popular. Set sail to Jost Van Dyke for legendary beach bars or to Anegada to snorkel past stunning reefs.

Best Beaches in the U.S. and British Virgin Islands

THE BATHS, VIRGIN GORDA

Massive granite boulders are piled along the shore and underwater at this unforgettable south shore beach, creating hidden grottoes that are perfect for swimming and snorkeling. The Cathedral Room, a cave formed by intersecting boulders over a shallow pool, is one of the most photographed sights in the BVI. *(Ch. 7)*

MAGENS BAY, ST. THOMAS

Located at the end of a long, rectangular bay, this is one of the most beautiful and popular beaches in the Caribbean. Part of a public park that also includes an arboretum, Magens Bay has calm, shallow waters patrolled by lifeguards, making it especially good for families. *(Ch. 3)*

SANDY POINT, ST. CROIX

At 2 miles (3 km) long, the beach at Sandy Point is the longest in the Virgin Islands and, as part of the Sandy Point National Wildlife Refuge, guaranteed to be a peaceful experience. Note, however, that the wildlife comes first: the beach is closed during peak sea turtle nesting season, usually March through June. *(Ch. 5)*

TRUNK BAY, ST. JOHN

Part of Virgin Islands National Park, Trunk Bay is stunning from above and below. Stop to enjoy the roadside view on the way to the park; then, throw down your towel on a gently arched quarter-mile of beach. An underwater snorkel trail follows a path alongside Trunk Cay, a small offshore island. *(Ch. 4)*

BUCK ISLAND, ST. CROIX

Tour boats operating from the Christiansted dock regularly make the 1½-mile (2½-km) trip out to Buck Island, the centerpiece of Buck Island Reef National Monument. From its wide ribbon of white sand on Turtle Beach, you can snorkel and remain close to the tour boats anchored just offshore. *(Ch. 5)*

LONG BAY BEACH, TORTOLA

The verdant hills of Tortola slope sharply down to a mile of sand at Long Bay. Swimming is best at the west end of the beach, and the surf is just lively enough for boogie boarding or, occasionally, surfing. *(Ch. 6)*

CANE GARDEN BAY, TORTOLA

Stake out a place on the sand and settle in for a day of swimming, snorkeling, and sunning at the shore, interrupted only by walks to nearby restaurants for drinks and snacks. As the sun settles over the horizon you can relocate to a beach bar to listen to live music or venture into town for dinner. (Ch. 6)

HAWKSNEST BEACH, ST. JOHN

If you're looking for a quiet alternative to the better-known Trunk Bay and Cinnamon Bay beaches in Virgin Island National Park, head to Hawksnest Beach on St. John's north shore for swimming and snorkeling in crystal clear waters. (Ch. 4)

WHITE BAY, JOST VAN DYKE

Boaters wading ashore at White Bay Beach to get frozen drinks gave the beach's most famous bar, the Soggy Dollar Bar, its name. But don't let the daily party at White Bay's beach bars overshadow the merits of the beach itself, which has soft white sand and dazzling blue-green waters. (Ch. 8)

Which Island Is Right for You?

ST. JOHN: FOR OUTDOORS ENTHUSIASTS

The Virgin Islands National Park occupies ⅔ of St. John, including most of the island's best beaches, an extensive network of over 20 hiking trails, and fascinating historic sites, including sugar-mill ruins and a trail marked with Taíno petroglyphs. *(Ch. 4)*

ST. CROIX: FOR FOODIES

St. Croix is full of small-town charm: even its two "cities," Christiansted and Frederiksted, are easily walkable. But the island has some big-time culinary talent paired with a well-established farm-to-table ethos, contributing to the best dining scene in the Virgin Islands—U.S. or British. *(Ch. 5)*

TORTOLA: FOR SOCIAL BUTTERFLIES

If you love the combination of surf, sand, beach bars, and nightlife, make Cane Garden Bay on Tortola your destination. Beachfront restaurants serve local seafood, Myett's bar has Bushwhacker cocktails, and there's live music most nights at Quito's. *(Ch. 6)*

VIRGIN GORDA: FOR EXPLORERS

Caving and diving—sometimes both at the same time—are the attractions at The Baths, a beach where giant, volcano-thrown boulders create a labyrinth onshore and an offshore playground for marine life. Navigating the caves on the beach is rewarded with hidden pools and quiet stretches of sand, while divers and snorkelers patrol the waters and venture into sunken caves in search of tropical fish and live corals. At the opposite end of the island is Gorda Peak National Park, where visitors can hike to the highest point on the "Fat Virgin" for views of North Sound and the other British Virgin Islands from the 1,370-foot summit. *(Ch. 7)*

ANEGADA: FOR TRENDSETTERS

A low-lying coral island surrounded by reefs, Anegada is both distant and, for sailors unfamiliar with the local waters, dangerous to reach. But the isolation is a big part of the island's charm. Rent a Mini Moke for the day and set off on the dusty roads of the 14-square-mile island to discover rock iguanas at Bones Bight, cold drinks at Cow Wreck Beach and the Big Bamboo Beach Bar, and high dunes and wild waves at the Anegada Beach Club. Wreck diving is popular on the surrounding reefs, where mounds of pink conch shells make a memorable highlight of a guided snorkeling trip. *(Ch. 8)*

1

Experience the U.S. and British Virgin Islands   WHICH ISLAND IS RIGHT FOR YOU?

ST. THOMAS: FOR SHOPPERS

St. Thomas's capital city, Charlotte Amalie, is one of the best duty-free ports in the Caribbean, with narrow, Danish-era streets and alleys jammed with shops and galleries selling jewelry, liquor, rare coins pulled from shipwrecks, and locally made gifts. *(Ch. 3)*

NORMAN ISLAND: FOR TREASURE SEEKERS

Norman Island has a real-life history as a pirates' hideout—people still search the island's caves for buried treasure. You're more likely to discover shimmering fish than gold, but it's worth lingering to enjoy the nearby Pirate's Bight restaurant and *Willy T* floating bar. *(Ch. 8)*

GUANA ISLAND: FOR NATURE LOVERS

Access to a world-renowned nature sanctuary and conservation program is included in the price of a stay at Guana Island, a luxury all-inclusive resort with private villas scattered across a lush island covered in rainforest. Guests can meet the locals (green iguanas, geckos, flamingos, and red-legged tortoises) while hiking the island's 12 miles of hiking trails or relaxing at one of seven beaches. *(Ch. 8)*

COOPER ISLAND: FOR RUM DRINKERS

One of the best rum bars in the Caribbean resides at Cooper Island's small ecoresort across Sir Francis Drake channel from Tortola. Visitors can sample from a collection of more than 280 rums and chase it with a beer from the on-site Cooper Island Brewing Company. *(Ch. 8)*

JOST VAN DYKE: FOR BAR CRAWLERS

No yacht tour of the BVI would be complete without anchoring at Jost Van Dyke for a pub crawl of the island's beach bars. The Soggy Dollar in White Bay is the famous home of the potent Painkiller rum punch; Foxy's in Great Harbour has great live music. *(Ch. 8)*

Weddings and Honeymoons

There's no question that the Virgin Islands is a bucket-list destination for a honeymoon. Romance is in the air here, and the white, sandy beaches, turquoise water, swaying palm trees, balmy tropical breezes, and perpetual summer sunshine put people in the mood for love. It's easy to understand too why the Virgin Islands are fast becoming a popular wedding destination. They are easy to reach from the United States and offer a soup-to-nuts selection of hotels and resorts. A destination wedding is no longer exclusive to celebrities and the superrich. You can plan a simple ceremony directly on the beach or use your resort's ballroom or gardens. Every large resort has a wedding planner, and there are independent wedding planners as well. Although the procedures in the British Virgin Islands are a little different, planning your wedding is relatively simple regardless of where you are.

GETTING MARRIED IN THE USVI

You must first apply for a marriage license at the Superior Court (in either St. Thomas or St. Croix; St. John has no court office). The fee for the application and license is $200. You have to wait eight days after the clerk receives the application to get married, and licenses must be picked up in person on a weekday, though you can apply by email. To make the process easier, most couples hire a wedding planner. If you plan to get married at a large resort, most have planners on staff to help you with the paperwork and all the details, but if you're staying in a villa, at a small hotel or inn, or are arriving on a cruise ship, you'll have to hire your own.

The wedding planner will help you organize your marriage license application and arrange for a location, flowers, music, refreshments, and whatever else you want to make your day memorable. The wedding planner will also hire a clergyman if you'd like a religious service or a nondenominational officiant if you prefer. Indeed, many wedding planners are licensed by the territory as nondenominational officiants and will preside at your wedding.

GETTING MARRIED IN THE BVI

Getting married in the BVI is a breeze, but you must make advance plans. To make things go more smoothly, hire a wedding planner to guide you through the ins and outs of the BVI system. Many hotels also have wedding planners on staff to help organize your event. Hotels often offer packages that include the ceremony; accommodations for you, your wedding party, and your guests; and extras like massages, sailboat trips, and Champagne dinners.

You must apply in person for your license ($220) on weekdays at the Registrar General's office in Road Town, Tortola, and wait three days to pick it up at the registrar's office there. If you plan to be married in a church, announcements (called *banns* locally) must be published for three consecutive Sundays in the church bulletin. Only the registrar or clergy can perform ceremonies. The registrar charges $120 at the office and $220 at another location. No blood test is required.

HOW TO DRESS

In the Virgin Islands, basically anything goes, from long, formal dresses with trains to white bikinis. Floral sundresses are fine, too. For the men, tuxedos are not the norm; a pair of solid-colored slacks with a nice shirt is. If you're planning a wedding on the beach, barefoot is the way to go.

If you decide to marry in a formal dress and tuxedo, you're better off making your selections at home and hand-carrying them aboard the plane. Yes, it can be a pain, but ask your wedding-gown retailer to provide a special carrying bag. After all, you don't want to chance losing your wedding dress in a wayward piece of luggage. And when it comes to fittings, again, that's something to take care of before you arrive in the Virgin Islands.

YOUR HONEYMOON

Do you want Champagne and strawberries delivered to your room each morning? A breathtaking swimming pool in which to float? A five-star restaurant in which to dine? Then a resort is the way to go. If you're on a tight budget or don't plan to spend much time in your room, there are also plenty of cheaper small inns and hotels throughout the USBVI to choose from. On the other hand, maybe you want your own private home in which to romp naked—or just laze around recovering from the wedding planning. Maybe you want your own kitchen in which to whip up a gourmet meal for your loved one. In that case, a private villa rental is the answer. That's another beautiful thing about the Virgin Islands: the lodging accommodations are almost as plentiful as the beaches, and there's bound to be one to match your tastes and your budget.

POPULAR HONEYMOON RESORTS

If you are looking for some serious time together with few distractions, you can always head to one of the private-island resorts in the BVI. **Guana Island** is luxurious, but **Cooper Island Beach Club** offers both privacy and moderate prices.

Many honeymooners choose the laid-back style of **Estate Lindholm** on St. John or the **Rosewood Little Dix Bay** on Virgin Gorda. Those looking for more creature comforts might consider the **Ritz-Carlton** on St. Thomas or the **Buccaneer Beach & Golf Resort** on St. Croix (which has a good golf course). The **Sugar Mill Hotel** on Tortola is simple and small but still gracious, while the **Scrub Island Resort** on Scrub Island, a 10-minute ferry ride from Tortola's Trellis Bay dock, offers the privacy advantages of a villa with some hotel amenities. St. Thomas's **Bolongo Bay Beach Resort,** though also popular with families, has an on-site wedding coordinator and is the island's only true all-inclusive resort.

Ferry Routes and Travel Times

ATLANTIC OCEAN

Great Harbour

JOST VAN DYKE
Inter Island Boat Service
New Horizon

ST. THOMAS

CHARLOTTE AMALIE–CRUZ BAY
Varlack Ventures

Cyril E. King International Airport

CHARLOTTE AMALIE

45 min.

35 min.

50 min.

ST. JOHN

MARRIOTT
Marriott Frenchman's Cove

Cruz Bay

Crown Bay

10 min.

Phillip's Landing

Marriott
12 min.

Red Hook
15 min.

RED HOOK–CRUZ BAY
PASSENGER ONLY
   Varlack Ventures
CAR BARGE
   Boyson Inc.
   Global Marine
   Love City

WATER ISLAND
Water Island Ferry

45 min.

120 min.

PUERTO RICO
Transportation Services STT
(not scheduled on a regular basis)

ST. THOMAS-ST.CROIX
QEIV Ferry

0   6 miles
0   9 km

*St. Croix Island is made to fit for this diagram. It is not true to scale.

ST. CROIX

Christiansted

ANEGADA
Road Town Fast Ferry

Setting Point

ROAD TOWN
Road Town Fast Ferry
Native Son
Smith's Ferry
Speedy's

*Beef Island
International
Airport*

*Virgin Gorda
Airport*

TORTOLA

East End

BEEF IS.
10 min.

45 min.

Spanish
Town

VIRGIN GORDA
Inter Island Boat Service
Smith's Ferry
Speedy's

ROAD TOWN

Hannah Bay

West End

20 min.

WEST END
Inter Island
Boat Service
Native Son
Smith's Ferry

The Bight

NORMAN ISLAND
Norman Island Ferry

C a r i b b e a n   S e a

Island Finder

	ST. THOMAS	ST. JOHN	ST. CROIX	TORTOLA	VIRGIN GORDA	JOST VAN DYKE	ANEGADA
APPEAL							
Crowds	●	◐	◐	◐	○	◐	○
Urban development	●	◐	●	◐	○	○	○
Family-friendly	●	●	◐	●	◐	○	◐
BEACHES							
Beautiful	◐	●	◐	◐	◐	●	●
Deserted	○	●	◐	◐	●	◐	●
ENTERTAINMENT							
Cultural and historic sights	●	◐	◐	◐	○	○	○
Fine dining	●	◐	◐	◐	◐	○	○
Nightlife	◐	◐	◐	◐	○	●	○
Shopping	●	◐	◐	◐	○	○	○
Casinos	●	◐	○	○	○	◐	○
LODGING							
Luxury resorts	●	◐	◐	◐	●	○	○
Moderately-priced resorts	●	○	●	◐	◐	◐	◐
Small inns	●	◐	●	◐	○	○	◐
NATURE							
Wildlife	◐	●	◐	◐	●	◐	◐
Ecotourism	◐	●	◐	◐	●	○	○
SPORTS							
Golf	●	○	◐	○	○	○	○
Scuba diving	●	◐	●	●	●	◐	●
Snorkeling	●	●	◐	●	●	●	●
Fishing	●	◐	●	◐	●	○	◐

● : noteworthy; ◐ : some; ○ : little or none

Chapter 2

TRAVEL SMART

Updated by
Carol Bareuther

★ **CAPITAL**
USVI: Charlotte Amalie,
St. Thomas
BVI: Road Town, Tortola

👫 **POPULATION**
USVI: 87,000
BVI: 31,000

💬 **LANGUAGE**
English

$ **CURRENCY**
USVI and BVI: U.S. dollar

☎ **AREA CODE**
USVI: 340
BVI: 284

⚠ **EMERGENCIES**
USVI: 911
BVI: 911 or 999

🚗 **DRIVING**
USVI and BVI: On the left

⚡ **ELECTRICITY**
USVI: 120 volts/60 cycles;
plugs are U.S. standard two-
and three-prong

BVI: 110 volts/60 cycles;
plugs are standard two- and
three-prong

🕐 **TIME**
Atlantic Standard Time zone
(one hour later than EST; the
same during daylight savings
time)

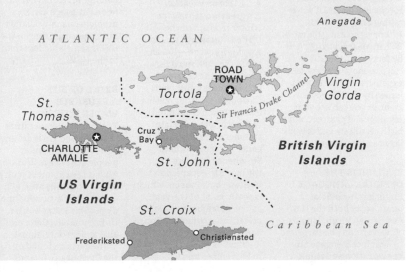

Know Before You Go

The U.S. Virgin Islands—St. Thomas, St. Croix, and St. John—operate under the American flag as a U.S. territory, while the British Virgin Islands—Tortola, Virgin Gorda, Jost Van Dyke, Anegada, and surrounding islands—are part of the British Commonwealth. Yet, the proximity between the two countries (at one point less than a mile, between St. John and Tortola), and centuries of cultural ties mean there are many characteristics all the islands have in common. Here's what you need to know before your trip.

YOU MIGHT NEED A PASSPORT

U.S. citizens don't need a passport to enter the U.S. Virgin Islands, but it's important to carry some type of government-issued photo ID like a driver's license or an original birth certificate (not a photocopy). However, U.S. and U.K. citizens must have a passport to enter the British Virgin Islands. Even if you're planning to stay in the U.S. Virgin Islands, the passport requirement for the BVI applies if you're taking a day sail, fishing trip, or sightseeing tour to a BVI. If you travel to the BVI by ferry from the USVI, you can use one of the new, less expensive Passport Cards issued by the U.S. government, or you can use your regular valid passport. But a birth certificate and driver's license are no longer enough.

ENGLISH IS THE OFFICIAL LANGUAGE

English is the official language of both the U.S. and British Virgin Islands. However, don't be surprised to hear locals engaged in conversation and think they are speaking a foreign language. Virgin Islands Creole is based on the English language, but it's a dialect all its own. You might hear "yuh chek?" (meaning "you know?"), "donkey years" (meaning a very long time ago), or "cheese 'n' bread" (the sound of being surprised or exasperated).

DON'T JUST VACATION IN HIGH SEASON

A Caribbean vacation is a great way to escape winter in much of the United States, but this is also high season—December 15 through April 15, especially the year-end holiday weeks. But wait! Caribbean weather doesn't change much from month to month, although late summer and early fall are generally more humid. So, whenever you're in the mood to escape, don't hesitate. Low season, which is really most of the year, can be quiet, but with lower prices for accommodations and flights. The only caveat: hurricanes are at their peak in September and October.

CORAL REEF–SAFE SUNSCREEN IS A MUST

In fact, it's the law in the Virgin Islands as of 2020. Coral reefs are dying at an alarming rate, and one of the major contributors is sunscreen, more specifically the chemicals oxybenzone and octinoxate. Luckily, numerous companies like Sun Bum, Blue Lizard, and Thinksport offer reef-safe alternatives. If you forget to pack sunscreen, reef-safe products are available at drug, department, and grocery stores. Either way, check those labels before you buy your next bottle.

IS IT SAFE?

Crime certainly happens in the Virgin Islands, and there are sections of Charlotte Amalie, St. Thomas, and Christiansted, St. Croix, that you would not want to walk through even during the day. But, for the most part, crime in the USVI and BVI is much lower than in most large U.S. cities. Petty theft of belongings from your car or on the beach can be a problem on many islands, but in general crime in the BVI is somewhat less than in the USVI.

BRING OR BUY A REUSABLE WATER BOTTLE

The average temperature in the Caribbean is around 80ºF, so it's no wonder people are always drinking (this is the capital of fruity, frozen cocktails after all), and using plastic cups and disposable water bottles. Unfortunately, these are also major contributors to the garbage found on the Caribbean's famous beaches. Plastic straws were banned in the Virgin Islands in 2019, and numerous properties are starting to offer alternatives to plastic water bottles. But why not bring your own bottle or buy one as a souvenir to use on vacation and take home?

BRING U.S. DOLLARS

The U.S. dollar is the official currency of both the U.S. and British Virgin Islands. Many vendors, even in the BVI, won't accept pounds or euros.

RENT A VEHICLE

If you're staying in a remote location, but plan to explore, eat out, or visit distant sights or beaches, consider renting a vehicle—car, jeep, or scooter. Be aware, though, that driving can be a challenge on narrow, winding roads on mountainous islands—especially at night. Taxis and inexpensive public buses (or private vans that operate like buses called "dollar buses") are always an option. These drivers are generally well-informed and will take you where you want to go, when you want to go, for as long as you wish, at an hourly rate. There are no ride-share services like Lyft or Uber in the USBVI.

DRIVE ON THE LEFT

Like currency, it's one size fits all in both the U.S. and British Virgin Islands: drive on the left side of the road. In the USVI, this is a holdover from when the Danes owned the islands. In the BVI, it's the norm from the United Kingdom. However, cars in both territories are typically imported from the United States, meaning although driving is on the left side of the road, the steering wheel is on the left, too.

USE FORMAL GREETINGS

Always start any encounter with a "good morning," "good afternoon," "good day," or "good night" before you ask a question. Virgin Islanders like formality and respect. Most also like to be called by their surname rather than first name. If you do use someone's first name, it's nice to put a Ms., Mrs., or Mr. in front of it. Do this, and you'll experience Virgin Islanders legendary friendliness and hospitality.

YES, YOU SHOULD TIP

Sometimes you'll see a service charge of about 10% on your restaurant bill (especially in the BVI); when this is the case, tip a little extra (about 5%). Otherwise, tip as you would at home, about 15% to 20%. Many hotels and resorts in the Virgin Islands add a hefty service charge of 10% to 15%, but that money doesn't always find its way to the staff. It's not inappropriate to leave $2 or $3 per day for the maid or to give $1 per bag to the bellhop. Tip taxi drivers in the USVI about 15% of the fare.

FOOD IS EXPENSIVE

You should expect to pay at least 30% more for groceries in the Virgin Islands than you would at home, and on some of the smaller islands, you'll pay an even larger premium. But there are good, U.S.–style supermarkets on St. Thomas and St. Croix, and decent markets on St. John and Tortola.

THERE'S JUST ONE ALL-INCLUSIVE RESORT

The Bolongo Bay Beach Resort on St. Thomas is the only true all-inclusive resort in the Virgin Islands. Some of the private-island resorts in the BVI do offer full-meal or all-inclusive plans, but they are as far from the typical all-inclusive resort experience as you could possibly imagine. Few resorts (even those that do offer meal plans) include alcoholic drinks, as you'd find at an all-inclusive resort in the Dominican Republic or Jamaica.

THERE ARE NO NUDE BEACHES

Be sure to pack more than your birthday suit. It's against the law in both the U.S. and British Virgin Islands to go nude in public places like the beaches. The beaches are where many local families, especially those with young children, go to spend the day.

Getting Here and Around

While St. Croix has a four-lane highway and St. Thomas has multiple lanes running along the Charlotte Amalie waterfront, the other islands in the region have only paved two-lane main roads that twist and turn up and down the hillsides. Potholes are common. Once you get into neighborhoods, most roads are paved, but particularly on St. John and in the British Virgin Islands, you may find some that are still dirt or gravel. Planes connect the larger islands but travel to St. John and the smaller BVI is only by ferry. Ferries also connect the larger islands with the smaller ones and with each other.

■TIP➡ **Ask the local tourist board about hotel and local transportation packages that include tickets to special events.**

Air

It's fairly easy to get to St. Thomas from the United States, with many nonstop flights. From New York to St. Thomas or San Juan, Puerto Rico, it takes about four hours; from Miami to St. Thomas or San Juan it's about three hours. There's no air service to St. John. For St. Croix, you usually connect in either Miami, San Juan, or St. Thomas. Air service to the British Virgin Islands is to Tortola either direct from Miami or via a connecting flight on a smaller plane from St. Thomas or San Juan. Flights between St. Thomas and Tortola take 15 minutes.

Reconfirming your flights on interisland carriers is a good idea, particularly when you're traveling to the smallest islands. You may be subjected to a carrier's whims: if no other passengers are booked on your flight, you may be asked

to take another flight later in the day, or your plane may make unscheduled stops to pick up more passengers or cargo. It's all part of the excitement—and unpredictability—of travel in the Caribbean. In addition, regional carriers use small aircraft with limited baggage space, and they often impose weight restrictions; travel light, or you could be subject to outrageous surcharges or delays on very large or heavy luggage, which may have to follow on another flight.

AIRPORTS
The major USVI airports are the Cyril E. King Airport on St. Thomas and Henry Rohlsen Airport on St. Croix, which is on the southwestern side of the island, near Frederiksted. St. John does not have an airport. In the BVI, the Terrance B. Lettsome International Airport is on Beef Island, Tortola. There are very small airports on Virgin Gorda and Anegada only for interisland flights.

➪ *Ground transportation options are covered in the Essentials sections in individual island chapters.*

FLIGHTS

There are nonstop and connecting flights, usually through San Juan, Puerto Rico, from the U.S. mainland to St. Thomas and St. Croix, with connecting ferry service from St. Thomas to St. John. There is one nonstop flight to the BVI from Miami. Or, you can connect in San Juan or St. Thomas for the short hop over to Tortola, Virgin Gorda, or Anegada.

American Airlines is the biggest air carrier to the Virgin Islands, with several nonstop flights a day from Boston, New York, and Miami to St. Thomas and several connecting flights through San Juan. American also offers nonstop service to St. Croix from Miami. The frequency of flights is seasonal.

Delta Air Lines flies direct to St. Thomas from Atlanta and New York, and to St. Croix from Atlanta. JetBlue has air service between Boston and St. Thomas and via San Juan to many points on the mainland, while Spirit Airlines flies nonstop every day from Fort Lauderdale. United Airlines offers direct flights from Chicago, Dulles, and Newark.

Although American offers a daily nonstop flight from Miami to Tortola, you can also fly from St. Thomas and St. Croix to Tortola and Virgin Gorda on Air Sunshine and Cape Air. Seaborne flies direct from San Juan to St. Thomas, St. Croix, and Tortola, and between St. Thomas and St. Croix.

Some islands in the British Virgin Islands are accessible only by small planes operated by local or regional carriers. International carriers will sometimes book those flights for you as part of your overall travel arrangements, or you can book directly with the local carrier.

Boat and Ferry

Ferries travel between St. Thomas and St. John as well as between St. Thomas and St. Croix. You can also travel by ferry from both St. Thomas and St. John to the British Virgin Islands, and between the British Virgin Islands themselves. The companies run regularly scheduled trips, departing from Charlotte Amalie or Red Hook on St. Thomas; Cruz Bay on St. John; West End, Road Town, or Beef Island on Tortola; Spanish Town or North Sound on Virgin Gorda; and Jost Van Dyke. There's also regularly scheduled service between Tortola, Virgin Gorda, and Anegada a few times a week. Schedules change, so check with the ferry companies directly, or your hotel or villa manager to find out the latest. The ferry companies are all regulated by the U.S. Coast Guard, and prices are about the same, so there's no point in trying to organize your schedule to take one company's ferries rather than another's. Just show up at the dock to buy your ticket on the next ferry departing for your destination. If it all seems confusing—and it can be very confusing for travel to or around the BVI—just ask a local who's also buying a ticket. They know the ropes.

Although you might save a few dollars flying into St. Thomas if you're headed to the BVI, it's much easier to connect through San Juan for a flight to Tortola or Virgin Gorda. If you're headed to St. John or to points like North Sound, Anegada, or Jost Van Dyke, you'll have to hop on a ferry regardless. If you're splitting your vacation between the U.S. and British Virgin Islands, ferries are the perfect way to get from one to another. You'll also get a bonus: views of the many small islands that dot the ferry route.

Getting Here and Around

Dolphin Water Taxi runs from St. Thomas to St. John and many points in the BVI. You'll avoid the often crowded ferries, the crew will handle your luggage and navigate customs in the BVI, and you'll arrive at your destination feeling relaxed; however, you'll pay significantly more for the convenience.

There's frequent daily service from both Red Hook (15 to 20 minutes, $8.15 each way plus $4 for each piece of luggage) and Charlotte Amalie (45 minutes, $13 each way plus $4 for each piece of luggage) to Cruz Bay. The more frequent ferry from Red Hook to St. John leaves at 6:30 am and hourly starting at 8 am, the last at midnight; from St. John back to Red Hook, the first ferry leaves at 6 am, the last at 11 pm. About every hour there's a car ferry, which costs $50 (plus $3 port charges) round-trip; you should arrive at least 25 minutes before departure. From Charlotte Amalie the first ferry to St. John leaves at 10 am, the last at 5:30 pm; from St. John to Charlotte Amalie, the first ferry leaves at 8:45 am, the last at 3:45 pm. The ferry between Charlotte Amalie and St. John is prone to cancellations, particularly in the slower fall months.

The Water Island ferry departs from the Crown Bay Marina on St. Thomas starting at 8:15 am on the hour until 6:15 pm on Mondays through Saturdays, and operates hourly from 9 am to 6 pm on Sunday and holidays. The 10-minute ride is $15 round-trip for adults, and $2 for each piece of luggage.

There's daily service between Charlotte Amalie or Red Hook, on St. Thomas, and West End or Road Town, Tortola, BVI, by either Smith's Ferry, Road Town Fast Ferry, or Native Son, and to Virgin Gorda, BVI, by Smith's Ferry. The round-trip fare is $55–$65 and the trip from Charlotte Amalie takes 45 minutes to an hour to West End and up to 90 minutes to Road Town; from Red Hook the trip is only a half hour. These prices do not include the $10 per person Customs & Immigration fees to enter the USVI by sea and the $20 per person departure tax to return to the USVI.

There's also frequent service from Cruz Bay to Tortola aboard an Inter-Island Boat Service ferry. The half-hour trip costs $55 round-trip; bring your passport if you plan to go to BVI (it's now required for all travel there).

The 1½-hour trip from Charlotte Amalie to Virgin Gorda costs $90 one way and $150 round-trip. From Red Hook and Cruz Bay, Inter-Island offers service on Thursday; Speedy's offers service on Saturday.

On Sundays, Tuesdays, and Fridays a ferry operates between Red Hook, Cruz Bay, and Jost Van Dyke; the trip takes 45 minutes and costs $120 per person round-trip.

Car

RENTAL CARS

Unless you plan to spend all your days at a resort or plan to take taxis everywhere, you'll need a rental car at least for a few days. While driving is on the left, you'll drive an American-style car with the steering wheel on the left. Traffic doesn't move all that fast in most USBVI locations, so driving on the left is not that difficult to master.

If you're staying on St. Thomas or St. Croix and don't plan to venture far off the main roads, you won't need a four-wheel-drive vehicle. On St. John and in the BVI, a four-wheel-drive vehicle is useful to get up steep roads when it rains. Many rental homes in St. John and the BVI are on unpaved roads, so a four-wheel-drive vehicle with high clearance may be a necessity if you rent a villa. While rental agencies don't usually prohibit access to certain roads, use common sense; if the road looks too bad, turn around.

Most car-rental agencies won't rent to anyone under age 25 or over age 75.

Some car-rental agencies offer infant car seats for about $5 a day, but check and check again right before you leave for your trip to make sure one will be available. If you don't use one, you may get a ticket since the law requires their use. You might consider bringing your own car seat from home.

Book your rental car well in advance during the winter season. Vehicles are particularly scarce around the busy Christmas to New Year's and Presidents' Day holidays. If you don't reserve, you might find yourself without wheels. Prices will be higher during the winter season.

Rates range from $90 a day ($630 a week) for an economy car with air-conditioning, automatic transmission, and unlimited mileage to as much as $150 a day ($1,050 a week) for a four-wheel-drive vehicle. Both the USVI and the BVI have major companies (with airport locations) as well as numerous local companies (near the airports, in hotels, and in the main towns), which are sometimes cheaper. Most provide pick-up service; some ask that you take a taxi to their headquarters.

A driver's license from the United States is fine in the USVI. A temporary driver's license is needed in the BVI and costs $10 per person, per day.

RENTAL CAR INSURANCE

Everyone who rents a car wonders whether the insurance that the rental companies offer is worth the expense. No one—including us—has a simple answer. If you own a car, your personal auto insurance may cover a rental to some degree, though not all policies protect you abroad; always read your policy's fine print. If you don't have auto insurance, then seriously consider buying the collision- or loss-damage waiver (CDW or LDW) from the car-rental company, which eliminates your liability for damage to the car. Some credit cards offer CDW coverage, but it's usually supplemental to your own insurance and rarely covers SUVs, minivans, luxury models, and the like. If your coverage is secondary, you may still be liable for loss-of-use costs from the car-rental company. But no credit-card insurance is valid unless you use that card for *all* transactions, from reserving to paying the final bill. All companies exclude car rental in some countries, so be sure to find out about the destination to which you are traveling. It's sometimes cheaper to buy insurance as part of your general travel insurance policy.

A car gives you mobility. You'll be able to spend an hour browsing at that cozy out-of-the-way shop instead of the 10 minutes allotted by your tour guide. You can beach-hop without searching for a ride, and you can sample that restaurant you've heard so much about that's half an hour (and an expensive taxi ride) away. On parts of some of the islands, you may need to rent a four-wheel-drive vehicle to really get out and about. Paved roads are generally good, but you may encounter a pothole or two (or three). Except for one divided highway on St. Croix, roads are narrow, and in hilly locations twist and

Getting Here and Around

turn with the hill's contours. The roads on the north side of Tortola are particularly serpentine, with scary drop-offs that will send you plummeting down the hillside if you miss the turn. Drive slowly. Many villas in St. John and the BVI are on unpaved roads. A four-wheel drive could be a necessity if it rains. A higher-clearance vehicle will help you get safely over the rocks that may litter the road.

GASOLINE

Gas is up to $1 to $2 more per gallon than in the United States. USVI stations sell gas by the gallon; BVI stations sell it by the liter or the gallon, depending on the station. Most stations accept major credit cards, but don't count on that. Some stations have a pump-it-yourself policy, but it's still easy to find one with attendants, except on St. John. There's no need to tip unless they change a tire or do some other quick mechanical chore. You'll have to ask for a handwritten receipt if you're not paying by credit card. On smaller islands, stations may be closed on Sunday.

PARKING

Parking can be tight in towns across the USBVI. Workers grab up the street parking, sometimes arriving several hours early to get prime spaces. It's particularly difficult to find parking in Cruz Bay, St. John. There are free public lots scattered around town, but they're usually filled by folks taking the ferry to St. Thomas. You can often find a spot in the public lot across from the tennis courts, but it's a 10-minute walk to the heart of Cruz Bay. Your rental-car company will probably allow you to park in its lot. Charlotte Amalie, St. Thomas, has a paid parking lot next to Fort Christian. An attendant takes your money—$2 for the first hour

and $5 for all day. This lot is closed for a month—from early April to early May—when the lot turns into the Carnival Village with rides, a stage, and food booths. In Christiansted, St. Croix, you'll find a public parking lot on Strand Street. Since the booth isn't staffed, there's no charge. There's also a public lot near Fort Christiansvaern, but that lot is locked at 4:30 pm. It costs $2 for the first hour and $5 for all day. Tortola has several free parking lots near the waterfront, but daytime parking is a nightmare unless you get there early. On Virgin Gorda, there's a free lot at Virgin Gorda Yacht Harbor. There are no parking meters anywhere in the USBVI. Even if you're desperate for a parking space in the USVI, don't park in a handicapped space without a sticker—unless you want to pay a $1,000 fine.

ROADSIDE EMERGENCIES

To reach police, fire, or ambulance, dial ☎ 911 in the USVI and ☎ 911 or 999 in the BVI. There are no emergency-service companies such as AAA in the USBVI. Before driving off into the countryside, check your rental car for tire-changing equipment, including a spare tire in good condition.

ROAD CONDITIONS

Island roads are often narrow, winding, and hilly. Those in mountainous regions that experience heavy tropical rains are also potholed and poorly maintained. Streets in towns are narrow, a legacy of the days when islanders used horse-drawn carts. Drive with extreme caution, especially if you venture out at night. You won't see guardrails on every curve, although the drops can be frighteningly steep. And pedestrians and livestock often share the roadway with vehicles.

You'll face rush-hour traffic on St. Thomas (especially in Charlotte Amalie); on St. Croix (especially in Christiansted and on Centerline Road); and on Tortola (especially around Road Town). All the larger towns have one-way streets. Although they're marked, the signs may be obscured by overhanging branches and other obstacles.

RULES OF THE ROAD
Driving in the Virgin Islands can be tricky. Traffic moves on the left in *both* the USVI and BVI. Almost all cars are American, which means the driver sits on the side of the car next to the road's edge, a position that makes some people nervous.

Buckle up before you turn the key. Police in the USVI are notorious for giving $75 tickets to unbelted drivers and front-seat passengers. The police are a bit lax about driving under the influence, but why risk it? Take a taxi or appoint a designated driver when you're out on the town.

Traffic moves at about 10 mph in town; on major highways you can fly along at 50 mph. On other roads, the speed limit may be less. Main roads in the USVI carry route numbers, but they're not always marked, and locals may not know them. (Be prepared for such directions as, "Turn left at the big tree.") Few USVI secondary roads have signs; BVI roads aren't very well marked either.

 Ride-Sharing

There are no formal ride-share companies operating in the Virgin Islands at this time.

 Scooter

Scooters can be a fun way to get around these islands, and many places offer day rates. Just remember to pay attention to road rules: on both island groups you drive on the left—and wear sunblock and a helmet. A valid driver's license and cash deposit or credit card may be required.

 Taxi

Taxi rates are set by the government, and you'll pay extra for your bags. Fares vary by destination and the number of people in the taxi, but count on paying $9 per person from Cyril E. King Airport on St. Thomas to Charlotte Amalie; $24 per person from Henry Rohlsen Airport on St. Croix to Christiansted; and $27 per person from Terrance E. Lettsome Airport on Beef Island, Tortola, to Road Town. Tip taxi drivers 15%.

Essentials

Dining

Everything from fast food to fine cuisine in elegant settings is available in the USBVI, and prices run about the same as what you'd pay in New York or any other major city. You'll find global chains such as McDonald's, Pizza Hut, KFC, and more on St. Thomas and St. Croix alongside authentic nonchain restaurants with kid-friendly menus. Resorts that cater to families always have a casual restaurant, but there are delis and other restaurants across the USBVI that offer something for everyone on their menus. Most chefs at top-of-the-line restaurants and even some small spots went to a major culinary school, which means innovative and interesting cuisine. Don't be afraid to sample local dishes at roadside restaurants and food trucks on all the islands. More and more restaurants have vegetarian offerings on their menus, though true vegetarian restaurants are hard to find. The restaurants we list are the cream of the crop in each price category.

Unless otherwise noted, the restaurants listed are open daily for lunch and dinner.

RESERVATIONS AND DRESS
In many places in the Caribbean reservations are expected, particularly at nicer restaurants. We mention reservations only when they are essential (there's no other way you'll ever get a table) or when they're not accepted. For popular restaurants, book as far ahead as you can (often a month or more), and reconfirm as soon as you arrive. Large parties (8 or more) should always call ahead to check the reservations policy. We mention dress only when men are required to wear a jacket or a jacket and tie. Beach attire is universally frowned upon in restaurants throughout the Caribbean.

WINES, BEER, AND SPIRITS
Top-notch restaurants offer good selections of fine wines. Beer and spirits are available on all islands at all kinds of restaurants and roadside stands, but you may not find the brand you prefer. Cruzan Rum, manufactured in St. Croix, is available across the USBVI, and there are local craft breweries throughout the islands. Alcoholic beverages are available from the smallest corner rum shop to the fanciest resort at all hours of the day and night. The only prohibition comes during the day on Good Friday, when no one can sell drinks until after 4 pm in the USVI and after 6 pm in the BVI.

➕ Health

Water in the USBVI is generally safe to drink. Mosquitoes can be a problem here, particularly after a spate of rain showers. Insect repellent is readily available, but you may want to bring something from home, because it's more expensive in the Virgin Islands. Dengue fever and the Chikungunya virus are a particular concern.

Less dangerous, but certainly a nuisance, are the little pests from the sand-flea family known as no-see-ums. You don't realize you're being had for dinner until it's too late, and these bites itch, and itch, and itch. No-see-ums start getting hungry around 3 pm and are out in force by sunset. They're always more numerous in shady and wooded areas. Take a towel along for sitting on the beach, and keep reapplying insect repellent.

Beware of the manchineel tree, which grows near the beach and has green apple-like fruit that is poisonous and bark and leaves that burn the skin.

Even if you've never been sunburned in your life, believe the warnings and use sunscreen in the USBVI. Start with at least an SPF of 15 and keep it on. Rays are most intense between 11 am and 2 pm, so move under a seagrape tree (although you can still burn here) or, better yet, take a shady lunch break. You can also burn in this part of the world when it's cloudy, so putting sunscreen on every day no matter what the weather is the best strategy. When packing sunscreen, be sure it's reef safe or a product without any of the three O's: oxybenzone, octinoxate, and octocrylene, as the USVI banned use of these products.

COVID-19

A novel coronavirus brought all travel to a virtual standstill in the first half of 2020. Like many places in the world, COVID-19 cases are now minimal in the USBVI with a majority of the residents vaccinated.

Given how abruptly travel was curtailed in March 2020, it is wise to consider protecting yourself by purchasing a travel insurance policy that will reimburse you for any costs due to COVID-19–related cancellations.

OVER-THE-COUNTER REMEDIES

Over-the-counter medications like aspirin, Tylenol, and Mylanta are readily available in the USBVI. You can find a big selection of these products at grocery and drug stores across the USBVI. You can find a smaller selection (and considerably higher prices) on the smaller islands.

IMMUNIZATIONS

No vaccinations are required to visit the USBVI. The most serious tropical disease prevalent here is dengue fever, which has no vaccine.

Lodging

Decide whether you want to pay the extra price for a room overlooking the ocean or the pool. At less expensive properties location may mean a difference in price of only $10 to $20 per night; at luxury resorts, however, it could amount to as much as $100 or more per night. Also find out how close the property is to a beach. At some hotels you can walk barefoot from your room onto the sand; others are across a road or a 10-minute drive away.

Nighttime entertainment is often alfresco in the USBVI, so if you go to bed early or are a light sleeper, ask for a room away from the dance floor. Air-conditioning isn't a necessity on all islands, many of which are cooled by trade winds, but it can be a plus if you enjoy an afternoon snooze, are bothered by humidity, or visit during the summer months. Breezes are best on upper floors, particularly corner rooms. If you like to sleep without air-conditioning, make sure that windows can be opened and have screens; also make sure there are no security issues with leaving your windows open. If you're staying away from the water, make sure the room has a ceiling fan and that it works. Even in the most luxurious resorts, there are times when things simply *don't* work; it's a fact of Caribbean life. No matter how diligent the upkeep, humidity and salt air quickly take their toll, and cracked tiles, rusty screens, and chipped paint are common everywhere.

The lodgings we list are the cream of the crop in each price category. When pricing accommodations, always ask what's included and what costs extra.

Essentials

APARTMENT AND VILLA RENTALS

Villas—whether luxurious or modest—are popular lodging options on all the Virgin Islands.

Renting a villa lets you settle in. You can have room to spread out, you can cook any or all of your meals, and you can have all the privacy you desire. Since most villas are in residential neighborhoods, your neighbors probably won't appreciate late-night parties or your children playing too loudly in the swimming pool. And you may be disturbed by your neighbor's weekend yard maintenance. That said, there's no better way to experience life in the USBVI.

Many villas are set up specifically for the rental market with bedrooms at opposite ends of the house. This makes them perfect for two couples who want to share an accommodation but still prefer some privacy. Others with more bedrooms are sized right for families. Ask about the villa layout to make sure young children won't have to sleep too far away from their parents. Villas with separate bedroom buildings are probably not a good idea unless your children are in their teens.

Most villas are owned by people who live somewhere else but hire a local management company to attend to the details. Depending on the island and the rental, the manager will either meet you at the ferry or airport or will give you directions to your villa. Most companies offer the same services with similar degrees of efficiency.

You can book your villa through the numerous agencies that show up on the Internet, but they're usually not based on the island you want to visit. Booking through an island-based manager means that you can talk to a person who knows the villa and can let you know whether it meets your specifications. Your villa manager can also arrange for a maid, a chef, and other staffers to take care of myriad other details to help make your vacation go smoothly. They're only a phone call away when something goes wrong or you have a question.

Catered To Vacation Homes focuses on St. John. Vacation St. Croix is based on St. Croix. McLaughlin-Anderson has rentals across the USBVI.

HOTELS

Hotels range from luxury beachfront resorts, where the staff caters to your every whim and where you'll find plenty of activities to keep you busy, to small, locally owned hillside hotels with great views that cater to more independent-minded visitors. They're priced accordingly. At the smaller inland properties you'll probably want to rent a car to get out to the island's best beaches and interesting restaurants.

The USBVI are quite Americanized thanks to television and the influx of U.S. visitors, but some traditional Caribbean customs still apply. Common courtesy is particularly important in the islands, so always say hello when you enter a store and make some small talk before getting down to business. Also, watch out for cars that stop suddenly in the middle of the road for chats with passersby and be aware that nothing, and we mean nothing, ever starts on time.

$ Money

Prices quoted are in U.S. dollars, which is the official currency on all the islands. Major credit cards are accepted at many establishments.

⇨ *Prices in this guide are given for adults. Reduced fees are almost always available for children.*

ATMS AND BANKS

You can find ATMs at most banks in the USBVI. The ATM at FirstBank, the only one on St. John, sometimes runs out of cash on long holiday weekends.

CREDIT CARDS

It's a good idea to inform your credit-card company before you travel, even if you're going to the USBVI. Otherwise, the company might put a hold on your card owing to unusual activity —not a good thing halfway through your trip. Record all your credit-card numbers—as well as the phone numbers to call if your cards are lost or stolen—in a safe place, so you're prepared should something go wrong. Both MasterCard and Visa have general numbers you can call (collect if you're abroad) if your card is lost, but you're better off calling the number of your issuing bank, since MasterCard and Visa usually just transfer you to your bank; your bank's number is usually printed on your card.

If you plan to use your credit card for cash advances, you'll need to apply for a PIN at least two weeks before your trip. It's usually cheaper (and safer) to use a credit card in the USBVI for major purchases (so you can cancel payments or dispute the charge if there's a problem).

▭ Packing

A pocket LED flashlight to deal with the occasional power outage, bug repellent for mosquitoes, sunglasses, a hat, and sunscreen are essentials for any USBVI vacation. If you forget something, those items are available at stores across the USBVI, but are usually more expensive than what you would pay at home. Pharmacies can fill prescriptions with a call to your home drug store, but this may be the week the drug shipment didn't arrive. It's always safer to bring everything you need. Dress is casual even at the most expensive resorts, but men are usually required to wear a collared shirt in dining rooms. For dinner out women typically wear what the locals call "island fancy" (a flowy skirt and nice top will do). Bring your bathing suit, a cover-up, sandals, sturdy walking shoes if you're a hiker, beach shoes if you plan on strolling those luscious strands of sand, and a sweater or fleece if you're visiting in the winter when the nights are cool. In these days of packing light, rent snorkel gear on the island rather than bringing it unless you have a prescription mask. Shorts and T-shirts will do everywhere during the day. Don't forget a good book for whiling away those afternoons in the beach chair and your camera for bringing home those USBVI memories.

Essentials

● Passports and Visas

For U.S. citizens, a passport is *not* required to visit the U.S. Virgin Islands, though you must still provide proof of citizenship by showing an original birth certificate with a raised seal as well as a government-issued photo ID. There are no immigration procedures upon arriving in St. Thomas or St. Croix for anyone arriving on planes from the U.S. mainland or Puerto Rico, but on your return you will clear immigration and customs before boarding your flight.

If you visit the BVI by ferry from the USVI, you must go through customs and immigration procedures and prove your citizenship. U.S. citizens must have a passport to enter the BVI by ferry.

If you fly into the BVI, you must go through customs and immigration upon arrival and have a valid passport. Aside from paying the departure tax, there are no special departure procedures.

● Safety

In the USBVI ask hotel staff members about the wisdom of venturing off the beaten path. Although it may seem like a nice night for a stroll back to your hotel from that downtown restaurant, it's better to take a taxi than face an incident.

Follow the same precautions that you would anywhere. Look around before using the ATM. Keep tabs on your wallet or bag; put it on your lap—not the back of your chair—in restaurants. Stow valuable jewelry or other items in the hotel safe when you leave your room; hotel and villa burglaries do occur infrequently. Deserted beaches on St. John and the BVI are usually safe, but think twice about stopping at that strand of lonely sand on St. Croix and St. Thomas. Hotel or public beaches are your best bets. Never leave your belongings unattended at the beach or on the seats of your rental car. Be sure to lock the doors on your rental villa or hotel room.

● Taxes

There's no sales tax in the USVI, but there's a 12.5% hotel-room tax; most hotels also add a 10% service charge to the bill. The St. John Accommodations Council members ask that hotel and villa guests voluntarily pay a $1 per day surcharge to help fund school and community projects and other good works. Many hotels add additional energy surcharges and the like, so ask about any additional charges, but these are not government-imposed taxes.

In the BVI the departure tax is $20 per person by boat and $20 per person by plane. There is also a $15 departure tax from the USVI when traveling to the BVI. There are separate booths at the airport and at ferry terminals to collect this tax, which must be paid in cash in U.S. currency. Most hotels in the BVI add a service charge ranging from 10% to 18% to the bill. A few restaurants and some shops tack on an additional 10% charge if you use a credit card. There's no sales tax in the BVI. However, there's a 10% government tax on hotel rooms.

💲 Tipping

Many hotels in the USVI add a 10% to 15% service charge to cover the services of your housekeeping and other staff. However, some hotels use part of that money to fund their operations, passing only a portion of it on to the staff. Check to determine the hotel's policy. If you discover you need to tip, give bellhops and porters $1 to $2 per bag and housekeepers $3 or $5 per day. Special errands or requests of hotel staff always require an additional tip. At restaurants bartenders and waiters expect a 15% to 20% tip, but always check your tab to see whether service is included. Taxi drivers in the USVI should get a 15% tip.

In the BVI tip porters and bellhops $1 per bag. Sometimes a service charge of 15% is included on restaurant bills; it's customary to leave another 5% if you liked the service. If no charge is added, 15% is the norm. Cabbies normally aren't tipped because most own their cabs; add 10% to 15% if their service is great.

📍 Visitor Information

Stop by the tourism department's local offices for brochures on things to do and places to see. The offices are open only weekdays from 8 to 5, so if you need information on the weekend or on one of the territory's many holidays, you're out of luck.

⇨ *For locations, see Visitor Information in the Essentials section of each chapter.*

When to Go

The Caribbean high season is traditionally winter—from December 15 to April 15—when you're guaranteed the most entertainment at resorts and the most people with whom to enjoy it. It's also the most fashionable, the most expensive, and the most popular time to visit—and most hotels are heavily booked. You must make reservations at least two or three months in advance for the very best places (sometimes a year in advance for the most exclusive spots). Hotel prices can drop 20% to 50% after April 15; airfares and cruise prices also fall. Saving money isn't the only reason to visit the Caribbean during the off-season. Many islands now schedule their carnivals, music festivals, and other events during the off-season. Late August, September, October, and early November are the least crowded—but the weather then is the most unpredictable. Some resorts and restaurants actually close during September and October.

CLIMATE

The Caribbean climate is fairly constant. The average year-round temperatures for the region are 78°F to 88°F. The temperature extremes are 65°F low, 95°F high; but, as everyone knows, it's the humidity, not the heat, that makes you suffer—especially when the two go hand in hand. The high-season months of December through April generally provide warm, sunny days with little humidity. The off-season months, particularly August through November, are the most humid. As part of the late-fall rainy season, hurricanes occasionally sweep through

Essentials

the Caribbean. Check the news daily and keep abreast of brewing tropical storms. The rainy season consists mostly of brief showers interspersed with sunshine. You can watch the clouds thicken, feel the rain, then have brilliant sunshine dry you off, all while remaining on your lounge chair. A spell of overcast days or heavy rainfall is unusual.

HURRICANE SEASON

The Atlantic hurricane season lasts from June 1 through November 30, but it's fairly rare to see a large storm in either June or November. Most major hurricanes occur between August and October, with the peak season in September.

Avoiding storms. Keep in mind that hurricanes are more common the farther north in the Caribbean you go. The U.S. and British Virgin Islands experienced first-ever back-to-back Category 5 hurricanes in 2017. Tourism departments in both jurisdictions are good about keeping tabs on visitors' safety and security and organizing evacuations both prior to and after major storms.

Airlines. Airports are usually closed during hurricanes and flights are canceled, which results in a disruption of the steady flow of tourists in and out of affected islands. If you are scheduled to fly into an area where a hurricane is expected, check with your airline regularly and often. If flights are disrupted, airlines will usually allow you to rebook for a later date. You will not get a refund if you have booked a nonrefundable ticket nor, in most cases, will you be allowed to change your ticket to a different destination; rather, you will be expected to reschedule your trip for a later date.

Hotels and resorts. If a hurricane warning is issued and flights to your destination are disrupted, virtually every USBVI resort will waive cancellation and change penalties and allow you to rebook your trip for a later date. Some will allow you to cancel if a hurricane threatens to strike, even if flights aren't canceled. Some will give you a refund if you have prepaid for your stay, while others will expect you to rebook your trip for a later date.

Travel insurance. If you plan to travel to the USBVI during the hurricane season, it is wise to buy travel insurance that allows you to cancel for any reason. This kind of coverage can be expensive (up to 10% of the value of the trip); but if you have to prepay far in advance for an expensive vacation package, the peace of mind may be worth it. Just be sure to read the fine print; some policies don't kick in unless flights are canceled and the hurricane strikes, something you may not be assured of until the day you plan to travel. To get a complete cancellation policy, you must usually buy your insurance within a week of booking your trip. If you wait to purchase insurance until after the hurricane warning is issued, it will be too late.

Hurricane tracking. To keep a close eye on the Caribbean during hurricane season, several websites track hurricanes as they progress: ⊕ *www.nhc.noa.gov/cyclones, www.weather.com/storms/hurricanes, stormcarib.com.*

On the Calendar

The USBVI's top seasonal events are listed here, and any one of them could provide the stuff of lasting memories. Contact local tourism authorities for exact dates and for more information.

January

Bordeaux Farmers Rastafari Agricultural & Cultural Vegan Food Fair. On St. Thomas, this annual three-day event over the Martin Luther King Jr. holiday weekend features locally grown produce, vegan foods, handicrafts, live music, and much more.

February

Celebration of Love. On Valentine's Day, St. John always hosts a free vow-renewal ceremony right on the beach at Trunk Bay.

St. Croix Agriculture and Food Fair. Every February, St. Croix celebrates its natural bounty with this food fair, also called "AgriFest." ⊕ www.viagrifest.org.

Sweetheart of the Caribbean and Classic Yacht Regatta. The BVI's West End Yacht Club hosts this regatta over Valentine's Day weekend. ⊕ www.westendyacht-clubbvi.com.

March

BVI Spring Regatta and Sailing Festival. More than 60 boats from the Caribbean, the United States, and Europe participate in three days of racing, with parties and sailing competitions on Tortola and Virgin Gorda. ⊕ www.bvispringregatta.org.

St. Patrick's Day Parade. Locals and visitors alike gather in downtown Christiansted on St. Croix for the annual parade, complete with floats, bands, and green-costumed, stilt-walking Mocko Jumbies.

St. Thomas International Regatta. During late March, the St. Thomas Yacht Club hosts this regatta, which pulls in yachties from all over. ⊕ stthomasinternationalregatta.com.

VI Jam Fest. Musicians from all over play for three days in venues across the U.S. Virgin Island of St. John. ⊕ www.vijamfest.com.

April

Carnival, St. Thomas. Expect to see plenty of Mocko Jumbies, St. Thomas's otherworldly stilt walkers, during Carnival, which takes place right after Easter. ⊕ www.vicarnivalschedule.com/stthomas.

St. Croix Food and Wine Experience. Foodies will prosper when local restaurateurs get together for this four-day celebration of all things food related. One of the highlights is "A Taste of St. Croix," a special one-night event when the top restaurants on the island serve up their top dishes; the event often sells out the same day the highly coveted tickets become available. ⊕ stxfoodandwine.com.

May

Leverick Bay Poker Run. North Sound, Virgin Gorda, is the start and finish of the run, where over 200 powerboats participate, culminating with a big beach party and live music at the finish.

On the Calendar

June

International Optimist Regatta. The regatta happens on St. Thomas, with over 100 8- to 15-year-old junior sailors from around the world racing their 8-foot single-sail dinghies. ⊕ *stthomasyachtclub.org.*

July

Carnival, St. John. The island celebrates with plenty of street celebrations and a huge parade on the 4th of July. ⊕ *www.vicarnivalschedule.com/stjohn.*

Bastille Day Kingfish Tournament. The Northside Sport Fishing Club hosts this event on the Sunday closest to Bastille Day, July 14. Lines are in the water at 5:30 am with weigh-in at Noon at Hull Bay; there is a party with live bands afterward. There are prizes for the largest kingfish and other species, for men, women, and junior anglers. ⊕ *www.vigfc.com.*

August

Emancipation Festival, BVI. Also known as August Festival, the event celebrates the abolition of slavery in the Danish West Indies in 1848.

Texas Society of the Virgin Islands Chili Cookoff. St. Thomas's Brewers Bay Beach fills with themed booths on the third Sunday of the month for this annual cookoff.

October

The Moorings Interline Regatta, BVI. Kick off the boat-racing season with this annual regatta in the Caribbean's sailing capital. ⊕ *www.moorings.com/regattas-and-events/interline-regatta.*

November

Annual Coral Bay Thanksgiving Regatta. On Thanksgiving weekend, the regatta brings together boat owners for a two-day race event sponsored by the Coral Bay Yacht Club.

Beauty & The Beast Triathlon. The St. Croix event attracts international-class athletes as well as amateurs for a 1.24-mile (2-km) swim, a 13.1-mile (21-km) run, and a 56-mile (90-km) bike ride; it includes a climb up the Beast on Route 69. ⊕ *www.stxtriathlon.com.*

BVI Food Fete. From rum fests to seafood soirees and tastes of all the islands, the monthlong party is paradise for food lovers. ⊕ *bvifoodfete.com.*

December

Crucian Christmas Festival, St. Croix. A nearly monthlong celebration coincides with the island's Christmas Carnival, ending January 6 with a huge parade. ⊕ *www.vicarnivalschedule.com.*

Foxy's Old Year's Night Celebration. Ring in the New Year at Foxy's on Jost Van Dyke, where the annual party has been consistently ranked as one of the top 10 New Year's Eve parties in the world.

Contacts

Air

AIRPORT INFORMATION
Cyril E. King Airport. (*STT*).
✉ *Rte. 30, Lindbergh Bay*
☏ *340/774–5100* ⊕ *www.
vlport.com/cekastt.* **Henry
Rohlsen Airport.** (*STX*).
✉ *Airport Rd., off Rte. 66,
Christiansted* ☏ *340/778–
1012* ⊕ *www.viport.com.*

INTERISLAND CARRIERS
Air Sunshine. ☏ *800/327–
8900, 954/434–8900,
954/434–8900 in
Tortola, 954/434–8900
in BVI, 954/434–8900
in Virgin Gorda* ⊕ *www.
airsunshine.com.* **Cape
Air.** ☏ *800/227–3247,
508/771–6944 outside the
U.S./USVI* ⊕ *www.capeair.
com.* **Fly BVI.** ☏ *284/340–
1747 in BVI* ⊕ *flybvi.com.*
LIAT. ☏ *888/844–5428,
268/480–5601/2* ⊕ *www.
liat.com.* **Seaborne Airlines.**
☏ *801/401–9100* ⊕ *www.
seaborneairlines.com.*

🚗 Car

Cool Breeze Car Rental.
✉ *Cruz Bay* ☏ *340/776–
6588, 340/693–3232*
⊕ *www.coolbreeze
carrental.com.* **iTGO
Car Rental.** ✉ *Mill Mall,
Wickham's Cay I, Road
Town* ☏ *284/494–5150,
284/494–2639* ⊕ *www.
itgobvi.com.* **L&S Jeep
Rental.** ☏ *284/495–5297*
⊕ *landsjeeprentalstax-
iandtours.com.* **Judi of
Croix.** ☏ *340/773–2123,
877/903–2123* ⊕ *www.
judiofcroix.com.* **St. John
Car Rental.** ✉ *Bay St., near
Whartside Village, Cruz
Bay* ☏ *340/776–6103*
⊕ *www.stjohncarrental.
com.*

Ferry

Dolphin Water Taxi. ✉ *American Yacht Harbor, Red
Hook, Hwy. 32, Rod Hook*
☏ *340/774–2628* ⊕ *www.
dolphinshuttle.com.*
Inter Island Boat Services.
☏ *340/776–6597* ⊕ *www.
interislandboatservices.
com.*

🛏 Lodging

**VILLA MANAGEMENT
COMPANIES Catered to
Vacation Homes.** ✉ *Cruz
Day* ☏ *340/776–6641,
800/424–6641* ⊕ *www.
cateredto.com.* **Vacation
St. Croix.** ✉ *400 La Grande
Princess, Christiansted*
☏ *340/718–0361* ⊕ *www.
vacationstcroix.com.*
**McLaughlin-Anderson
Luxury Caribbean Vil-
las.** ☏ *340/776–0635,
800/537–6246* ⊕ *www.
mclaughlinanderson.com.*

📍 Visitor
Information

USVI Tourist Board.
☏ *800/372–8784* ⊕ *www.
visitusvi.com.* **BVI Tourist
Board.** ☏ *800/835–8530 in
the U.S., 284/852–6020
Tortola, 284/495–5181
Virgin Gorda* ⊕ *www.
bvitourism.com.*

Chapter 3

ST. THOMAS

3

Updated by
Carol Bareuther

👁 Sights	🍴 Restaurants	🛏 Hotels	🛍 Shopping	🍸 Nightlife
★★★☆☆	★★★★☆	★★★★☆	★★★★★	★★☆☆☆

WELCOME TO ST. THOMAS

TOP REASONS TO GO

★ **Shop 'til you drop:** Find great deals on duty-free jewelry, timepieces, and electronics along Charlotte Amalie's Main Street—but don't forget to pick up some locally made crafts as well.

★ **Tell fish stories:** Go in search of magnificent blue marlin and other trophy-worthy fish in the waters around St. Thomas from June through October.

★ **Get your sea legs:** Charter a yacht (or just take a regularly scheduled day sail) to cruise between the islands any time of year. It's a short hop to the British Virgin Islands from St. Thomas.

★ **Step back in time:** Take a self-guided walking tour of the historic sights in Charlotte Amalie, including Fort Christian, Government House, and the Synagogue, to imagine life when Denmark ruled the islands.

★ **Take a dip:** Swim at Magens Bay, considered by many to be one of the most beautiful beaches in the world.

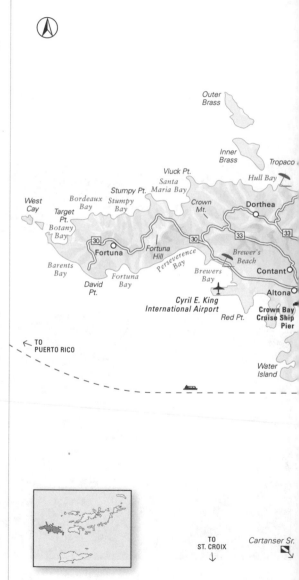

ATLANTIC OCEAN

Hans Lollick

Picara Pt.

Magens Bay

Lovelund Bay

Mahogany Run Golf Course

The General Rogers

Thatch Cay

Grass Cay and Congo Cay

Mandal Pt.

Signal Hill

Magens Bay

Tutu Bay

Mandal

Coki Beach

Mafolie

42

French-town

Charlotte Amalie

40

Frydendal

Lindquist Beach

Cabes Pt.

38

St. Thomas Harbor

Paradise Pt.

38

Tutu

Sapphire Beach

Redhook Bay

Hassel Island

32

Vessup Beach

TO ST. JOHN

Morning Star Beach

Nadir

30

Red Hook

Cow and Calf Rocks

Limestone Bay

Coculus Pt.

Jersey Bay

Secret Harbour

Great Bay

Great St. James Island

St. James Bay

Long Pt.

Little St. James Island

TO ST. JOHN

Frenchcap

Caribbean Sea

0   2 miles

0   3 km

EATING AND DRINKING WELL IN THE VIRGIN ISLANDS

Take a mix of local and imported ingredients—everything from papaya to salt cod. Blend this with the cooking styles of the indigenous Ciboney, Carib, and Arawak peoples, plus those who immigrated from Africa, Europe, Asia, and beyond, and you have the rich melting pot that is traditional Virgin Islands cuisine.

Despite its American-flag status and the abundant fast-food and Continental-style restaurants that dominate the islands, the traditional cuisine of the Virgin Islands still maintains a foothold here. The best places to sample the authentic flavors of the islands are local restaurants, bakeries, and mobile food vans, as well as the many food fairs and fish fries that take place throughout the year. When you order an entrée—a "plate of food" as a meal is called—it will often be accompanied by a green salad and a choice of three filling, starchy side dishes, all packed with fresh ingredients and bold flavors.

SNACKS

Be sure to try the popular **Caribbean pate** *(pah-teh)*, a triangular fried pastry stuffed with spicy ground beef, conch, or salted fish. And nothing beats **mangoade, passion fruit punch,** or **soursop juice** to tame the heat (pates often boast a touch of fiery Scotch bonnet peppers among their ingredients). For a tamer snack, look for **Johnny Cakes** (fried cornmeal cakes) or hushpuppy-like **conch fritters.** Another refresher is **coconut water,** the nectar of cracked coconuts.

FRUIT

Tropical fruits are abundant throughout the islands. Make sure to sample juicy, sweet mangoes, floral-scented papaya (great with a squeeze of lime), tart star fruit (bite into it or slice it up), and finger-long fig bananas, which are sweeter than stateside-purchased varieties. Other favorites include soursop, passion fruit, coconuts (both young and mature), guava, and pineapple.

VEGETABLES

Common vegetables include okra, spinach and other greens, sweet potatoes, eggplants, green plantains, and gnarly root vegetables like tannia, cassava, and boniato. *Kallaloo* is a popular soupy vegetable stew made with spinach and okra, seasoned with fresh herbs, and further flavored with crab, fish, or ham.

SEAFOOD

Popular fish varieties include snapper, grouper, yellowtail, mahi mahi, and wahoo, which are often fried or grilled and served whole. Lobster and conch also are prevalent, the latter appearing in everything from ceviche salads to soups. The unofficial national dish for the Virgin Islands is "fish and fungi," simmered fish with a side of okra-studded cornmeal-like polenta.

3

St. Thomas EATING AND DRINKING WELL IN THE VIRGIN ISLANDS

MEAT

Meat plays a prominent role in soups on the islands. Goat water (mutton stew) and souse (pig-foot stew) make hearty meals, and are typically served with dumplings or bread. Curried goat is a classic dish worth a taste. For something less spicy, try simply prepared chicken and rice.

STARCHES

Don't be thrown off by unexpected naming conventions. For example, "peas and rice" may be made with red beans, kidney beans, or black beans (no peas). Potato stuffing, a mix of mashed white potatoes, tomato sauce, and seasonings, isn't used to stuff anything. And "fungi" (fun-gee) is not mushrooms, but a polenta-like dish of African origin made from cornmeal flecked with chopped okra.

DRINKS

Rum, made from sugarcane, has a significant history in the Virgin Islands, dating back to the rise of sugarcane plantations in the mid-1700s. Rum is still produced here, and it's available in numerous styles (and flavors). Try a local brew at one of the microbreweries in Frenchtown and Havensight. For a lower-proof sipper, try *mauby,* a bitter root beer-like drink made from the bark of the mauby tree.

As the transportation hub of the Virgin Islands, St. Thomas serves as the landing spot for most visitors even if they don't linger. Visitors who stay longer may be drawn by the legendary shopping and the wide variety of water sports, activities, beaches, and accommodations. The bustling port of Charlotte Amalie is the main town, while Red Hook sits on the eastern tip. The west end of the island is relatively wild, and hotels and resorts rim the southern and eastern shores.

If you fly to the 32-square-mile (83-square-km) island of St. Thomas, you land at its western end; if you arrive by cruise ship, you come into one of the world's most beautiful harbors. Either way, one of your first sights is the town of Charlotte Amalie. From the harbor you see an idyllic-looking village that spreads into the lower hills. If you were expecting a quiet hamlet with its inhabitants hanging out under palm trees, you've missed that era by about 300 years. Although other islands in the USVI developed plantation economies, St. Thomas cultivated its harbor, and it became a thriving seaport soon after it was settled by the Danish in the 1600s.

The success of the naturally perfect harbor was enhanced by the fact that the Danes—who ruled St. Thomas with only a couple of short interruptions from 1666 to 1917—avoided involvement in some 100 years' worth of European wars. Denmark was the only European country with colonies in the Caribbean to stay neutral during the War of the Spanish Succession in the early 1700s. Accordingly, products of the Dutch, English, and French islands—sugar, cotton, and indigo—were traded through Charlotte Amalie, along with regular shipments of enslaved peoples (emancipation came in 1848). When the Spanish wars ended, trade fell off, but by the end of the 1700s Europe was at war again; Denmark again remained neutral and St. Thomas continued to prosper. Even into the 1800s, while the economies of St. Croix and St. John foundered with the market for sugarcane, St. Thomas's economy remained vigorous. This prosperity led to the development of shipyards, a well-organized banking system, and a large merchant class. In 1845, Charlotte

Amalie had 101 large importing houses owned by the English, French, Germans, Haitians, Spaniards, Americans, Sephardim, and Danes.

Charlotte Amalie is still one of the world's most active cruise-ship ports. On almost any day at least one and sometimes as many as eight cruise ships are tied to the docks or anchored outside the harbor. Gently rocking in the shadows of these giant floating hotels are just about every other kind of vessel imaginable: sleek sailing yachts that will take you on a sunset cruise complete with rum punch and a Jimmy Buffett soundtrack, private megayachts that spirit busy executives away, and barnacle-bottom sloops—with laundry draped over the lifelines—that are home to world-cruising ramblers. Huge container ships pull up in Subbase, west of the harbor, bringing in everything from breakfast cereals to tires. Anchored right along the waterfront are down-island barges that ply the waters between the Greater Antilles and the Leeward Islands, transporting goods like refrigerators and disposable diapers.

The waterfront road through Charlotte Amalie was once part of the harbor. Before it was filled in to build the highway, the beach came right up to the back door of the warehouses that now line the thoroughfare. Two hundred years ago those warehouses were filled with indigo, tobacco, and cotton. Today the stone buildings house silk, crystal, linens, and leather. Fragrances are still traded, but by island beauty queens in air-conditioned perfume palaces instead of through open market stalls. The pirates of old used St. Thomas as a base from which to raid merchant ships of every nation, though they were particularly fond of the gold- and silver-laden treasure ships heading to Spain. Pirates are still around, but today's versions use St. Thomas as a drop-off for their contraband: illegal immigrants and drugs.

Planning

Getting Here and Around

AIR
American, Delta, JetBlue, Spirit, and United fly to St. Thomas from the United States. Cape Air and Seaborne Airlines fly from San Juan.

BUS
On St. Thomas the island's large buses make public transportation a very comfortable—though slow—way to get from east and west to Charlotte Amalie and back (service to the north is limited). Buses run about every 30 minutes from stops that are clearly marked with Vitran signs. Fares are $1 between outlying areas and town and 75¢ for journeys within town. Some open-air safari cabs also follow the bus routes, and these drivers charge $1 for short trips in town—hence their nickname "dollar buses"—or $2 for longer trips to places like Tutu or Red Hook.

CAR
You will want to rent a car if you are staying in a private villa, but if you are staying in a hotel on the beach, you can usually get by with taxis, though getting a taxi every day can be expensive. If you are a family or group of four, then a car can be a more cost-effective solution since taxi rates are per person.

Traffic can be bad, especially in Charlotte Amalie at rush hour (7 to 9 and 4:30 to 6). If you need to get from an East End resort to the airport during these times, find the alternate route (starting from the East End, Route 38 to 42 to 40 to 33) that goes up the mountain and then drops you back onto Veterans Highway. All drivers should get a copy of *Road Map St. Thomas–St. John;* it's available on the island anywhere you find maps and guidebooks. In addition, most GPS units will work in the Virgin Islands and some car-rental agencies will rent out GPS devices.

CAR RENTALS

Major car-rental companies, including Avis, Budget, and Hertz, have locations at the airport; Avis and Budget also have branch offices. Local rental companies include Dependable, Discount, and Paradise Rental Car.

CONTACTS Avis. ⊠ *Cyril E. King Airport, 70 Lindbergh Bay, Lindbergh Bay* ✛ *4 miles (6½ km) west of Charlotte Amalie* ☎ *340/774–1468* ⊕ *www.avis. com.* **Budget.** ⊠ *Cyril E. King Airport, 70 Lindbergh Bay, Lindbergh Bay* ✛ *4 miles (6½ km) west of Charlotte Amalie* ☎ *340/776–5774* ⊕ *www.budgetstt. com.* **Discount Car Rental.** ⊠ *Cyril E. King Airport, 70 Lindbergh Bay* ✛ *4 miles (6½ km) west of Charlotte Amalie; car rental is located adjacent to the entrance road of the airport, 1 min from the terminal* ☎ *340/776–4858, 877/478–2412* ⊕ *www. discountcar.vi.* **Hertz.** ⊠ *Cyril E. King Airport, 70 Lindbergh Bay, Lindbergh Bay* ✛ *4 miles (6½ km) west of Charlotte Amalie* ☎ *340/774–1879* ⊕ *www.hertzstt. com.* **Paradise Rental Car.** ⊠ *Cyril E. King Airport, 70 Lindbergh Bay, Contant* ☎ *340/643–2692* ⊕ *www.pdiseinc.com.*

ScooterVI

Scooters and motorbikes rent by the day ($75–80) or week ($300–315). Rental fee includes helmet, tank of gas, and island map. ⊠ *9717 Estate Thomas No. 1, Rte. 30, Havensight* ✛ *Across from the main Havensight Mall gate, between Al Cohen Mall and Guardian Insurance Plaza* ☎ *340/774–5840* ⊕ *www.scootervi.com.*

FERRY

There's frequent service from St. Thomas to St. John and Tortola, and less frequent service to St. Croix, Jost Van Dyke, Virgin Gorda, and Anegada. Virgin Islands ferry schedules are published in the free *Virgin Islands This Week* magazine and on ⊕ *www.VInow.com.* There's also a ferry from the Crown Bay Marina west of Charlotte Amalie to Water Island. In St. Thomas, ferries leave from both Charlotte Amalie and Red Hook. Remember that a passport is now required to travel between the USVI and BVI by ferry. Schedules change, so you should confirm current schedules with the ferry companies.

CONTACTS VInow.com. ⊕ *www.vinow. com.*

TAXI

USVI taxis charge per person and have set prices. Drivers usually take multiple fares, especially from the airport, ferry docks, and the cruise-ship terminal. Most taxis are either safari-style or enclosed, air-conditioned vans. They can be hailed on the street (especially in town and near major shopping malls and attractions) and can also be called by telephone. There are taxi stands in Charlotte Amalie across from Emancipation Garden (in front of Little Switzerland, behind the post office) and along the waterfront. V.I. Taxi Association has exclusive rights to pick up customers at Cyril E. King Airport, Havensight Cruise Ship Dock, Yacht Haven Grande, and Sapphire Beach Resort.

■ TIP➔ **There is no Uber, Lyft, or other ride-share option here.**

CONTACTS VITRAN Plus. ⊠ *Knud Hansen Complex, 1303 Hospital Ground, adjacent to Lionel Roberts Stadium* ☎ *340/774–5678.* **East End Taxi.** ⊠ *Urman Victor Fredericks Marine Terminal, 6117 Red Hook Quarters, off Rte. 38, Red Hook* ☎ *340/775–6974* ⊕ *eastendtaxivi.com.* **Islander Taxi Services.** ⊠ *Fortress Storage, Bldg. K, Suite 2025, at the intersection of Rtes. 313 and 38, Charlotte Amalie* ☎ *340/774–4077* ⊕ *www.islandertaxi-service.com.* **Virgin Islands Taxi Association.** ⊠ *68A Estate Contant, Charlotte Amalie* ☎ *340/774–4550, 340/774–7457 Radio Dispatch* ⊕ *vitaxiassociation.com.*

Beaches

All 44 St. Thomas beaches are open to the public, although you can reach some of them only by walking through a resort. Hotel guests frequently have access to lounge chairs and floats that are off-limits to nonguests; for this reason, you may feel more comfortable at one of the beaches not associated with a resort, such as Magens Bay (which charges an entrance fee to cover beach maintenance) or Coki Beach. Whichever one you choose, remember to remove your valuables from the car and keep them out of sight when you go swimming.

Hotels

You can let yourself be pampered at a luxurious resort on the eastern end of the island, many of which are self-contained and feel like islands unto themselves. Or, if your means are more modest, you can find cheaper hotels in lovely settings throughout the island. There are also guesthouses and inns with great views (if not a beach at your door) and great service at about half the cost of what you'll pay at the beachfront pleasure palaces. Many of these are west and north of Charlotte Amalie or in the overlooking hills—ideal if you want the peace and quiet afforded by a lush, junglelike landscape. There are also inexpensive lodgings (most right in town) that are perfect if you just want a clean room to return to after a day of exploring or beach bumming. East End condominium complexes are popular with families and are close to the ferry dock in Red Hook, which makes island-hopping to St. John or the British Virgin Islands a breeze. Although condos are pricey, they have full kitchens, and you can definitely save money by cooking for yourself—especially if you bring some of your own nonperishable food. Though you may spend some time laboring in the kitchen, many condos ease your burden

with daily maid service and on-site restaurants; a few also have resort amenities, including pools and tennis courts. There is also a selection of Airbnbs for rent, from studios to five- and six-bedroom homes.

⇨ *Hotel prices are the lowest cost of a standard double room in high season.*

WHAT IT COSTS in U.S. Dollars			
$	$$	$$$	$$$$
HOTELS			
under $276	$276– $375	$376– $475	over $475

PRIVATE VILLAS

St. Thomas has a wide range of private villas, from modest two-bedroom houses to luxurious five-or-more-bedroom mansions. Most will require that you book for seven nights during high season, five in low season. A minimum stay of up to two weeks is often required during the holiday season.

You can arrange private villa rentals through various agents that represent luxury residences and usually have both websites and brochures that show photos of the properties they represent. Some are suitable for travelers with disabilities, but be sure to ask specific questions regarding your own needs.

Calypso Realty. ☎ *340/774–1620* ⊕ *www.calypsorealty.com.* **McLaughlin-Anderson Luxury Caribbean Villas.** ☎ *340/776–0635, 800/537–6246* ⊕ *www.mclaughlinanderson.com.*

Nightlife

On any given night, especially in season, you can find steel-pan orchestras, rock and roll, piano music, jazz, broken-bottle dancing (actual dancing atop broken glass), disco, and karaoke. Pick up a free copy of the bright-yellow *Virgin Islands This Week* magazine when you arrive (it can be found at the airport, in stores, and in hotel lobbies). The back pages list who's playing where. The Friday edition of the *Virgin Islands Daily News* carries complete listings for the upcoming weekend.

Restaurants

The beauty of St. Thomas and its sister islands has attracted a cadre of professionally trained chefs who know their way around fresh fish and local fruits. You can dine on everything from terrific cheap local dishes such as goat water (a spicy stew) and fungi (a cornmeal polenta-like side dish) to imports such as hot pastrami sandwiches and raspberries in crème fraîche.

Restaurants are spread all over the island, although fewer are found in the west and northwest sections. Most restaurants out of town are easily accessible by taxi and have ample parking. If you dine in Charlotte Amalie, take a taxi. Parking close to restaurants can be difficult to find.

Dining on St. Thomas is informal. Few restaurants require a jacket and tie. Still, shorts and T-shirts are inappropriate for dinner at snazzier places; men would do well to wear slacks and a shirt with a collar and buttons. Dress codes on St. Thomas rarely require women to wear skirts, but you can never go wrong with something flowing.

⇨ *Restaurant prices are the average cost of a main course at dinner or, if dinner is not served, at lunch.*

WHAT IT COSTS in U.S. Dollars			
$	$$	$$$	$$$$
RESTAURANTS			
under $13	$13–$20	$21–$30	over $30

Safety

To be safe, keep your hotel or vacation villa door locked at all times, stick to well-lighted streets at night, and use the same kind of street sense that you would in any unfamiliar territory. Don't wander the streets of Charlotte Amalie alone at night. If you plan to carry things around, rent a car—not an open-air vehicle—and lock possessions in the trunk. Keep your rental car locked wherever you park. Don't leave cameras, purses, and other valuables lying on the beach while you snorkel for an hour (or even for a minute), no matter how many people are nearby.

Shopping

St. Thomas lives up to its billing as a duty-free shopping destination. Even if shopping isn't your idea of how to spend a vacation, you still may want to slip in on a quiet day (check the cruise-ship listings—Monday and Sunday are usually the least crowded) to browse. Among the best buys are liquor, linens, china, crystal (most stores will ship), and jewelry. The amount of jewelry available makes this one of the few items for which comparison shopping is worth the effort. Local crafts include shell jewelry, carved calabash bowls, straw brooms, woven baskets, and dolls. Spice mixes, hot sauces, and tropical jams and jellies are other native products.

On St. Thomas, stores on Main Street in Charlotte Amalie are open weekdays and Saturdays from 9 am to 5 pm. The hours of the shops in the Havensight Mall (next to the cruise-ship dock) and the Crown Bay Commercial Center (next to the Crown Bay cruise-ship dock) are the same, though occasionally some stay open until 9 pm on Friday, depending on how many cruise ships are anchored nearby. You may also find some shops open on Sunday if cruise ships are in port. Hotel shops are usually open evenings as well.

There's no sales tax in the USVI, and you can take advantage of the $1,600 duty-free allowance per family member (remember to save your receipts). Although you can find the occasional sales clerk who will make a deal, bartering isn't the norm.

Sights

To explore outside Charlotte Amalie, rent a car or hire a taxi. Your rental car should come with a good map and perhaps a GPS unit; if not, pick up the pocket-size *Road Map St. Thomas–St. John* at a tourist information center. Roads are marked with route numbers, but they're confusing and seem to switch numbers suddenly. Roads are also identified by signs bearing the St. Thomas–St. John Hotel and Tourism Association's mascot, Tommy the Starfish. More than 100 of these color-coded signs line the island's main routes. Orange signs trace the route from the airport to Red Hook; green signs identify the road from town to Magens Bay; Tommy's face on a yellow background points from Mafolie to Crown Bay through the north side; red signs lead from Smith Bay to Four Corners via Skyline Drive; and blue signs mark the route from the cruise-ship dock at Havensight to Red Hook. These color-coded routes are not marked on most visitor maps, however. Allow yourself a day to explore, especially if you want to stop to take pictures or to enjoy a light bite or refreshing swim. Most gas stations are in town or on the island's more populated eastern side, so fill up before heading to the north side. And remember to drive on the left!

Visitor Information

CONTACTS U.S. Virgin Islands Hotel and Tourism Association. ☎ *340/774–6835* ⊕ *usvihta.com.* **USVI Department of Tourism.** ✉ *74B & 75 Kronprindsens*

Gade, Charlotte Amalie ✛ Downtown, behind the old USO building and public restrooms ☎ *340/774–8784, 800/372–8784* ⊕ *www.visitusvi.com.*

BANKS
The major banks on St. Thomas are First Bank, Banco Popular, and Oriental (formerly Scotia Bank), each of which has several branches in convenient locations.

Charlotte Amalie

Look beyond the pricey shops, T-shirt vendors, and bustling crowds for a glimpse of the island's history. The city served as the capital of Denmark's outpost in the Caribbean until 1917, an aspect of the island often lost in the glitz of the shopping district.

Emancipation Gardens, right next to the fort, is a good place to start a walking tour. Tackle the hilly part of town first: head north up Government Hill to the historic buildings that house government offices and have incredible views. Several regal churches line the route that runs west back to the town proper and the old-time market. Virtually all the alleyways that intersect Main Street lead to eateries that serve frosty drinks, sandwiches, and West Indian fare. There are public restrooms in this area, too. Allow an hour for a quick view of the sights.

A note about the street names: in deference to the island's heritage, the streets downtown are labeled by their Danish names. Locals will use both the Danish name and the English name (such as Dronningens Gade and Norre Gade for Main Street), but most people refer to things by their location ("a block toward the Waterfront off Main Street" or "next to the Little Switzerland Shop"). You may find it more useful if you ask for directions by shop names or landmarks.

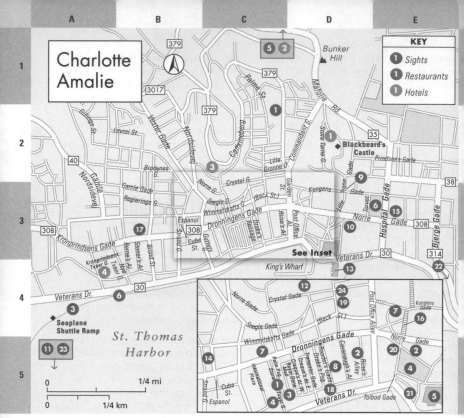

Charlotte Amalie

KEY
1 Sights
1 Restaurants
1 Hotels

St. Thomas Harbor

Seaplane Shuttle Ramp

See Inset

0   1/4 mi
0   1/4 km

Sights ▼

1 All Saints Episcopal Church **C2**
2 Educators Park........... **E5**
3 Edward Wilmoth Blyden IV Marine Terminal **A4**
4 Emancipation Garden ... **E5**
5 Fort Christian **E5**
6 Franklin D. Roosevelt Memorial Park **E3**
7 Frederick Evangelical Lutheran Church......... **E4**
8 Gallery Camille Pissarro **D5**
9 Government House..... **D3**
10 Grand Hotel.............. **D3**
11 Hassel Island............ **A5**
12 Hebrew Congregation of St. Thomas............ **D4**
13 Legislature Building **D4**
14 Market Square........... **C5**
15 Memorial Moravian Church **E3**
16 99 Steps.................... **E4**

17 Saints Peter and Paul Cathedral **B3**
18 St. Thomas Historical Trust Museum........... **D5**
19 St. Thomas Reformed Church....... **D4**
20 U.S. Post Office **E5**
21 Vendors Plaza............ **E5**
22 Virgin Islands Children's Museum...... **E4**
23 Water Island............. **A5**
24 Weibel Museum **D4**

Restaurants ▼

1 Amalia Café **C5**
2 Café Amici............... **D5**
3 Gladys' Cafe............. **D5**
4 Greenhouse Bar and Restaurant........... **C5**
5 Mafolie Restaurant...... **C1**
6 Texas Pit BBQ........... **B4**
7 Virgilio's................... **C5**

Hotels ▼

1 The Green Iguana **D2**
2 Mafolie Hotel............. **C1**
3 Villa Santana **C2**
4 Windward Passage Hotel...................... **A4**

Fort Christian (1872–80), the oldest surviving structure in St. Thomas

Sights

All Saints Episcopal Church

RELIGIOUS BUILDING | Built in 1848 from stone quarried on the island, the church has thick, arched window frames lined with the yellow brick that came to the islands as ballast aboard ships. Merchants left the brick on the waterfront when they filled their boats with molasses, sugar, mahogany, and rum for the return voyage. The church was built in celebration of the end of slavery in the USVI. ⊠ *13 Commandant Gade, near the Emancipation Garden U.S. Post Office, Charlotte Amalie* ☎ *340/774–0217.*

Educators Park

MONUMENT | A peaceful place amid the town's hustle and bustle, the park has memorials for three famous Virgin Islanders: educator Edith Williams, J. Antonio Jarvis (a founder of *The Virgin Islands Daily News*), and educator and author Rothschild Francis. The last gave many speeches here. ⊠ *Main St., across from Emancipation Garden post office, Charlotte Amalie.*

Edward Wilmoth Blyden IV Marine Terminal

MARINA/PIER | Locally called Tortola Wharf, this is where you can catch the *Native Son* and other ferries to the BVI. The restaurant upstairs is a good place to watch the Charlotte Amalie harbor traffic and sip an iced tea. Next door is the Charles F. Blair Jr. Seaplane Terminal, where Seaborne Airlines offers service to St. Croix. ⊠ *Veterans Dr., across from the Windward Passage Hotel, Charlotte Amalie* ☎ *340/774 1629* ⊕ *www.viport.com.*

Emancipation Garden

MONUMENT | A bronze bust of a freed enslaved person blowing a conch shell commemorates slavery's end in 1848—the garden was built to mark emancipation's 150th anniversary in 1998. The gazebo here is used for official ceremonies. One other monument shows a scaled-down model of the U.S. Liberty Bell, with a plaque remembering the Virginia-bound English settlers who stopped here in 1607, a month before they established Jamestown. ⊠ *Between Tolbod Gade and Fort Christian, next to Vendor's Plaza, Charlotte Amalie.*

Fort Christian

MILITARY SIGHT | FAMILY | St. Thomas's oldest existent structure, this remarkable building was built between 1672 and 1680 and is now a U.S. National Historic Landmark. Over the years, it was used as a jail, governor's residence, town hall, courthouse, and church. In 2005, a multimillion-dollar renovation project started to stabilize the structure and halt centuries of deterioration. This project was completed in 2017 in time to commemorate the centennial of the U.S. purchase of the territory from Denmark in 1917. You can tour the museum inside on your own or take a guided tour at 10 am or 1:45 pm. Outside, look for historic features, like the four renovated faces of the famous 19th-century clock tower. ⊠ *Forte Strande and Waterfront Hwy., Adjacent to Emancipation Garden, Charlotte Amalie* 🕾 *340/714–3678* 🖃 *$10* 🕐 *Closed weekends.*

Franklin D. Roosevelt Memorial Park

CITY PARK | FAMILY | The former Coconut Park was renamed in honor of Franklin D. Roosevelt in 1945. It's a great place to put your feet up and people-watch. Five granite pedestals represent the five branches of the military, bronze urns commemorate special events and can be lighted, and inscribed bronze plaques pay tribute to the territory's veterans who died defending the United States. There's also a children's playground. ⊠ *Intersection of Norre Gade and Rte. 35, adjacent to the Memorial Moravian Church, Charlotte Amalie.*

Frederick Evangelical Lutheran Church

RELIGIOUS BUILDING | This historic church has a massive mahogany altar, and its pews—each with its own door—were once rented to families of the congregation. Lutheranism is the state religion of Denmark, and when the territory was without a minister, the governor—who had his own elevated pew—filled in.

⊠ *7 Norre Gade, across from Emancipation Garden, Charlotte Amalie* 🕾 *340/776-1315* ⊕ *www.felcvi.org* 🕐 *Sunday Service starts at 9 am weekly.*

Gallery Camille Pissarro

NOTABLE BUILDING | Housing an antiques shop and an art gallery, this was the birthplace and childhood home of the acclaimed 19th-century impressionist painter Camille Pissarro, who lived for most of his adult life in France. The art gallery on the second floor contains three original pages from Pissarro's sketchbook and two pastels by Pissarro's grandson, Claude. ⊠ *14 Dronningens Gade (Main St.), between Raadets Gade and Trompeter Gade, Charlotte Amalie* 🕾 *340/774–4621.*

Government House

GOVERNMENT BUILDING | Built in 1867, this neoclassical, white, brick-and-wood structure houses the offices of the governor of the Virgin Islands. Outside, the bright red Danish-style guardhouse is a perfect place for a photo. The view of the harbor is picture-postcard pretty from the First Lady's garden directly across the street. ■TIP→ **The inside of the building is currently closed to visitors.** ⊠ *Government Hill, 21–22 Kongens Gade, Charlotte Amalie* ✛ *On the hill above the Frederick Lutheran Church* 🕾 *340/774–0001.*

Grand Hotel

NOTABLE BUILDING | This imposing building stands at the head of Main Street. Once the island's premier hotel, it has been converted into offices, shops, and a restaurant. It houses the Hamilton & Lafayette Rum Cafe and Boutique, which hosts guided tours of its micro-distillery. ⊠ *43-46 Norre Gade, at intersection of Tolbod Gade, adjacent to Emancipation Garden, Charlotte Amalie* 🕾 *340/774–7282.*

In Search of Pirates

The line between fact and fiction is often fluid, and it ebbs and flows according to who is telling the tale. So it is with the swashbuckling seafarers of St. Thomas, such as Bluebeard, Blackbeard, and Sir Francis Drake. But you'll find the story—we don't promise that it's completely true—if you follow the pirate trail.

Start atop Bluebeard's Hill to the east of Charlotte Amalie. Today this is the site of Bluebeard's Castle hotel. According to legend, it was Bluebeard—in reality Eduard de Barbe-Bleue—who picked this prime location to build a stone watchtower from which he could keep an eye on approaching enemies. Bluebeard kept his most prized booty, the lovely Señorita Mercedes, prisoner in the tower. That is, of course, until Mercedes broke free and discovered his gold-filled treasure chests along with gushing love letters to several other young ladies. Mercedes invited all of Bluebeard's paramours to the tower to pillage his plunder.

High atop Blackbeard's Hill, rising north of Fort Christian and Government House, is Blackbeard's Castle. No one knows if Blackbeard—better known as Edward Teach—ever visited this site, but historians agree that this infamous pirate did indeed sail the Caribbean Sea in the early 18th century.

Drive over the hill to find Drake's Seat. Named for the English privateer Sir Francis Drake, this popular scenic overlook is supposedly where Drake spied ships approaching from what are now the British Virgin Islands. Don't let anyone tell you that the wooden bench is where Drake sat, however. Scholars have a hard enough time trying to prove that Drake really stood on this spot.

Finally, head back into downtown Charlotte Amalie and to Royal Dane Mall. This winding trio of brick-and-stone-paved alleyways is home to a couple of bronze plaques inscribed with historical facts about the island. One of them tells about buried pirate treasure. Some doubt it's really here. Others never stop dreaming of the day they'll find it.

Hassel Island

ISLAND | East of Water Island in Charlotte Amalie harbor, Hassel Island is part of the Virgin Islands National Park. On it are the ruins of a British military garrison (built during a brief British occupation of the USVI during the 1800s) and the remains of a marine railway (where ships were hoisted into dry dock for repairs). The St. Thomas Historical Trust leads 2- to 2½-hour walking tours, with boat transportation to and from St. Thomas, by advance request. ⊠ *Charlotte Amalie Harbor* 🕾 *340/774–5541 St. Thomas Historical Trust, 340/244–2546 Tour Guide Doc Palancia* ⊕ *www.stthomashistorical-trust.org* 🕾 *$75 cash per person* ⚶ *Tours are given only by request. Reservations are required with 3-day advance notice.* ☞ *Minimum 2 persons.*

Hebrew Congregation of St. Thomas

RELIGIOUS BUILDING | The synagogue's Hebrew name, *Beracha Veshalom Vegmiluth Hasidim,* translates as the Congregation of Blessing, Peace, and Loving Deeds. The small building's white pillars contrast with rough stone walls, as does the rich mahogany of the pews and altar. The sand on the floor symbolizes the exodus from Egypt. Since

Did You Know?

Charlotte Amalie is the busiest cruise port in the Caribbean and one of the busiest in the world. As many as eight cruise ships have called in a single day.

the synagogue first opened its doors in 1833, it has held a weekly service, making it the oldest synagogue building in continuous use under the American flag and the second-oldest (after the one on Curaçao) in the western hemisphere. Guided tours can be arranged. Brochures detailing the key structures and history are also available. Next door the Weibel Museum showcases Jewish history on St. Thomas. ⊠ *Synagogue Hill, 15 Crystal Gade, Charlotte Amalie* ☎ *340/774–4312* ⊕ *www.synagogue.vi.*

Legislature Building

GOVERNMENT BUILDING | Its light yellow colonial-style exterior is the face of the vociferous political wrangling of the Virgin Islands Senate. Constructed originally by the Danish as a police barracks, the building was later used to billet U.S. Marines, and much later it housed a public school. You're welcome to sit in on sessions in the upstairs chambers. ⊠ *Waterfront Hwy. (aka Rte. 30), across from Fort Christian, Charlotte Amalie* ☎ *340/774–0880* ⊕ *www.legvi.org.*

Market Square

MARKET | Locals gather daily—especially by 4 am on Saturday mornings—at what was once a slave market in the 18th-century, to sell local fruits such as mangoes and papayas, root vegetables, and bunches of fresh herbs. Sidewalk vendors offer brightly colored fabrics, tie-dyed clothing, and handicrafts at good prices. A smaller number of vendors set up shop here all week long. ⊠ *Main St., at Strand Gade, Charlotte Amalie* ☎ *340/774–5182.*

Memorial Moravian Church

RELIGIOUS BUILDING | Built in 1884, this church was named to commemorate the 150th anniversary of the Moravian Church in the Virgin Islands. ⊠ *17 Norre Gade, next to Roosevelt Park, Charlotte Amalie* ☎ *340/776–0066* ⊕ *www.memorialmoravianvi.org.*

Big Event

April is a great time to visit St. Thomas, as the island comes alive for Carnival. The celebrations—steel-drum music, colorful costumes, and dancing in the streets—culminate the last weekend of the month.

99 Steps

STREET | This staircase "street," built by the Danes in the 1700s, leads to the residential area above Charlotte Amalie. Although historic Blackbeard's Castle, at the top, is closed, the splendid views are worth the trek. If you count the stairs as you go up, you'll discover, as thousands have before you, that there are more than the name implies. ⊹ *Look for steps heading north from Government Hill.*

Saints Peter and Paul Cathedral

RELIGIOUS BUILDING | This building was consecrated as a parish church in 1848, and serves as the seat of the territory's Roman Catholic diocese. The ceiling and walls are covered with 11 murals depicting biblical scenes; they were painted in 1899 by two Belgian artists, Father Leo Servais and Brother Ildephonsus. The marble altar and walls were added in the 1960s. Over a dozen statues of handcrafted saints represent the many nationalities of the congregants who worship here. Guided tours available. ⊠ *22-AB Kronprindsens Gade, 1 block west of Market Sq., Charlotte Amalie* ☎ *340/774–0201* ⊕ *www.cathedralvi.com* ☞ *Sunday Mass in English at 10:30 am and in Spanish at 12:30 pm weekly.*

St. Thomas Historical Trust Museum

HISTORY MUSEUM | Tours of the museum, which are by appointment only, take 30 minutes and include a wealth of pirate artifacts, as well as West Indian antique furniture and art (some of which dates to the 1600s), old-time postcards, and historic books. The Trust office, also at the museum, is where you can book 2- to 2½ hour historic Charlotte Amalie walking tours and three-hour Hassel Island tours. ⊠ *5332 Raadets Gade, Charlotte Amalie* ☎ *340/774–5541* ⊕ *www.stthomashistoricaltrust.org* ✉ *Free, but donations appreciated* ⊗ *Open by appointment only.*

St. Thomas Reformed Church

RELIGIOUS BUILDING | This church has an austere loveliness that's amazing considering all it's been through. Founded in 1744, it's been rebuilt twice after fires and hurricanes. The unembellished cream-color hall is quite peaceful. The only other color is the forest green of the shutters and the carpet. Call ahead if you wish to visit at a particular time, as the doors are sometimes locked. Services are held at 10 am each Sunday. ⊠ *5 Crystal Gade at Nye Gade, Charlotte Amalie* ⊹ *1½ blocks north of Main St.* ☎ *340/776–8255* ⊕ *www.strchurch.org* ☞ *Sunday services start at 10 am weekly.*

U.S. Post Office

GOVERNMENT BUILDING | While you buy stamps, contemplate the murals of waterfront scenes by *Saturday Evening Post* artist Stephen Dohanos. His art was commissioned as part of the Works Project Administration in the 1930s. ⊠ *Tolbod Gade and Main St., 5046 Norre Gade, next to Emancipation Garden, Charlotte Amalie* ☎ *340/774–1950* ⊗ *Closed Sun.*

Vendors Plaza

MARKET | **FAMILY** | Red-roofed, pastel-painted kiosks house vendors selling everything from T-shirts to leather goods. Look for local crafts and art among the ever-changing selections at this busy market. ⊠ *Waterfront, west of Fort Christian, Charlotte Amalie.*

★ Virgin Islands Children's Museum

CHILDREN'S MUSEUM | **FAMILY** | Giant bubble makers, a rainbow-colored gear table, and a larger-than-life abacus are just a few of the interactive exhibits at this indoor, family-friendly, play-and-learn museum. Science was never so fun! ⊠ *Buccaneer Mall, Rte. 30, Havensight* ⊹ *Across from the cruise ship dock* ☎ *340/643–0366* ⊕ *www.vichildrensmuseum.org* ✉ *$10* ⊗ *Closed Mon.*

★ Water Island

ISLAND | **FAMILY** | This island, the fourth largest of the U.S. Virgin Islands, sits about a ¼ mile (½ km) out in Charlotte Amalie harbor. A ferry between Crown Bay Marina and the island ($15 round-trip) operates several times daily, Monday through Saturday from 7 am to 6 pm and Sunday and holidays from 8 am to 6 pm. From the ferry dock, rent a golf cart for $55 a day and drive or hike the less than half a mile distance to Honeymoon Beach (though you have to go up a big hill), where Brad Pitt and Cate Blanchett filmed a scene of the movie *The Curious Case of Benjamin Button*. Get lunch from a food truck or Dinghy's Beach Bar & Grill on the far south side of the beach. ⊠ *Charlotte Amalie harbor* ☎ *340/690–4159 for ferry info* ⊕ *www.waterislandferry.com* ✉ *$15 round-trip.*

Weibel Museum

HISTORY MUSEUM | This museum is in the back foyer of the Synagogue of Beracha Veshalom and showcases 300 years of Jewish history on St. Thomas. The small gift shop sells a commemorative silver coin celebrating the anniversary of the Hebrew congregation's establishment on the island in 1796. There are also tropically inspired items, such as menorahs painted to resemble palm trees. ⊠ *Synagogue Hill, 15 Crystal Gade, Charlotte Amalie* ⊹ *From Main St., walk up Raadets Gade (H. Stern is on the corner) to the top of the hill; turn left and it's the 2nd bldg. on the right* ☎ *340/774–4312* ⊕ *www.synagogue.vi* ✉ *Free* ⊗ *Closed weekends.*

🍴 Restaurants

★ Amalia Café

$$$$ | SPANISH | A great place to take a break and get a bite while shopping, this open-air café tucked into the alleyway of Palm Passage serves authentic Spanish cuisine for lunch and dinner. Try tapas such as mussels in brandy sauce, escargots with mushrooms and herb butter, or Galician-style octopus and baby eels served in a sizzling garlic sauce. **Known for:** authentic paella; Spanish tapas; caramel flan. [$] *Average main: $32* ✉ *Palm Passage, 24 Dronningens Gade, facing the Waterfront, Charlotte Amalie* ☎ *340/714–7373* 🌐 *www.amaliacafe.com* 🕒 *Closed Sun.*

Café Amici

$$ | ITALIAN | Within the historic stonework and cascading tropical blossoms of A.H. Riise Alley, this charming open-air eatery will pull you in by the nose and send you straight to the wood-burning brick-oven pizza. **Known for:** pizza, subs, and pasta; popular with the local business crowd; alfresco seating. [$] *Average main: $20* ✉ *37 Main St., in the A.H. Riise Mall, Charlotte Amalie* ☎ *340/779–9000* 🌐 *www.cafeamicistthomas.com* 🕒 *No dinner. Closed Sun.*

★ Gladys' Cafe

$$ | CARIBBEAN | This cozy alleyway restaurant is rich in atmosphere, with its mahogany bar and native stone walls, making dining a double delight. Try the local specialties like conch in butter sauce, jerk pork, or panfried yellowtail snapper. **Known for:** service with a smile; homemade hot sauce; local West Indian cuisine. [$] *Average main: $19* ✉ *5600 Royal Dane Mall, Suite 9, Charlotte Amalie* ☎ *340/774–6604* 🌐 *www.gladyscafe.com* 🕒 *No dinner.*

Greenhouse Bar and Restaurant

$$ | AMERICAN | FAMILY | Fun-lovers come to this waterfront restaurant to eat, listen to music, and play games, including video lottery terminals. Even the most finicky eater should find something to please on the eight-page menu that offers burgers, salads, and pizza all day long, along with peel-and-eat shrimp, Caribbean lobster tail, Alaskan king crab, and Black Angus filet mignon for dinner. **Known for:** family-friendly vibe; live music; eight-page menu with huge selection of American-style fare. [$] *Average main: $20* ✉ *Waterfront Hwy. at Store Tvaer Gade, Charlotte Amalie* ☎ *340/774–7998* 🌐 *www.thegreenhouserestaurant.com.*

Mafolie Restaurant

$$$$ | CARIBBEAN | Enjoy a romantic meal with an iconic bird's-eye view of the Charlotte Amalie harbor. For starters, try the kallaloo soup (shrimp and crab in a thick, creamy spinach broth). **Known for:** sublime key lime pie; tropical flavors; sweeping views. [$] *Average main: $38* ✉ *7091 Estate Mafolie, off Rte. 35, Charlotte Amalie* ☎ *340/774–2790* 🌐 *mafolie.com.*

Texas Pit BBQ

$$ | AMERICAN | The smell of smoky barbecue ribs, beef brisket, and chicken wafts enticingly from these mobile stands, which set up daily around 4 pm. Austin native and longtime Virgin Islands resident Bill Collins perfected his signature sauce, which received a thumbs-up from the late culinary great James Beard. **Known for:** barbecue; coleslaw and potato salad; no seating (head to the beach for a picnic). [$] *Average main: $16* ✉ *Waterfront, across from Windward Passage Hotel, Charlotte Amalie* ☎ *340/776–9579* 💳 *No credit cards* 🕒 *No lunch. Closed Sun.*

Virgilio's

$$$$ | ITALIAN | For the island's best northern Italian cuisine, don't miss this intimate, elegant hideaway that's on a quiet side street. Come here for more than 40 homemade pastas topped with superb sauces, like capellini with fresh tomatoes and garlic or peasant-style spaghetti in a rich tomato sauce with mushrooms and prosciutto. **Known for:** tender osso

Where to Shop for Groceries 🍴

High food prices in Virgin Islands supermarkets are enough to dull anyone's appetite. According to a report by the U.S. Virgin Islands Department of Labor, food is around 30% more expensive than on the mainland.

Although you'll never match the prices back home, you can shop around for the best deals. If you're traveling with a group, it pays to stock up on the basics at warehouse-style stores like Pricesmart (membership required) and Cost-U-Less. Even the non-bulk food items here are sold at lower prices than in the supermarkets or convenience stores. Good buys include beverages, meats, produce, and spirits.

After this, head to supermarkets such as Plaza Extra, Pueblo, and Food Center. Although the prices aren't as good as at the big-box stores, the selection is better.

Finally, if you want to splurge on top-quality meats, exotic produce and spices, and imported cheeses and spirits, finish off your shopping at high-end shops like Moe's Fresh Market and Gourmet Gallery.

The Fruit Bowl is the place for fresh produce. The prices and selection are unbeatable.

For really fresh tropical fruits, vegetables, and seasoning herbs, visit the farm stands near Ft. Mylner (daily), on the Charlotte Amalie waterfront (daily), at Market Square (Saturday mornings), and in Estate Bordeaux (second and fourth Sunday of every month).

buco; rich creamy tiramisu; eclectic art and décor. [$] *Average main: $34* ✉ *18 Dronningens Gade, Charlotte Amalie* ☎ *340/776–4920* 🌐 *www.virgiliosvi.com* 🕑 *Closed Sun.*

🛏 Hotels

Accommodations in town and near town offer the benefits of being close to the airport, shopping, and a number of casual and fine-dining restaurants. The downside is that this is the most crowded and noisy area of the island. Crime can also be a problem. Don't go for a stroll at night in the heart of town. Use common sense, and take the same precautions you would in any major city. Properties along the hillsides are less likely to have crime problems; plus, they command a steady breeze from the cool trade winds. This is especially important if you're visiting in summer and early fall.

The Green Iguana

$ | **HOTEL** | Atop Blackbeard's Hill, this value-priced small hotel offers the perfect mix of gorgeous harbor views, proximity to shopping (five-minute walk), and secluded privacy provided by the surrounding showy trees and bushy hibiscus. **Pros:** personalized service; near the center of town; laundry on premises. **Cons:** not too many frills; need a car to get around; noise from town, especially during events. [$] *Rooms from: $160* ✉ *1002 Blackbeard's Hill, Charlotte Amalie* ☎ *340/776–7654* 🌐 *www.thegreeniguana.com* 🛏 *9 rooms* 🍴 *No Meals.*

★ **Mafolie Hotel**

$$$ | **B&B/INN** | The view and the value are the selling points of this simply furnished family-run hotel perched 800 feet above Charlotte Amalie's harbor. **Pros:** fantastic views; nice restaurant and bar; friendly staff. **Cons:** small pool; on a busy street;

need a car to get around. $ *Rooms from: $410* ✉ *7091 Estate Mafolie, off Rte. 35, Charlotte Amalie* ☎ *340/774–2790* ⊕ *www.mafolie.com* ⟿ *22 rooms, including 5 suites* ❧ *Free Breakfast.*

Villa Santana

$ | **HOTEL** | Built by exiled General Antonio López Santa Anna of Mexico, this 1857 landmark provides a panoramic view of the harbor and plenty of West Indian charm, which will make you feel as if you're living in a slice of Virgin Islands history. **Pros:** historic charm; plenty of privacy; modern amenities like good Wi-Fi. **Cons:** not on a beach; no restaurant; need a car to get around. $ *Rooms from: $250* ✉ *2602 Bjerge Gade, 2D Denmark Hill, Charlotte Amalie* ☎ *340/776–1311* ⊕ *www.villasantana.com* ⟿ *6 rooms* ❧ *No Meals.*

Windward Passage Hotel

$ | **HOTEL** | Business travelers, tourists on their way to the British Virgin Islands, and laid-back vacationers who want the convenience of being able to walk to duty-free shopping, sights, and restaurants favor this harbor-front hotel. **Pros:** walking distance to Charlotte Amalie; nice harbor views; across from BVI ferry terminal. **Cons:** basic rooms; on a busy street; no water sports, but dive shop is on property. $ *Rooms from: $250* ✉ *Veterans Dr., Charlotte Amalie* ☎ *340/774–5200, 800/524–7389* ⊕ *www.windwardpassage.com* ⟿ *180 rooms* ❧ *No Meals.*

Nightlife

Greenhouse Bar and Restaurant

BARS | Once this popular eatery puts away the salt-and-pepper shakers after 10 pm on the weekends, it becomes a rock-and-roll club with a DJ or live reggae bands bringing the weary to their feet. ✉ *Waterfront Harbor, Charlotte Amalie* ☎ *340/774–7998* ⊕ *www.thegreenhouserestaurant.com.*

Shopping

The prime shopping area in Charlotte Amalie is between Post Office and Market squares; it consists of two parallel streets that run east–west (Waterfront Highway and Main Street) and the alleyways that connect them. Particularly attractive are the historic A. H. Riise Alley, Royal Dane Mall, and Palm Passage.

Vendors Plaza, on the waterfront side of Emancipation Gardens in Charlotte Amalie, is a central location for vendors selling handmade earrings, necklaces, and bracelets; straw baskets and handbags; T-shirts; fabrics; African artifacts; and local fruits. Look for the many brightly colored kiosks.

ART GALLERIES
Camille Pissarro Art Gallery

ART GALLERIES | This second-floor gallery, at the birthplace of St. Thomas's famous artist, offers a fine collection of original paintings and prints by local and regional artists. ✉ *14 Main St., Charlotte Amalie* ☎ *340/774–4621.*

CAMERAS AND ELECTRONICS
Royal Caribbean

ELECTRONICS | Find a wide selection of cameras, camcorders, stereos, watches, and clocks at this store. There is also a branch at the Crown Bay Center. ✉ *33 Main St., Charlotte Amalie* ☎ *340/776–4110* ⊕ *www.royalcaribbeanvi.com.*

CHINA AND CRYSTAL
The Crystal Shoppe at A. H. Riise

CERAMICS | This retailer specializes in all that glitters, from Swarovski and Waterford crystal to figurines by Hummel, Daum, and Royal Copenhagen, and china by Belleek, Kosta Boda, and several Limoges factories. There's also a large selection of Lladró figurines. ✉ *37 Main St., at Riise's Alley, Charlotte Amalie* ☎ *340/777–2222, 800/323–7232* ⊕ *www.ahriise.com.*

Charlotte Amalie is filled with back alleys and interesting shops.

Little Switzerland

GLASSWARE | This popular Caribbean chain carries crystal from Baccarat, Waterford, and Orrefors; and china from Kosta Boda, Rosenthal, and Wedgwood. There's also an assortment of Swarovski cut crystal animals, gemstone globes, and many other affordable collectibles. The Main Street location features separate boutiques showcasing timepieces from Omega, TAG Heuer, Patek Philippe, David Yurman, and Breitling. A branch at the Crown Bay Center is open when ships are in port, and locations are in Havensight Mall and at the Ritz Carlton. ☒ *5182 Dronningens Gade, Charlotte Amalie* ☎ *248/809–5560 ext. 10110* ⊕ *www. littleswitzerland.com.*

CLOTHING

Local Color

WOMEN'S CLOTHING | This St. Thomas chain has clothes for men, women, and children among its brand names, which include Jams World, Fresh Produce, and Urban Safari. You can also find St. John artist Sloop Jones's colorful, hand-painted island designs on cool dresses, T-shirts, and sweaters. The tropically oriented accessories include big-brimmed straw hats, bold-color bags, and casual jewelry. There's another location at the Havensight Mall. ☒ *5332–5333 Raadets Gade, Charlotte Amalie* ☎ *340/774–2280* ⊕ *www.localcolorvi.com.*

FOODSTUFFS

Belgian Chocolate Factory

FOOD | FAMILY | This store makes its beautiful chocolates before your eyes. Specialties include triple-chocolate rum truffles. You can find imported chocolates here as well. Both the homemade and imported delectables come in decorative boxes, so they make great gifts. ☒ *Hibiscus Alley, 5093 Dronningens Gade, Suite 3, Charlotte Amalie* ☎ *340/777–5247.*

Pueblo Supermarket

FOOD | This Caribbean chain carries stateside brands of most products—but at higher prices because of shipping costs to the islands. ☒ *Subbase, ½ mile (¾ km) east of Crown Bay Marina, Charlotte Amalie* ☎ *340/774–4200.*

HANDICRAFTS
Made in the U.S. Virgin Islands

CRAFTS | This pop-up shop is open from Thanksgiving until early January each year and is located in a historic building across from Fort Christian. Inside, you'll find a treasure trove for bona fide made-in-the-Virgin Islands arts, crafts, and local food products that make the perfect gifts. There are soaps, hot sauces, hand-tied palm brooms, native dolls, books by local authors, T-shirts, jewelry, and much more. Signs next to displays tell you about the respective artists. There are also some local handicrafts such as soaps in kiosks at Vendor's Plaza. ⊠ *23 Dronningens Gade, across from Fort Christian, Charlotte Amalie* ☎ *340/714–1700.*

JEWELRY
★ Cardow Jewelers

JEWELRY & WATCHES | You can get gold in several lengths, widths, sizes, and styles, along with jewelry made of diamonds, emeralds, and other precious gems from this small chain's main store. You're guaranteed 40% to 60% savings off U.S. retail prices, or your money will be refunded within 30 days of purchase. There's also a line of classy commemorative Virgin Islands watches made on-site. Branches located at the Cyril E. King Airport; Ritz-Carlton, St. Thomas; and Crown Bay Center. ⊠ *5195 Dronningens Gate, across from Emancipation Garden, Charlotte Amalie* ☎ *340/776–1140* ⊕ *www.cardow.com.*

Diamonds International

JEWELRY & WATCHES | At this large chain with several outlets on St. Thomas, just choose a diamond, emerald, or tanzanite gem and a mounting, and you can have your dream ring set in an hour. Famous for having the largest inventory of diamonds on the island, this shop welcomes trade-ins, has a U.S. service center, and includes diamond earrings with every purchase. Branches located at Crown Bay Center and Havensight Mall. ⊠ *31 Main St., Charlotte Amalie*

☎ *340/774–3707* ⊕ *www.diamondsinternational.com.*

Rolex Watches at A. H. Riise

JEWELRY & WATCHES | A. H. Riise is the official Rolex retailer of the Virgin Islands and this shop offers one of the largest new and pre-owned selections of these fine timepieces in the Caribbean. An After Sales Service Center helps you keep your Rolex ticking for a lifetime. ⊠ *37 Main St., at Riise's Alley, Charlotte Amalie* ☎ *340/777–6789* ⊕ *www.ahriise.com.*

Trident Jewels and Time

JEWELRY & WATCHES | Fine gems and exquisite timepieces are the draw at this second-generation family-owned boutique. You'll find loose diamonds, sapphires, emeralds, and tanzanite as well as name-brand watches such as Ulysse Nardin, Harry Winston, Franck Muller, Bovet, Jaquet Droz, Bell & Ross, U-Boat, and Graham. ⊠ *9 Main St., Charlotte Amalie* ☎ *340/776–7152* ⊕ *www.tridentjewels.com.*

LEATHER GOODS
★ Zora's

LEATHER GOODS | This store specializes in fine, made-to-order leather sandals. There's also a selection of locally made backpacks, purses, and briefcases in durable, brightly colored canvas. ⊠ *34 Norre Gade, across from Roosevelt Park, Charlotte Amalie* ☎ *340/774–2559.*

LINENS
Fabric & Fashion Playroom

FABRICS | Silks and fancy fabrics share space with colorful batiks, African Kente and Caribbean madras prints, ribbons, and accessories in this small shop off the beaten path. ⊠ *5412 Store Gade, Charlotte Amalie* ✛ *½ block north of the Greenhouse Restaurant* ☎ *340/714–4410*

Mr. Tablecloth

FABRICS | This store has prices to please, and the friendly staff here will help you choose from the floor-to-ceiling selection of linens, which include Tuscan lace

Red Hook stretches over a rolling coastline on the East Side of St. Thomas.

tablecloths and Irish linen pillowcases. ⊠ *6 Main St., Charlotte Amalie* ☎ *340/774–4343* ⊕ *www.mrtablecloth-vi.com.*

LIQUOR AND TOBACCO

A. H. Riise Liquors and Tobacco

TOBACCO | This giant duty-free liquor outlet carries a large selection of tobacco (including imported cigars), as well as cordials, wines, and rare vintage Armagnacs, cognacs, ports, and Madeiras. It also stocks fruits in brandy and harware from England. Enjoy rum samples at the tasting bar. ⊠ *37 Main St., at Riise's Alley, Charlotte Amalie* ☎ *340/777–2222* ⊕ *www.ahriise.com.*

East End

Although the eastern end has many major resorts and spectacular beaches, don't be surprised if a cow, a herd of goats, or even a deer crosses your path as you drive through the relatively flat, dry terrain. You can pick up sandwiches from the market in the Red Hook area if you want a picnic lunch.

◉ Sights

★ Coral World Ocean Park

AQUARIUM | FAMILY | This interactive aquarium and water-sports center lets you experience a variety of sea life and other animals. In the 2-acre dolphin habitat, you can swim with these graceful creatures. There are also several outdoor pools where you can pet baby sharks, feed stingrays, touch starfish, and view endangered sea turtles. During the Sea Trek Helmet Dive, you walk along an underwater trail wearing a helmet that provides a continuous supply of air. You can also try Snuba, a cross between snorkeling and scuba diving. Swim with a sea lion for the chance to play ball or get a big, wet, whiskered kiss. The park also has an offshore underwater observatory, an 80,000-gallon coral reef exhibit (one of the largest in the world), and a nature trail with native ducks and tortoises. Daily feedings take place at most exhibits.

✉ *6450 Estate Smith Bay, Estate Smith Bay* ✛ *Coki Point Rd. north of Rte. 38* ☎ *340/775–1555* ⊕ *www.coralworldvi.com* 🎫 *$23.50* ⊘ *Closed Fri. and Sat.*

Red Hook

MARINA/PIER | The IGY American Yacht Harbor marina here has fishing and sailing charter boats, a dive shop, and powerboat-rental agencies. There are also several bars and restaurants, including the Caribbean Saloon, The Tap & Still, Island Time Pub, Raw Sushi & Sake Bar, and Duffy's Love Shack. Other services include mail service, drug and grocery stores, and medical services. Ferries depart from here to St. John and the BVI. ✉ *Red Hook, Rtes. 38 and 32, Red Hook.*

Beaches

Coki Beach

BEACH | **FAMILY** | Funky beach huts selling local foods such as pates (fried turnovers with a spicy ground-beef filling), quaint vendor kiosks, and a brigade of hair braiders and taxi men make this beach overlooking picturesque Thatch Cay feel like a carnival. But this is the best place on the island to snorkel and scuba dive. Fish—including grunts, snappers, and wrasses—are like an effervescent cloud you can wave your hand through. **Amenities:** local food and drink; lifeguards; parking; showers; toilets; water sports. **Best for:** partiers; snorkeling; learning to scuba dive. ✉ *End of Rte. 388, off Rte. 38, Estate Smith Bay* ✛ *Next to Coral World Ocean Park.*

Lindquist Beach

BEACH | **FAMILY** | This public beach has a serene sense of wilderness that isn't found on the more crowded beaches. A lifeguard is on duty between 8 am and 5 pm and picnic tables and restrooms are available. Try snorkeling over the offshore reef. **Amenities:** lifeguards; parking; toilets. **Best for:** swimming; snorkeling. ✉ *Rte. 38, Estate Smith Bay* ✛ *At end of*

a paved road, adjacent to a paved parking lot ☎ *340/777–6300* 🎫 *$5.*

Sapphire Beach

BEACH | **FAMILY** | A steady breeze makes this beach a windsurfer's paradise. The swimming is great, as is the snorkeling, especially at the reef near Pettyklip Point. Beach volleyball is big on the weekends as is a Sunday live music beach jam. There's a small restaurant serving breakfast and lunch. **Amenities:** parking; toilets. **Best for:** snorkeling; swimming; windsurfing. ✉ *Rte. 38, Sapphire Bay* ✛ *½ mile (1 km) north of Red Hook.*

Secret Harbour

BEACH | Placid waters make it easy to stroke your way out to a swim platform offshore from the Secret Harbour Beach Resort & Villas. Nearby reefs give snorkelers a natural show. There's a bar and restaurant as well as a dive shop where you can rent beach lounge chairs. **Amenities:** food and drink; parking; toilets; water sports. **Best for:** snorkeling; sunset; swimming. ✉ *Rte. 322, Nazareth* ✛ *Take 1st right off Rte. 322.*

Vessup Beach

BEACH | This wild, undeveloped beach is lined with sea grape trees and century plants. It's close to Red Hook harbor, so you can watch the ferries depart. The calm waters are excellent for swimming. It's popular with locals on weekends. **Amenities:** parking; water sports. **Best for:** swimming. ✉ *Off Rte. 322, Nazareth.*

🍴 Restaurants

Caribbean Saloon

$$$ | **AMERICAN** | Sports on wide-screen TVs and live music on weekends are two added attractions at this hip sports bar that's in the center of the action in Red Hook. The menu ranges from finger-licking barbecue ribs to more sophisticated fare, such as the signature filet mignon wrapped in bacon and smothered in melted Gorgonzola cheese. **Known for:** fresh catch of the day; late-night menu;

ive music on the weekends. $ *Average main: $28* ⊠ *American Yacht Harbor, Bldg. B, Rte. 32, Red Hook* ☎ *340/775–7060* ⊕ *www.caribbeansaloon.com.*

Duffy's Love Shack

$$ | ECLECTIC | If the floating bubbles don't attract you to this zany eatery billed as the "ultimate tropical drink shack," the lime-green shutters, loud rock music, and fun-loving waitstaff just might. The menu has a selection of burgers, tacos, burritos, and salads, and bartenders shake up such exotic concoctions as the Love Shack Volcano—a 50-ounce flaming extravaganza. **Known for:** grilled fish tacos; the Caribbean Pu-Pu platter sampler; tropical cocktails. $ *Average main: $19* ⊠ *Red Hook Shopping Center, Rte. 32 and 6500 Red Hook Plaza, Red Hook* ⊹ *In the parking lot* ☎ *340/779–2080* ⊕ *www.duffysloveshack.com.*

★ Old Stone Farmhouse

$$$$ | ECLECTIC | At this beautifully restored plantation house, guests can dine on sophisticated starters such as pastrami-cured duck confit or foie gras in nutmeg crepes and simply elegant surf-and-turf selections like grass-fed filet mignon or butter-poached lobster. Splurge on an order of California Oestra Cavier served with all the fixings like blinis, egg yolks, and cream fraiche. **Known for:** excellent service; elegant setting; well-prepared dishes. $ *Average main: $48* ⊠ *Rte. 42, Lovenlund* ⊹ *1 mile (1½ km) west of entrance to Mahogany Run Golf Course* ☎ *340/777–6277* ⊕ *www. oldstonefarmhouse.net* ⊗ *Closed Mon. and Tues.*

★ Pizza Pi

$$ | PIZZA | FAMILY | Sail up in a boat, paddle by in a kayak, or drive out in a dinghy to pick up freshly made New York–style pizza from this "floating" food truck. This 37-foot motor sailor is an authentic brick-oven pizzeria, serving pizzas topped with locally grown basil and fresh lobster. **Known for:** one-of-a-kind location; delicious pizza; inventive toppings.

$ *Average main: $16* ⊠ *Christmas Cove, Great St. James Island* ⊹ *Across from Cowpet Bay, on the east end of St. Thomas* ☎ *340/643–4674* ⊕ *www. pizza-pi.com.*

3 Palms Restaurant

$$$$ | AMERICAN | Come early to sip a craft cocktail on the comfy outdoor deck couches overlooking the American Yacht Harbor Marina. Inside, you'll find an ever-changing menu focusing on freshly caught seafood and locally grown veggies, fruits, and microgreens. **Known for:** local seafood; craft cocktails; harbor view. $ *Average main: $32* ⊠ *American Yacht Harbor complex, 6100 Red Hook Road, Red Hook* ☎ *340/643–3429* ⊕ *3palmsvi.com.*

★ XO Bistro

$$$$ | CONTEMPORARY | Tucked into a Red Hook shopping center, this down-home eatery has a congenial atmosphere and well-prepared sandwiches, flatbreads, and entrées that make it popular with local professionals. Come early for a seat at the bar and get the scoop on local island news. **Known for:** more upscale food than surrounding restaurants; theme nights; friendly waitstaff with island knowledge. $ *Average main: $36* ⊠ *6501 Red Hook Plaza, Red Hook* ☎ *340/779–2069* ⊕ *www.xobistro.net.*

🛏 Hotels

You can find most of the large, luxurious beachfront resorts on St. Thomas's East End. The downside is that these properties are about a 30-minute drive from town and a 45-minute drive from the airport (substantially longer during peak hours). On the upside, these properties tend to be self-contained; plus, there are a number of good restaurants, shops, and water-sports operators in the area. Once you've settled in, you don't need a car to get around.

Point Pleasant Resort
$$$ | **RESORT** | Hilltop suites give you an eagle's-eye view of the East End and beyond, and those in a building adjacent to the reception area offer incredible sea views, but the sea-level junior suites, where the sounds of lapping waves lull you to sleep, are smaller. **Pros:** there's a resort shuttle; convenient kitchens; pleasant pools. **Cons:** steep climb from beach; need a car to get around; some rooms need refurbishing. [$] *Rooms from: $475* ✉ *6600 Estate Smith Bay, off Rte. 38, Estate Smith Bay* ☎ *340/775–7200, 888/619–4010* 🌐 *www.pointpleasantresort.com* 🛏 *128 suites* 🍴 *No Meals.*

Ritz-Carlton, St. Thomas
$$$$ | **RESORT** | **FAMILY** | Everything sparkles at the island's most luxurious resort, from the in-room furnishings and amenities to the infinity pool, white-sand, eco-friendly Blue Flag–designated beach, and turquoise sea beyond. **Pros:** gorgeous views; great water-sports facilities; beautiful beach; airport shuttle. **Cons:** steep resort fee; food and drink is expensive ($29 hamburger, $15 piña colada); half-hour or more drive to town and airport. [$] *Rooms from: $1,525* ✉ *6900 Estate Great Bay, off Rte. 317, Estate Great Bay* ☎ *340/775–3333, 800/241–3333* 🌐 *www.ritzcarlton.com* 🛏 *180 rooms* 🍴 *No Meals.*

Secret Harbour Beach Resort
$$$ | **RESORT** | There's not a bad view from these low-rise studio, one-, and two-bedroom condos, which are either beachfront or perched on a hill overlooking an inviting cove. **Pros:** beautiful beach and great snorkeling; good restaurant; secluded location. **Cons:** some rooms are small; car needed to get around; condo owners are territorial about beach chairs. [$] *Rooms from: $475* ✉ *Rte. 317, 6280 Estate Nazareth, Nazareth* ☎ *340/775–6550, 800/524–2250* 🌐 *www.secretharbourvi.com* 🛏 *49 suites* 🍴 *Free Breakfast.*

Two Sandals by the Sea
$$ | **B&B/INN** | This cozy bed-and-breakfast feels like a home away from home because of its casual ambience, picturesque setting overlooking Red Hook Harbor, and the friendliness of the owners. **Pros:** quaint and clean; close to beaches; breakfast included in price. **Cons:** a little too intimate for some; need a car to get around; no pool. [$] *Rooms from: $350* ✉ *On Ridge Rd., 6264 Estate Nazareth, Nazareth* ☎ *340/998–2395* 🌐 *www.twosandals.com* 🛏 *6 rooms* 🍴 *Free Breakfast.*

Shopping

Red Hook has **American Yacht Harbor,** a waterfront shopping area with a dive shop, a tackle store, clothing and jewelry boutiques, a bar, and a few restaurants.

Don't forget **St. John.** A ferry ride (an hour from Charlotte Amalie or 20 minutes from Red Hook) will take you to the charming shops of **Mongoose Junction** and **Wharfside Village,** which specialize in unusual, often island-made articles.

CLOTHING

Caribbean Surf Co.
MIXED CLOTHING | **FAMILY** | There's something for every beachgoer, surfer, and sunbather at this local, family-owned surf store. Billabong, Oakley, and Reef swimwear, sunglasses, and sandals are available for adults and children, as well as surfboards and surf gear. There is a second location at Havensight Mall. ✉ *6500 Red Hook Plaza, Suite 205, Red Hook* ☎ *340/774–3583.*

FOODSTUFFS

Food Center
FOOD | This supermarket sells fresh produce, meats, and seafood. There's also an on-site bakery and deli with hot and cold prepared foods, which are the big draw here, especially for those renting villas, condos, or charter boats in the East End area. ✉ *Rte. 32, 1 mile (2 km) west of Red*

look, Estate Frydenhoj ☎ 340/777–8806 ⊕ www.foodcentervi.com.

Moe's Fresh Market

FOOD | This gourmet market near the ferry to St. John has the best deli cheeses, prepared-to-order subs, and selection of organic foods, coffees, and wines on the island. Two other locations are at Yacht Haven Grande near the cruise ship dock in Havensight and at the corner of Waterfront Drive and Espanole Strade in Charlotte Amalie. ✉ *6502 Smith Bay Rd., Rte. 32, Red Hook* ☎ *340/693–0254* ⊕ *www.moesvi.com.*

JEWELRY

Little Switzerland

JEWELRY & WATCHES | Designer jewelry available in this major chain includes David Yurman, Bulgari, Chopard, and Penny Preville. There is also an extensive selection of watches. ✉ *Ritz-Carlton, St. Thomas, Rte. 322, Nazareth* ☎ *248/809–5560 ext. 10050* ⊕ *www.littleswitzerland. com.*

Tradewinds Galleria

JEWELRY & WATCHES | Caribbean Hook bracelets, made of sterling silver or 14k gold, are the pieces to buy at this marina-located shop. You can also find rings, necklaces, and pendants. ✉ *American Yacht Harbor Marina, 6100 Red Hook Qtr C14, Red Hook* ☎ *340/775–5595.*

South Shore

 Sights

French Heritage Museum

HISTORY MUSEUM | The museum houses fishing nets, accordions, tambourines, mahogany furniture, photographs, and other artifacts illustrating the lives of the island's French descendants during the 18th through 20th centuries. Admission is free, but donations are accepted. ✉ *Rue de St. Anne and rue de St. Barthélemy, next to Joseph Aubain Ballpark, Frenchtown* ☎ *340/714–2583*

⊕ *www.frenchheritagemuseum.com* ✉ *Free, donations accepted.*

Frenchtown

BUSINESS DISTRICT | Popular for its bars and restaurants, Frenchtown is also the home of descendants of immigrants from St. Barthélemy (St. Barth). You can watch them pull up their brightly painted boats and display their equally colorful catch of the day along the waterfront. If you chat with them, you can hear speech patterns slightly different from those of other St. Thomians. Get a feel for the residential district of Frenchtown by walking west to some of the town's winding streets, where tiny wooden houses have been passed down from generation to generation. ✉ *Turn south off Waterfront Hwy. (Rte. 30) at post office, Frenchtown.*

Skyride to Paradise Point

VIEWPOINT | **FAMILY** | Fly skyward in a seven-minute gondola ride to Paradise Point, an overlook with breathtaking views of Charlotte Amalie, the harbor, and the neighboring islands of St. Croix to the south and Vieques and Culebra, Puerto Rico, to the west. You'll find several shops, a bar (the specialty here is the Bushwacker, a creamy frozen cocktail), and a restaurant. Alternatively, you could skip the $25 gondola ride and take a taxi to the top for $7 per person from the Havensight Dock. ✉ *Rte. 30, across from Havensight Mall, Havensight* ☎ *340/774–9809* ⊕ *www.paradisepointvi. com* ✉ *$25.*

★ **Virgin Islands Children's Museum**

CHILDREN'S MUSEUM | **FAMILY** | Giant bubble makers, a rainbow-colored gear table, and a larger-than-life abacus are just a few of the interactive exhibits at this indoor, family-friendly, play-and-learn museum. Science was never so fun! ✉ *Buccaneer Mall, Rte. 30, Havensight* ⊹ *Across from the cruise ship dock* ☎ *340/643–0366* ⊕ *www.vichildrensmuseum.org* ✉ *$10* ⊙ *Closed Mon.*

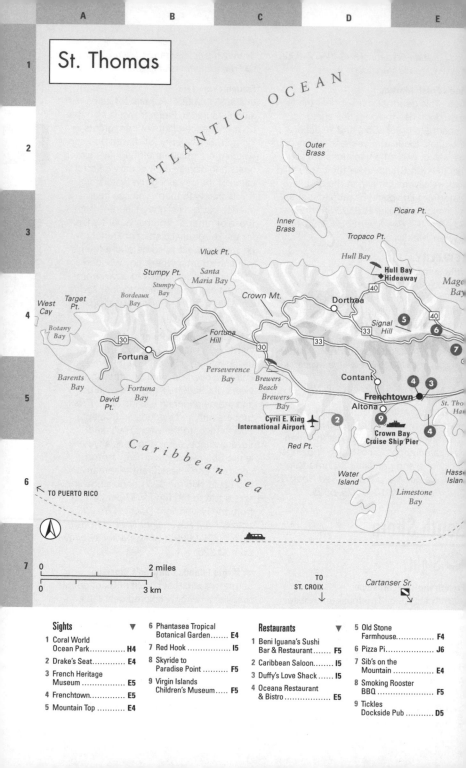

St. Thomas

ATLANTIC OCEAN

Outer Brass

Inner Brass

Picara Pt.

Tropaco Pt.

Hull Bay

Hull Bay Hideaway

Vluck Pt.

Stumpy Pt.

Santa Maria Bay

Crown Mt.

Dorthea

40

Signal Hill

5

40

6

7

Stumpy Bay

Bordeaux Bay

West Cay

Target Pt.

Botany Bay

30

Fortuna Hill

30

33

33

Fortuna

Mage Bay

Barents Bay

Perseverance Bay

Brewers Beach

Brewers Bay

Contant

Frenchtown

Altona

4 3

St. Tho Ha

David Pt.

Fortuna Bay

Cyril E. King International Airport

2

9

Crown Bay Cruise Ship Pier

4

Red Pt.

Caribbean Sea

Water Island

Limestone Bay

Hass Islan

TO PUERTO RICO

0   2 miles
0   3 km

TO ST. CROIX

Cartanser Sr.

Sights ▼

1 Coral World Ocean Park............. **H4**
2 Drake's Seat............. **E4**
3 French Heritage Museum **E5**
4 Frenchtown............. **E5**
5 Mountain Top **E4**
6 Phantasea Tropical Botanical Garden....... **E4**
7 Red Hook **I5**
8 Skyride to Paradise Point **F5**
9 Virgin Islands Children's Museum **F5**

Restaurants ▼

1 Beni Iguana's Sushi Bar & Restaurant **F5**
2 Caribbean Saloon........ **I5**
3 Duffy's Love Shack **I5**
4 Oceana Restaurant & Bistro **E5**
5 Old Stone Farmhouse................ **F4**
6 Pizza Pi..................... **J6**
7 Sib's on the Mountain **E4**
8 Smoking Rooster BBQ **F5**
9 Tickles Dockside Pub **D5**

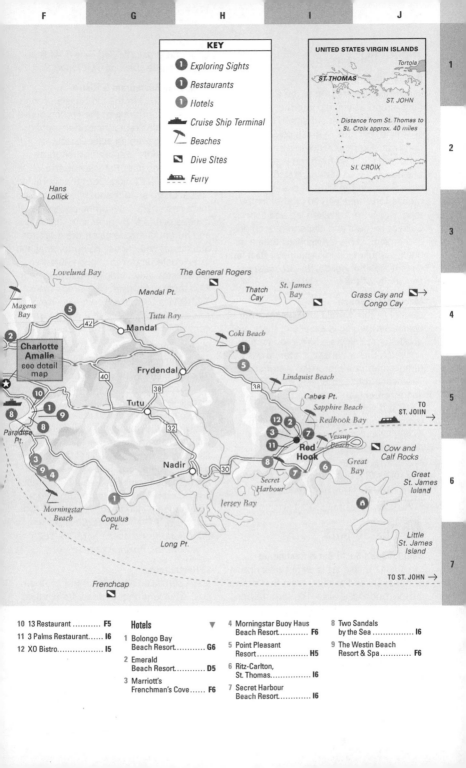

KEY

- ❶ Exploring Sights
- ❶ Restaurants
- ❶ Hotels
- Cruise Ship Terminal
- Beaches
- Dive Sites
- Ferry

UNITED STATES VIRGIN ISLANDS

Tortola

ST. THOMAS

ST. JOHN

Distance from St. Thomas to
St. Croix approx. 40 miles

ST. CROIX

Hans
Lollick

Lovelund Bay

Mandal Pt.

The General Rogers

Thatch
Cay

St. James
Bay

Grass Cay and
Congo Cay

Magens
Bay

Tutu Bay

Mandal

Coki Beach

Lindquist Beach

Charlotte
Amalie
see detail
map

Frydendal

Cabes Pt.

Sapphire Beach

TO
ST. JOHN

Tutu

Redhook Bay

Paradise
Pt.

Red
Hook

Vessup
Beach

Cow and
Calf Rocks

Nadir

Great
Bay

Great
St. James
Island

Secret
Harbour

Jersey Bay

Morningstar
Beach

Coculus
Pt.

Long Pt.

Little
St. James
Island

TO ST. JOHN →

Frenchcap

Beaches

Brewers Beach

BEACH | Watch jets land at the Cyril E. King Airport as you dip into the usually calm seas. Rocks at either end of the shoreline, patches of grass poking randomly through the sand, and shady tamarind trees 30 feet from the water give this beach a wild, natural feel. Civilization has arrived, in the form of one or two mobile food vans parked on the nearby road. Buy a fried-chicken leg and Johnny Cake or burgers and chips to munch on at the picnic tables. **Amenities:** food and drink; lifeguards; parking; toilets. **Best for:** sunset; swimming. ✉ *Rte. 30, west of University of the Virgin Islands.*

Morningstar Beach

BEACH | At this ¼-mile-long (½-km-long) beach, swimming is excellent; there are good-size rolling waves year-round, but do watch the undertow. Water sports rentals offer non-motorized water sports. The beachfront Salt Shack restaurant serves breakfast, lunch, and dinner. At 7 am and again at 5 pm, you can catch the cruise ships gliding majestically out to sea from the Charlotte Amalie harbor. **Amenities:** parking. **Best for:** surfing; swimming. ✉ *Rte. 315, Estate Bakkero* ✥ *2 miles (3 km) southeast of Charlotte Amalie, past Havensight Mall and cruise-ship dock.*

Restaurants

Beni Iguana's Sushi Bar & Restaurant

$$ | SUSHI | Edible art is an apt description of the sushi and sashimi feast that draws visitors and locals alike. The favorite here is steamed mussels in a house-made creamy sesame dressing dubbed "iguana sauce," which is, happily, not made from the spiny reptile that roams the island's hillsides and roadways. **Known for:** vegetarian options; fresh seafood; red snapper roll. [$] *Average main: $18* ✉ *Havensight Mall, West Indian Dock Rd., Bldg. IX, facing the cruise ship dock, Charlotte Amalie* ☎ *340/777–8744* 🌐 *beniiguanassushibar.com* 🕒 *Closed Sun.*

★ **Oceana Restaurant & Bistro**

$$$$ | ECLECTIC | In the old Russian consulate house at the tip of the Frenchtown peninsula, this restaurant offers superb views along with an eclectic array of dishes expertly prepared by longtime Virgin Islands chef Patricia LaCorte and her staff. Choose from the more casual bistro-style menu, which features taste-and-share charcuterie and artisanal cheese plates and entrées like flatbreads and burgers, or splurge on the more formal dinner selections like butter-poached local lobster and filet mignon. **Known for:** seaside view; indulgent dishes; near Frenchtown nightlife. [$] *Average main: $42* ✉ *Villa Olga, 8A Honduras, Frenchtown* ☎ *340/774–4262* 🌐 *www.oceanavi.com* 🕒 *No dinner Sun.*

Smoking Rooster BBQ

$$ | BARBECUE | House-smoked, hand-rubbed meats with a side of rum are the specialty here. Order the sampler platter for a taste of everything: choice of two meats like pulled pork and beef brisket, two sides such as potato mac salad (a mishmash of two favorites with a flavor all its own) and brisket beans, plus pickled veggies and Texas toast. **Known for:** barbecue with house-made dry rubs; artisan craft beer and huge rum selection; house-pickled veggie sides. [$] *Average main: $19* ✉ *Havensight Mall, Rte. 30, Charlotte Amalie* ☎ *340/715–2625* 🌐 *www.thesmokingrooster.com.*

13 Restaurant

$$$$ | SOUTHERN | A flavor of the southern U.S. is evident on the menu, from a fried green tomato appetizer to entrées like shrimp 'n grits and a southern fish fry with cornmeal-coated catfish. This same down-home theme is served for Sunday brunch. **Known for:** upscale twist on Southern favorites; casual local vibe; marina-front view. [$] *Average main: $34* ✉ *5304 Yacht Haven Grande, Route 30, Charlotte Amalie* ☎ *340/774–6800* 🌐 *13restaurant.com.*

Hotels

The south shore of St. Thomas connects to the east end of the island via a beautiful road that rambles along the hillside, with frequent peeks between the hills for views of the ocean, and, on a clear day, of St. Croix some 40 miles (60 km) to the south. The resorts here are on their own beaches. They offer several opportunities for water sports, as well as land-based activities, fine dining, and evening entertainment.

Bolongo Bay Beach Resort
$$$$ | **RESORT** | **FAMILY** | All the rooms at this family-run resort tucked along a palm-lined beach have balconies with ocean views; down the beach are nine condos with full kitchens. **Pros:** family-run property; on the beach; water sports abound. **Cons:** beach casual; on a busy road; need a car to get around. [$] *Rooms from: $550* ✉ *Rte. 30, Bolongo* ☎ *340/775–1800, 800/524–4746* 🌐 *www.bolongobay.com* 🛏 *74 rooms* 🍴 *All-Inclusive.*

Marriott's Frenchman's Cove
$$$$ | **TIMESHARE** | **FAMILY** | Not to be confused with neighboring Frenchman's Reef Hotel, this beachfront villa-style timeshare property offers the glitz of a resort with the comfort and amenities of a private club. **Pros:** infinity pool with waterslide; ferry service to Charlotte Amalie; secluded beach. **Cons:** limited parking for those with rental cars; only one restaurant on property; adjoining hotel property is closed, thus no current access to walking distance shops, restaurants, and an additional beach. [$] *Rooms from: $690* ✉ *7338 Estate Bakkeroe, Estate Bakkero* ☎ *340/693–4800* 🌐 *www.marriott.com* 🛏 *221 rooms* 🍴 *No Meals.*

Morningstar Buoy Haus Beach Resort
$$$$ | **RESORT** | There's a boutique-style intimate beach club vibe at this Frenchman's Reef oceanfront property where even garden view rooms in the five low-rise buildings are only steps away from the ¼-mile long white sand beach. **Pros:** room service; romantic setting; beachfront location. **Cons:** lots of walking; limited dining; need a taxi or rental car to explore the island. [$] *Rooms from: $1020* ✉ *2 Estate Bakkeroe* ☎ *340/249–0123, 800/228–9290 toll free* 🛏 *94 rooms, 2 suites* 🍴 *No Meals.*

The Westin Beach Resort & Spa
$$$$ | **RESORT** | Fully renovated and re-opened in 2023, this 8-floor, high-rise, family-friendly resort by Frenchman's Reef sits on a cliff overlooking the Charlotte Amalie harbor. **Pros:** oceanfront views; several dining options; plenty of activities. **Cons:** lots of walking; need a taxi or rental car to explore the island; can be a crowded cruise ship feel in peak season. [$] *Rooms from: $810* ✉ *5 Estate Bakkeroe* ☎ *888/236–2427 toll free, 340/249–0100* 🛏 *392 rooms, 28 suites* 🍴 *No Meals.*

Nightlife

Iggies Oasis
LIVE MUSIC | Bolongo Bay's poolside bar and restaurant offers live music on the weekends. ✉ *Bolongo Bay Beach Resort, Rte. 30, Bolongo* ☎ *340/775–1800* 🌐 *www.bolongobay.com.*

Performing Arts

The Forum
MUSIC | A mix of live musical performances, film festivals, and operas are held here from October through May each year. Tickets are $30 for adults and $5 for students, making this a fun and affordable way to spend an evening with the classics. ✉ *Prior-Jollek Hall, Antilles School, 7280 Frenchman's Bay Road, Off Rte 30* ☎ *646/725–2252* 🌐 *theforumusvi.com* ☞ *$30 for adults, $5 for students, free for children.*

Mocko Jumbie Magic

Mocko Jumbies, the island's other-worldly stilt walkers, trace their roots back to West Africa. The steps of the stilt walkers held religious significance in West Africa, but today's West Indian version is more secular—bending backward to gravity-defying lengths and high kicking to the pulsating beat of drums, bells, and whistles.

Today satins and sequins have replaced costumes made of grasses, shells, and feathers. Festive headpieces—braids of feathers, glittering crowns, tall hats, and even spiky horns—attract plenty of attention from onlookers. A mask completes the outfit, assuring that the dancer's identity is concealed from spectators, thus maintaining the magic of the Mocko Jumbie.

Beyond Carnival celebrations, the Mocko Jumbie is so popular that it's a mainstay at many hotels. Mocko Jumbie dancers also perform at store openings, when cruise ships dock, or even at weekend beach jams. Old-fashioned or newfangled, Mocko Jumbies will always be loved best for driving away "jumbie spirits," as they say in the islands.

🛍 Shopping

West of Charlotte Amalie, the pink-stucco **Nisky Center**, on Harwood Highway about ½ mile (¾ km) east of the airport, is more of a hometown shopping center than a tourist area.

At the Crown Bay cruise-ship pier, the **Crown Bay Center**, off the Harwood Highway in Subbase about ½ mile (¾ km) west of Frenchtown, has quite a few shops, but they only tend to be open on days when a cruise ship is docked at the Crown Bay Cruise Ship Pier.

Havensight Mall, next to the cruise-ship dock, may not be as charming as downtown Charlotte Amalie, but it does have more than 60 shops. It also has an excellent bookstore, a bank, a pharmacy, a gourmet grocery, and smaller branches of many downtown stores. The shops at **Port of Sale**, adjoining Havensight Mall (its buildings are pink instead of brown), sell discount goods. Next door to Port of Sale is the **Yacht Haven Grande** complex, a stunning megayacht marina with beautiful, safe walkways and many upscale shops.

East of Charlotte Amalie on Route 38, **Tillett Gardens** is an oasis of artistic endeavor across from the Tutu Park Shopping Mall.

Tutu Park Shopping Mall, across from Tillett Gardens, is the island's one and only enclosed mall. More than 30 stores and a food court are anchored by Kmart and Plaza Extra grocery store.

ART GALLERIES
Mango Tango

ART GALLERIES | This gallery sells and displays works by popular local artists—originals, prints, and note cards. There's a one-person or multiple-person show at least one weekend a month. ✉ 4003 Raphune Hill, off Rte. 38, Raphune Hill, above the Paint Depot, ½ mile (1 km) east of Charlotte Amalie, Raphune 📞 340/777–3060 ⊕ www.mangotangoart. com.

CAMERAS AND ELECTRONICS
Boolchand's

ELECTRONICS | This store sells brand-name cameras, audio and video equipment, and binoculars. ✉ Havensight Mall, Rte. 30, Bldg. II, Suite C, Havensight 📞 340/725–1614 ⊕ www.boolchand.com.

Royal Caribbean

ELECTRONICS | A wide selection of cameras, watches, and clocks are stocked here. The store has two outlets, one on Main Street in Charlotte Amalie and the other at the cruise ship pier in Crown Bay. The Crown Bay store, located 1-mile west of Frenchtown, is only open when a ship is in port. ⊠ *Crown Bay Commercial Center, Rte. 30, Charlotte Amalie* ☎ *340/ 779–6372* ⊕ *www.royalcaribbeanvi.com*

CLOTHING

White House/Black Market

WOMEN'S CLOTHING | This boutique sells sophisticated clothing for women. You'll find just the right party or evening-wear look in dresses, tops, and bottoms made out of everything from sequins to shimmering and satiny fabrics. Check out the perpetual sale rack in the back for the best deals. ⊠ *5316 Yacht Haven Grande, Suite 116, Charlotte Amalie* ☎ *340/776–5566* ⊕ *www.whitehouseblackmarket.com.*

FOODSTUFFS

Cost-U-Less

FOOD | This is the Caribbean equivalent of Costco and Sam's Club and it sells everything from soup to nuts—in giant sizes and case lots—without a membership fee. The meat-and-seafood department, however, has family-size portions. There's a well-stocked fresh-produce section and a case filled with rotisserie chicken and baked goods. ⊠ *Rte. 38, ¼ mile (½ km) west of Rte. 39 intersection, Estate Annas Retreat* ☎ *340/777–3588* ⊕ *www.costuless.com.*

★ Fruit Bowl

FOOD | This grocery store is the best place on the island to go for fresh fruits and vegetables. There are many ethnic, vegetarian, and health-food items as well as a fresh meat area, seafood department, and extensive salad and hot food bar. ⊠ *Wheatley Center, Intersection of Rtes. 38 and 313, Charlotte Amalie* ☎ *340/774–8565* ⊕ *www. thefruitbowlvi.com.*

Plaza Extra

FOOD | This large, U.S.–style supermarket sells everything you need from produce to meat, including fresh seafood, a deli, and a bakery. You can find Caribbean ingredients and there's a liquor department, too. ⊠ *Tutu Park Shopping Mall, Rte. 38, Tutu* ☎ *340/775–5646* ⊕ *www. plazaextratutu.com.*

PriceSmart

FOOD | This giant emporium carries everything from electronics to housewares in its members-only warehouse-size store. The meat, poultry, and seafood departments are especially popular. A small café in front sells pizzas, hot dogs, and chicken wings. ⊠ *4400 Estate Charlotte Amalie, Rte. 38 west of Fort Mylner, Tutu* ☎ *340/777–3430* ⊕ *www. pricesmart.com.*

JEWELRY

Cardow Jewelers

JEWELRY & WATCHES | This store sells gold in several lengths, widths, sizes, and styles, along with diamonds, emeralds, and other precious gems. You're guaranteed 40% to 60% savings off U.S. retail prices or your money will be refunded within 30 days of purchase. The flagship location is on Main Street. ⊠ *Crown Bay Center, Rte. 305, Crown Bay* ☎ *340/776–2038* ⊕ *www.cardow.com.*

Diamonds International

JEWELRY & WATCHES | At this major chain shop with three outlets on St. Thomas, just choose a diamond, emerald, or tanzanite gem and a mounting, and you can have your dream ring set in an hour. Famous for having the largest inventory of diamonds on the island, this shop welcomes trade-ins, has a U.S. service center, and offers free diamond earrings with every purchase. ⊠ *Havensight Mall, Rte. 30, Bldg. II, Havensight* ☎ *340/776–0040* ⊕ *www.diamondsinternational.com.*

Drake's Seat looks out over a panoramic view of the Virgin Islands.

LIQUOR AND TOBACCO

Duty Free St. Thomas

TOBACCO | This giant duty-free liquor outlet offers a large selection of tobacco (including imported cigars), as well as cordials, wines, and rare vintage Armagnacs, cognacs, ports, and Madeiras. It also stocks fruits in brandy and barware from England. Enjoy rum samples at the tasting bar. Prices are among the best in St. Thomas. ⊠ *Havensight Mall, Rte. 30, Bldg. II, Havensight* ☎ *340/776–2303, 800/315–1600.*

Tobacco Discounters

TOBACCO | This duty-free outlet carries a full line of discounted brand-name cigarettes, cigars, and tobacco accessories. ⊠ *9100 Port of $ale Mall, Rte. 30, next to Havensight Mall, Havensight* ☎ *340/774–2256.*

West End

The west end of the island is lusher and quieter—with fewer houses and less traffic. Here there are roller-coaster routes (made all the scarier because the roads have no shoulders) as well as incredible vistas. Leave time in the afternoon for a swim and enjoy a slice of pizza at Magens Bay before leaving. A day in the country will reveal the tropical pleasures that have enticed more than one visitor to become a resident.

Sights

Drake's Seat

VIEWPOINT | Sir Francis Drake was supposed to have kept watch over his fleet from this vantage point, looking for enemy ships. The panorama is especially breathtaking (and romantic) at dusk, and if you plan to arrive late in the day, you'll miss the hordes of day-trippers on taxi tours who stop here to take pictures.

✉ *Rte. 40, Mafolie* ✣ *Located ¼ mile (½ km) west of the intersection of Rtes. 40 and 35.*

Mountain Top

VIEWPOINT | **FAMILY** | Head out to the observation deck—more than 1,500 feet above sea level—to get a bird's-eye view that stretches from Puerto Rico's out-island of Culebra in the west all the way to the British Virgin Islands to the north. There's also a restaurant, restrooms, and duty-free shops that sell everything from Caribbean art to nautical antiques, ship models, and touristy T-shirts. ✉ *Estate St. Peter* ✣ *Head north off Rte. 33, look for signs* ☎ *340/774–2400* 🌐 *www.mountaintopvi.com* 🎟 *Free.*

Phantasea Tropical Botanical Garden

GARDEN | Orchids, palms, cactus, and bromeliads are a few of the stunning plants that bloom along the self-guided hiking trails. These gardens are the essence of peace and quiet; they are located high on the island's lush north side. There are critters here too: peacocks, hummingbirds, and hermit crabs, to name a few. ✉ *Bishop Dr. (intersection of Rtes. 334 and 33)* ✣ *On the road to Mountain Top* ☎ *340/774–2916* 🌐 *www.stthomasbotanicalgarden.com* 🎟 *$10* ⏰ *Mondays.*

⛱ Beaches

Hull Bay

BEACH | Watch surfers ride the waves here from December to March, when huge swells roll in from north Atlantic storms. The rest of the year, tranquility prevails at this picturesque neighborhood beach. Enjoy burgers, tacos, and a game of darts at the Shack at Hull Bay. The Hideaway at Hull Bay is the home of the annual Bastille Day Kingfish Tournament held each July. **Amenities:** food and drink; parking; water sports. **Best for:** swimming; snorkeling; partiers. ✉ *Hull Bay, Rte. 37, at end of road on north side, Estate Hull Bay.*

★ Magens Bay

BEACH | **FAMILY** | Deeded to the island as a public park, this heart-shaped stretch of white sand is considered one of the most beautiful in the world. The bottom of the bay is flat and sandy, so this is a place for sunning and swimming rather than snorkeling. On weekends and holidays, the sounds of music from groups partying under the sheds fill the air. There's a bar, snack shack, and beachwear boutique; bathhouses with restrooms, changing rooms, and saltwater showers are close by. Kayaks and paddleboards are available for rent at the water-sports kiosk. **Amenities:** food and drink; lifeguards; parking (fee); showers; toilets; water sports. **Best for:** partiers; swimming; walking. ✉ *Magens Bay, Rte. 35, at end of road on north side of island* ☎ *340/777–6300* 🌐 *www.magensbayauthority.com* 🎟 *Adults $5, parking $2.*

🍴 Restaurants

Sib's on the Mountain

$$ | **AMERICAN** | **FAMILY** | With live music and football on TV, Sib's is the perfect place for a casual dinner after a day at the beach. In addition to burgers, barbecue ribs and chicken, and beer, there's also a breakfast café outside with island-roasted coffees, including the signature "Bushwackercappuccino." **Known for:** casual American-style foods; historic locals hangout; gaming machines. [$] *Average main: $19* ✉ *Rte. 35, Mafolie* ☎ *340/774–8967* 🌐 *sibsonthemountain.com.*

Tickles Dockside Pub

$$ | **AMERICAN** | **FAMILY** | Nautical types and locals come here for casual fare with homey appeal: chicken-fried steak, meat loaf with mashed potatoes, and baby back ribs. Hearty breakfasts feature eggs and pancakes, and lunch is an array of burgers, salads, sandwiches, and soups. **Known for:** marina views; hearty food; Sunday brunch. [$] *Average main: $18* ✉ *8168 Crown Bay Marina, Suite 308,*

Did You Know?

With its flat, sandy bottom, Magens Bay is one of the best swimming beaches on St. Thomas. After your outing, stop by Udder Delights east of the beach for a milkshake, rum-spiked or not.

Contant ✥ off Rte. 304 ☎ *340/777–8792* 🌐 *www.ticklesdocksidepub.com.*

Hotels

A few lodging properties are on the beach to the west near the airport. Otherwise, this area of the island is more sparsely populated and residential.

Emerald Beach Resort

$ | **HOTEL** | You get beachfront ambience at this reasonably priced mini-resort tucked beneath the palm trees, but the trade-off is that it's directly across from a noisy airport runway. **Pros:** beachfront location; good value; great Sunday brunch. **Cons:** airport noise until 10 pm; on a busy road; limited water sports. [$] *Rooms from: $240* ✉ *8070 Lindbergh Bay, Lindbergh Bay* ☎ *340/777–8800* 🌐 *www.emeraldbeach.com* 🛏 *90 rooms* 🍴 *Free Breakfast.*

Activities

AIR TOURS

Caribbean Buzz Helicopters

AIR EXCURSIONS | Near to the UVI field, Caribbean Buzz Helicopters offers a 30-minute tour that includes St. Thomas, St. John, the west end of Tortola, Jost Van Dyke, and all the cays in between. It's a nice ride if you can afford the splurge (tours are from $750 for up to three people), but in truth, you can see most of the aerial sights from Paradise Point or Mountain Top, and there's no place you can't reach easily by car or boat. ✉ *Jet Port, 8202 Lindbergh Bay, Charlotte Amalie* ☎ *340/775–7335* 🌐 *www.caribbean-buzz.com.*

BOATING AND SAILING

Calm seas, crystal waters, and nearby islands (perfect for picnicking, snorkeling, and exploring) make St. Thomas a favorite jumping-off spot for day- or weeklong sails or powerboat adventures. With more than 100 vessels from which to choose, St. Thomas is the charter-boat center of the U.S. Virgin Islands. You can go through a broker to book a sailing vessel with a crew or contact a charter company directly. Crewed charters start at approximately $4,500 per person per week, while bareboat charters can start at as little as $3,000 per person for a 50- to 55-foot sailboat (but this doesn't include provisioning, fuel, and optional add-ons like water-toy rentals), which can comfortably accommodate up to six people. If you want to rent your own boat, hire a captain. (The cost of the service ranges from $100 to $150 per day, plus tip.) Most local captains are excellent tour guides.

Single-day charters are also a possibility. You can hire smaller boats for the day, including the services of a captain if you wish to have someone take you on a guided snorkel trip around the islands.

Island Yachts

BOATING | The sailboats from Island Yachts are available for charter with or without crews. ✉ *6100 Red Hook Quarter, 18B, Red Hook* ☎ *340/344–2143* 🌐 *www.iyc.vi.*

★ **Magic Moments**

BOATING | "Luxury" is the word at Magic Moments, where crews aboard the 45-foot Sea Rays offer pampered island-hopping snorkeling cruises for between $2,100 and $3,250 for up to six people. Nice touches include a chilled prawns-and-Champagne lunch and icy-cold eucalyptus-infused washcloths for freshening up. ✉ *American Yacht Harbor, 6501 Red Hook Plaza, Suite 201, Docks B and C, Red Hook* ☎ *340/775–5066, 800/734–7345* 🌐 *www.yachtmagicmoments.com.*

Stewart Yacht Charters

BOATING | Run by longtime sailor Ellen Stewart, this company is skilled at matching clients with yachts and crews for weeklong charter holidays. ✉ *6501 Red Hook Plaza, Suite 20, Red Hook* ☎ *340/775–1358, 800/432–6118.*

Did You Know?

Motoring around on an underwater scooter can be a leisurely alternative to traditional diving on St. Thomas.

DIVING AND SNORKELING

Popular dive sites include such wrecks as the *Cartanser Sr.*, a beautifully encrusted World War II cargo ship sitting in 35 feet of water, and the *General Rogers*, a Coast Guard cutter resting at 65 feet. Here you can find a gigantic resident barracuda. Reef dives offer hidden caves and archways at **Cow and Calf Rocks,** coral-covered pinnacles at **Frenchcap,** and tunnels where you can explore undersea from the Caribbean to the Atlantic at **Thatch Cay, Grass Cay,** and **Congo Cay.** Many resorts and charter yachts offer dive packages. A one-tank dive starts at $90; two-tank dives are $130 and up. Call the USVI Department of Tourism to obtain a free eight-page guide to Virgin Islands dive sites. There are plenty of snorkeling possibilities, too.

Admiralty Dive Center

SCUBA DIVING | Boat dives, rental equipment, and a retail store are available from this dive center. You can also get multiple-tank packages if you want to dive over several days. ⊠ *Frenchtown Marina, 59 Honduras St., Charlotte Amalie* ☎ *340/777–9802* ⊕ *www.admiralty-dive.com.*

B.O.S.S. Underwater Adventure

SCUBA DIVING | As an alternative to traditional diving, try an underwater motor scooter called a B.O.S.S., or Breathing Observation Submersible Scooter. A 3½-hour tour, including snorkel equipment, rum punch, and towels, is $135 per person. ⊠ *Crown Bay Marina, Rte. 304, Charlotte Amalie* ☎ *340/201–9352* ⊕ *www.bossusvi.com.*

Coki Dive Center

SCUBA DIVING | FAMILY | Snorkeling and dive tours in the fish-filled reefs off Coki Beach are available from this PADI Five Star outfit, as are classes, including one on underwater photography. It's run by the avid diver Peter Jackson. ⊠ *Rte. 388 at Coki Point, Estate Smith Bay* ☎ *340/775–4220* ⊕ *www.cokidive.com.*

Snuba of St. Thomas

SCUBA DIVING | FAMILY | In Snuba, a snorkeling and scuba-diving hybrid, a 20-foot air hose connects you to the surface. The cost is $89. Children must be age eight or older to participate. ⊠ *Rte. 388 at Coki Point, Estate Smith Bay* ☎ *340/693–8063* ⊕ *www.visnuba.com.*

St. Thomas Dive Center

SCUBA DIVING | FAMILY | This PADI Five Star center offers boat dives to the reefs around Buck Island and nearby offshore wrecks, as well as multiday dive packages. ⊠ *Bolongo Bay Beach Resort, Rte. 30, Bolongo* ☎ *340/776–2381* ⊕ *www.stthomasdivecenter.com.*

FISHING

Fishing here is synonymous with blue marlin angling—especially from June through October. Four 1,000-pound-plus blues, including three world records, have been caught on the famous North Drop, about 20 miles (32 km) north of St. Thomas. A day charter for marlin with up to six anglers costs from $1,750 to $2,000 for the day. If you're not into marlin fishing, try hooking sailfish in winter, dolphin (the fish, not the mammal) in spring, and wahoo in fall. Inshore trips for four hours range from $850 to $1,000. To find the trip that will best suit you, walk down the docks at either American Yacht Harbor or Sapphire Beach Marina in the late afternoon and chat with the captains and crews.

Abigail III

FISHING | Captain Red Bailey's *Abigail III* specializes in marlin fishing. ⊠ *Sapphire Beach Marina, Rte. 38, ¼ mile (½ km) northwest of Red Hook, Sapphire Bay* ☎ *340/775–6024* ⊕ *www.visportfish.com.*

★ Double Header Sportfishing

FISHING | FAMILY | This company offers trips out to the North Drop on its 40-foot sportfisher and half-day reef and bay trips aboard its two speedy 37-foot center consoles. ⊠ *Oasis Cove Marina, Rte. 32, Estate Frydenhoj* ☎ *340/777–7317* ⊕ *www.doubleheadersportfishing.net.*

GUIDED TOURS

VI Taxi Association St. Thomas City-Island Tour

DRIVING TOURS | The VI Taxi Association gives a two-hour tour for two people in an open-air safari bus or enclosed van. Aimed at cruise-ship passengers, this $29 tour includes stops at Drake's Seat and Mountain Top. Other tours include a three-hour trip to Coki Beach with a shopping stop in downtown Charlotte Amalie for $35 per person; a three-hour trip to the Coral World Ocean Park for $35 per person; and a five-hour beach tour to St. John for $35 per person. For $60 for two, you can hire a taxi for a customized three-hour drive around the island. Make sure to see Mountain Top, as the view is wonderful. ☎ 340/774–4550 ⊕ vitaxiassociation.com.

SEA EXCURSIONS

Landlubbers and seafarers alike will enjoy the wind in their hair and salt spray in the air while exploring the waters surrounding St. Thomas. Several businesses can book you on a snorkel-and-sail to a deserted cay for a half day that starts at $90 per person or a full day that begins at $140 per person. An excursion over to the British Virgin Islands starts at $145 per person, not including customs fees. A luxury daylong motor-yacht cruise complete with gourmet lunch is $450 or more per person.

St. Thomas Water Sports

BOATING | FAMILY | For a soup-to-nuts choice of sea tours including a stand-up paddleboard safari, full- and half-day sails, sunset cruises, fishing trips, powerboat rentals, and kayak tours, contact this reliable outfitter. ⊠ Marriott's Frenchman's Cove, Rte. 315, Estate Bakkero ☎ 340/473–5708, 340/998–6789 ⊕ www.watersportsvi.com.

SEA KAYAKING

★ **Virgin Islands Ecotours**

KAYAKING | FAMILY | Fish dart, birds sing, and iguanas lounge in trees as you paddle on three- or five-hour guided kayak trips in the Mangrove Lagoon, as well as excursions to Henley, Cas, and Patricia cays. There's also a three-hour stand-up paddleboard and snorkel tour of the lagoon. Three-hour trips include snacks; five-hour trips include lunch. ⊠ Mangrove Lagoon, Rte. 32, 2 miles (3 km) east of Rte. 30, Nadir ☎ 340/779–2155 ⊕ www.viecotours.com.

STAND-UP PADDLEBOARDING

St. Thomas Scuba & Snorkel Adventures

WATER SPORTS | There's a large variety of stand-up paddleboards to rent, something that can suit every family member. The waters off Hull Bay Beach are usually calm, protected by offshore reefs, and ideal for a paddle. ⊠ Hull Bay Hideaway, 10-1 Hull Bay, Estate Hull Bay ☎ 340/474–9332 ⊕ www.stthomasadventures.com ⊠ $60 per day for board; additional $50 for lesson and guide.

TENNIS

The Caribbean sun is hot, so be sure to hit the courts before 10 am or after 5 pm. (Many courts are lighted.) You can indulge in a set or two even if you're staying in a guesthouse without courts; most hotels rent time to nonguests.

Ritz-Carlton, St. Thomas

TENNIS | Two courts are available at the Ritz-Carlton, where nonguests can take lessons. ⊠ 6900 Great Bay, end of Rte. 317, Nazareth ☎ 340/775–3333 ⊕ www.ritzcarlton.com ⊠ $120 per hour and $60 per half hour.

Subbase

TENNIS | There are two public tennis courts, open on a first-come, first-served basis at no cost. Lights are on until 10 pm. ⊠ Rte. 306, next to Water and Power Authority, Charlotte Amalie.

WINDSURFING & KITE-BOARDING

Expect some spills, anticipate the thrills, and try your luck clipping through the seas. Most beachfront resorts rent Windsurfers and offer one-hour lessons for about $150.

Chapter 4

ST. JOHN

4

Updated by
Carol Bareuther

☉ Sights	🍴 Restaurants	🏨 Hotels	🛍 Shopping	🍸 Nightlife
★★★★★	★★★★★	★★★☆☆	★★☆☆☆	★★★☆☆

WELCOME TO ST. JOHN

TOP REASONS TO GO

★ **Beach-hopping:** Fill your cooler with cold drinks, grab the snorkeling gear, and stash your beach chair in the back of your car for a day spent at the beaches along St. John's North Shore Road.

★ **Hiking Reef Bay:** Opt for a trip with a ranger in Virgin Islands National Park. A safari bus takes you to the trailhead, and a boat brings you back.

★ **Snorkeling at Trunk Bay:** Trunk Bay is St. John's most popular snorkeling spot, and for good reason: a snorkeling trail teaches you about the local marine life.

★ **Relaxing in a villa:** There are about 1,000 vacation villas across the island in all sizes, prices, and locations; most will give you all the comforts of home.

★ **Exploring Cruz Bay:** Spend a half day poking around Cruz Bay's varied stores, shopping for that perfect gift for the folks back home.

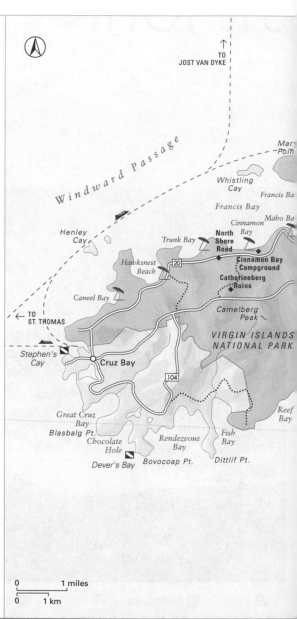

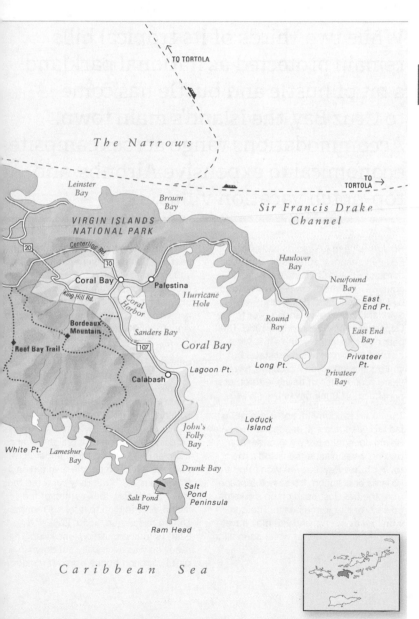

TO TORTOLA

The Narrows

TO
TORTOLA →

Leinster Bay

Brown Bay

Sir Francis Drake Channel

VIRGIN ISLANDS NATIONAL PARK

Centerline Rd.

20

10

Coral Bay

Palestina

Haulover Bay

Newfound Bay

King Hill Rd.

Coral Harbor

Hurricane Hole

East End Pt.

Bordeaux Mountain

Sanders Bay

Round Bay

East End Bay

Reef Bay Trail

107

Coral Bay

Privateer Pt.

Calabash

Lagoon Pt.

Long Pt.

Privateer Bay

Leduck Island

John's Folly Bay

White Pt.   *Lameshur Bay*

Drunk Bay

Salt Pond Peninsula

Salt Pond Bay

Ram Head

Caribbean   Sea

Only 3 miles (5 km) from St. Thomas but still a world apart, St. John is the least developed of the U.S. Virgin Islands. While two-thirds of its tropical hills remain protected as national parkland, a bit of hustle and bustle has come to Cruz Bay, the island's main town. Accommodations range across campsites economical to expensive Airbnbs, and top-notch vacation villas.

St. John's heart is Virgin Islands National Park, a treasure that takes up a full two-thirds of St. John's 20 square miles (53 square km). The park was spearheaded by Laurance S. Rockefeller and Frank Stick and was finally handed over to the Department of the Interior in 1956. The park helps keep the island's interior in its pristine and undisturbed state, but if you go at midday you'll probably have to share your stretch of beach with others, particularly at Trunk Bay.

The island is booming, and it can get a tad crowded at the ever-popular Trunk Bay Beach during the busy winter season; parking woes plague the island's main town of Cruz Bay, but you won't find traffic jams or pollution. It's easy to escape from the fray: just head off on a hike or go early or late to the beach. The sun won't be as strong, and you may have that perfect crescent of white sand all to yourself.

St. John doesn't have a major agrarian past like her sister island, St. Croix, but if you're hiking in the dry season, you can probably stumble upon the stone ruins of old plantations. The less adventuresome can visit the repaired ruins at the park's Annaberg Plantation.

In 1675 Jorgen Iverson claimed the unsettled island for Denmark. By 1733 there were more than 1,000 enslaved people working more than 100 plantations. In that year the island was hit by a drought, hurricanes, and a plague of insects that destroyed the summer crops. With famine as a real threat and the planters keeping them under tight rein, the enslaved people revolted on November 23, 1733. They captured the fort at Coral Bay, took control of the island, and held on to it for six months. During this period, about 20% of the island's total population was killed. The rebellion was eventually put down in part by French troops from Martinique.

lavery continued until 1848, when nslaved people in St. Croix marched on ederiksted to demand their freedom om the Danish government. This time was granted. After emancipation, St. ohn's inhabitants mostly made a living n small farms. Life continued in much e same way until the national park pened in 1956 and tourism became an dustry

f the three U.S. Virgin Islands, St. John, hich has 5,000 residents, has the rongest sense of community, which primarily rooted in a desire to protect e island's natural beauty. Despite the owth, there are still many pockets of anquility. Here you can truly escape e pressures of modern life for a day, a eek—perhaps forever.

Planning

Getting Here and Around

IR

t. John does not have an airport, so you ill need to fly into St. Thomas and then ke a ferry over.

US

lodern Vitran buses on St. John run om the Cruz Bay ferry dock through oral Bay to the far eastern end of the sland at Salt Pond, making numerous tops in between. The fare is $1 to any oint, but the service is slow and not ways reliable.

AR

ou will almost certainly need a car if you re staying in a villa or in Coral Bay, but ou might be able to get by with taxis if ou are staying elsewhere. The terrain St. John is very hilly, the roads are inding, and the blind curves numerous. lajor roads are well paved, but once you et off a specific route, dirt roads filled ith potholes are common. For such riving, a four-wheel-drive vehicle is your

best bet. Be aware that you can't bring all rental cars over to St. John from St. Thomas. Even more important, the barge service is very busy, so you can't always get a space.

St. John has only three gas stations, two in Cruz Bay and one mid-island, so make sure you're not near empty when you set out for Coral Bay.

■TIP→ **Parking in Cruz Bay is difficult, but if you can't find a spot, there's plenty of room at the lot near the public tennis courts. Your best bet is to rent a car from a company that allows you to park in its lot.**

Make sure you ask before you sign on the dotted line if you plan to spend time in Cruz Bay.

CAR RENTALS

All the car-rental companies in St. John are locally owned, and most are just a short walk from the ferry dock in Cruz Bay. Those located a bit farther away will pick you up.

CONTACTS Best. ⊠ *Near library, Cruz Bay* ☎ *340/690–0856* ⊕ *www.bestcar-rentalvi.com.* **Cool Breeze.** ⊠ *1 block east of the passenger ferry dock, Cruz Bay* ☎ *340/776–6588* ⊕ *www.coolbreezecar-rental.com.* **Courtesy.** ⊠ *Near St. Ursula's Church, Cruz Bay* ☎ *340/776–6650* ⊕ *www.courtesycarrental.com.* **Denzil Clyne.** ⊠ *North Shore Rd., across from creek, Cruz Bay* ☎ *340/776–6715.* **O'Connor Car Rental.** ⊠ *Rte. 104, near the roundabout, Cruz Bay* ☎ *340/776–6343* ⊕ *www.oconnorcarrental.com.* **St. John Car Rental.** ⊠ *Bay St., near Wharfside Village, Cruz Bay* ☎ *340/776–6103* ⊕ *www.stjohncarrental.com.*

FERRY

There's frequent daily service from both Red Hook and Charlotte Amalie on St. Thomas to Cruz Bay (the more frequent ferry is the one from Red Hook). There's also frequent service from Cruz Bay to Tortola and less frequent service to the other British Virgin Islands, including

You may meet a sea turtle while snorkeling in the waters of St. John.

Jost Van Dyke (some via Tortola). Virgin Islands ferry schedules are published on the website of the Virgin Islands Vacation Guide and Community. The actual schedules change, so you should check with the ferry companies to determine the current schedules. Remember that a passport is now required to travel between the USVI and BVI by ferry.

CONTACTS Virgin Islands Vacation Guide and Community. ⊕ *www.vinow.com.*

TAXI

Taxis meet ferries arriving in Cruz Bay. Most drivers use vans or open-air safari buses and you can find them congregated at the dock. There are taxi stands at Trunk Bay and Cinnamon Bay. You can also hail taxis anywhere on the road. Almost all trips will be shared, and prices are per person. Paradise Taxi will pick you up if you call, but most drivers don't provide that service. If you need one to pick you up at your rental villa, ask the villa manager to call or arrange a ride in advance.

CONTACTS Paradise Taxi. ⊠ *Waterfront, Cruz Bay* ☏ *340/714–7875.*

Beaches

St. John is blessed with many beaches, and all of them fall into the good, great, and don't-tell-anyone-else-about-this-place categories. Those along the north shore are all within the national park. Some are more developed than others—and many are crowded on weekends, holidays, and in high season—but by and large they're still pristine. Beaches along the south and eastern shores are quiet and isolated.

Hotels

St. John doesn't have many beachfront hotels, but that's a small price to pay for all the pristine sand. The island's one major resort—Westin St. John Resort & Villas—*is* on the beach but is 100% time share. Most villas are in the residential south-shore area, a 15-minute drive from the north-shore beaches. If you head east you come to the laid-back community of Coral Bay, where there are growing numbers of villas and cottages. If you're looking for village charm, there are a few inns in Cruz Bay. Your choice of accommodations also includes condominiums and cottages near town; ecoresorts and campgrounds; and luxurious villas, often with a pool or a hot tub (sometimes both) and a stunning view.

St. John attracts so many different kinds of travelers because accommodations come in all price ranges. Folks on a budget can find inexpensive digs via Airbnb and VRBO. Cruz Bay has a few moderately priced guesthouses and no-frills vacation villas. Those with fatter wallets will have no trouble finding a room at the island's resort or luxury vacation villas. St. John also has several resort-style condo complexes. Many of the island's condos are just minutes from the hustle and bustle of Cruz Bay, but you can find more scattered around the island. You need a car, since most lodgings are in the hills and very few are at the beach.

⇨ *Hotel prices are the lowest cost of a standard double room in high season.*

WHAT IT COSTS in U.S. Dollars

$	$$	$$$	$$$$
HOTELS			
under $276	$276–$375	$376–$475	over $475

Nightlife

St. John isn't the place to go for glitter and all-night partying. Still, after-hours Cruz Bay can be a lively little town in which to dine, drink, and dance. Notices posted on the bulletin board outside the Connections telephone center—up the street from the ferry dock—or listings in the island's print and online newspaper, the *St. John Tradewinds*

(⊕ *stjohntradewinds.com*), will keep you apprised of local events.

Restaurants

The cuisine on St. John seems to get better every year, with culinary school–trained chefs vying to see who can come up with the most imaginative dishes. There are restaurants to suit every taste and budget—from some of the more elegant establishments in Cruz Bay (where the only dress code is "no bathing suits") to the casual beach bars of Coral Bay. For quick lunches, try the West Indian food stands and food trucks in Cruz Bay Park and across from the post office. Some restaurants close for vacation in September and even October. If you have your heart set on a special place, call ahead to make sure it's open during these months. In the December to April peak season, reservations are often required.

With the exception of the grown-on-the-island greens, which you can find in salads at a wide variety of local restaurants, and an occasional catch of local fish, almost all the food served here is imported from the mainland. This means that you may find prices on restaurant menus and supermarket shelves on the high side, since the shipping costs are passed along to the consumer.

⇨ *Restaurant prices are the average cost of a main course at dinner or, if dinner is not served, at lunch.*

WHAT IT COSTS in U.S. Dollars

$	$$	$$$	$$$$
RESTAURANTS			
under $13	$13–$20	$21–$30	over $30

Safety

Although crime is not as prevalent on St. John as it is on St. Thomas and St. Croix, it does exist. Keep your hotel or vacation villa door locked at all times, even during the day if you are, say, out by the pool. Stick to well-lighted streets at night, and use the same kind of street sense that you would in any unfamiliar territory. It's not a good idea to walk around Cruz Bay late at night. If you don't have a car, plan on taking a taxi, which you should arrange in advance.

Tours

On St. John taxi drivers provide tours of the island, making stops at various sites, including Trunk Bay and Annaberg Plantation, for about $35 per person. Rangers at the V.I. National Park Visitors Center give several guided tours on- and offshore (some requiring reservations).

CONTACTS Virgin Islands National Park.
⊠ *North Shore Rd., at creek, Cruz Bay* ☎ *340/776–6201* ⊕ *www.nps.gov/viis.*

Visitor Information

CONTACTS USVI Division of Tourism.
⊠ *Henry Samuel St., next to post office, Cruz Bay* ☎ *340/776–6450* ⊕ *www. visitusvi.com.*

BANKS
St. John has two full-service banks, First Bank VI and Merchants Commercial Bank, located in Cruz Bay. Both banks have ATMs. There is also an ATM at The Marketplace in Cruz Bay, next to Starfish Market.

Cruz Bay and Environs

⊙ Sights

St. John's main town may be compact (it consists of only several blocks), but it's definitely a hub: the ferries from St. Thomas and the British Virgin Islands pull in here, and it's where you can get a taxi or rent a car to travel around the island. There are plenty of shops in which to browse, a number of watering holes where you can stop for a breather, many restaurants, and a grassy square with benches where you can sit back and take everything in. Look for the current edition of the handy, amusing "St. John Map" featuring Max the Mongoose.

★ Virgin Islands National Park
NATIONAL PARK | Covering more than two-thirds of St. John, Virgin Islands National Park preserves the island's natural environments and is a must if you're interested in bird-watching, snorkeling, camping, history, or just strolling in beautiful environs. At Francis Bay there's a boardwalk through the mangroves, where birds may be plentiful; Trunk Bay boasts an underwater snorkel trail while Salt Pond Bay offers pleasant snorkeling too; Cinnamon Bay's campground offers bare sites, eco-tents, and cottages; and you can explore plantation history at Annaberg Sugar Mill and Catherineberg Estate ruins.

There are more than 20 trails on the north and south shores, with guided hikes along the most popular routes. A full-day trip to Reef Bay is a highlight; it's an easy hike through lush and dry forest, past the ruins of an old plantation, and to a sugar factory adjacent to the beach. It can be a bit arduous for young kids, however. The nonprofit Friends of the Virgin Islands National Park runs a $75 per person ranger-guided tour to Reef Bay that includes a safari bus ride to the trailhead and a boat ride back to

Did You Know?

The Virgin Islands National Park makes up more than two-thirds of St. John and includes more than 5,000 acres underwater.

Cruz Bay

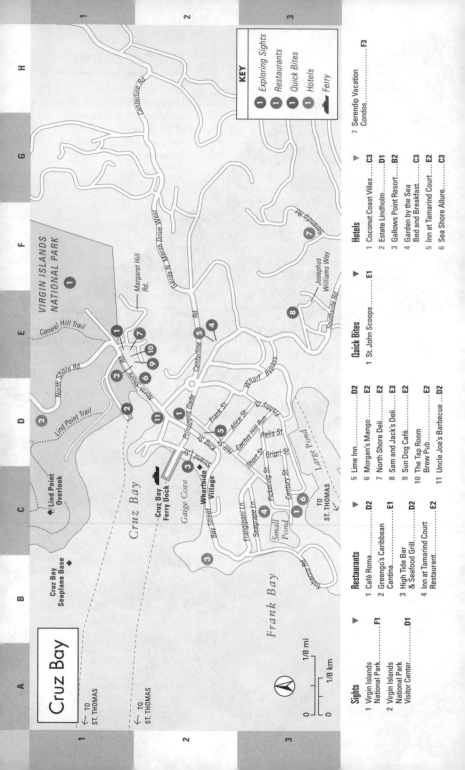

1/8 mi
1/8 km

← TO ST. THOMAS
← TO ST. THOMAS

TO ST. THOMAS

Frank Bay

Cruz Bay

Cruz Bay Seaplane Base ◆

◆ **Lind Point Overlook**

Lind Point Trail

Caneel Hill Trail

VIRGIN ISLANDS NATIONAL PARK

North Shore Rd.

Margaret Hill Rd.

Gerda N. Marsh Drive West

Centerline Rd.

Serendip Rd.

Centerline Rd.

Wharf Bypass

Frank St.

Alice St.

Relis St.

Grigri St.

Short St.

Cactus Hill Run

Fisher St.

Southside Rd.

Josephus Williams Way

Gage Cove

Wharfside Village ◆

Cruz Bay Ferry Dock

Bay Street Ln.

Frangipani Ln.

Seagrape Ln.

Pickering St.

Century St.

Tobacco Ln.

Bay St.

King St.

Princess Gade

Large Pond

Small Pond

Sights ▶
1 Virgin Islands National Park **F1**
2 Virgin Islands National Park Visitor Center **D1**

Restaurants ▶
1 Café Roma **D2**
2 Greengo's Caribbean Cantina **E1**
3 High Tide Bar & Seafood Grill **D2**
4 Inn at Tamarind Court Restaurant **E2**
5 Lime Inn **D2**
6 Morgan's Mango **E2**
7 North Shore Deli **E2**
8 Sam and Jack's Deli **E3**
9 Sun Dog Café **E2**
10 The Tap Room Brew Pub **E2**
11 Uncle Joe's Barbecue **D2**

Quick Bites ▶
1 St. John Scoops **E1**

Hotels ▶
1 Coconut Coast Villas **C3**
2 Estate Lindholm **D1**
3 Gallows Point Resort **B2**
4 Garden by the Sea Bed and Breakfast **C3**
5 Inn at Tamarind Court **E2**
6 Sea Shore Allure **C3**
7 Serendip Vacation Condos **F3**

KEY
1 Exploring Sights
1 Restaurants
1 Quick Bites
1 Hotels
Ferry

the visitor center. The schedule changes from season to season; call for times and to make reservations, which are essential. To pick up a useful guide to St. John's hiking trails, see various large maps of the island, and find out about current Park Service programs—including guided walks and cultural demonstrations—stop by the park visitor center at the western tip of the park in Cruz Bay on North Shore Road. ✉ *North Shore Rd., near creek, Cruz Bay* ☎ *340/776–6201* 🌐 *www.nps.gov/viis.*

Virgin Islands National Park Visitor Center
VISITOR CENTER | To pick up a useful guide to St. John's hiking trails, see various large maps of the island, and find out about current park service programs, including guided walks and cultural demonstrations, stop by the visitor center. ✉ *North Shore Rd., near creek, Cruz Bay* ☎ *340/776–6201* 🌐 *www.nps.gov/viis.*

🍴 Restaurants

Café Roma
$$$ | **ITALIAN** | **FAMILY** | This second-floor restaurant in the heart of Cruz Bay is *the* place for traditional Italian cuisine, so don't let the underwhelming ambience turn you away. The lasagna, spaghetti and meatballs, and seafood manicotti are all delicious, as are the small pizza—they're available at your table, but larger ones are for takeout or at the bar. **Known for:** authentic Italian cuisine; lively atmosphere; Raju Cajun (chicken and penne tossed in a Cajun sherry cream sauce). [$] *Average main: $27* ✉ *1-C King St., Cruz Bay* ☎ *340/776–6524* 🌐 *www.caferomastjohn.com* ⏲ *No lunch.*

Greengo's Caribbean Cantina
$$$ | **MEXICAN** | This is the place to go for Mexican food on St. John. You'll find nacho starters, tacos, burritos, and enchiladas as well as a half dozen margarita variations to wash it all down. **Known for:** fresh tortillas; infused tequila; cool murals. [$] *Average main: $26* ✉ *Mongoose Junction shopping center, North Shore Rd., Cruz Bay* ☎ *340/777–8226* 🌐 *greengosvi.com/st-john-vi.*

High Tide Bar & Seafood Grill
$$$ | **ECLECTIC** | **FAMILY** | This casual spot right at Cruz Bay Beach serves everything from hamburgers and mahi sandwiches to surf and turf and Caribbean lobster. At happy hour, order a Painkiller and watch the sunset over the bay. **Known for:** family-friendly atmosphere; beachfront setting; good happy hour. [$] *Average main: $30* ✉ *Wharfside Village, Strand St., Cruz Bay* ☎ *340/714–6169* 🌐 *www.hightidevi.com.*

Inn at Tamarind Court Restaurant
$$ | **MEXICAN** | Sit in the open-air courtyard of this locals' favorite eatery for reasonably priced Mexican staples like tacos, tostadas, and fajitas. The best bet is at breakfast. **Known for:** full selection of breakfast fare; quiet courtyard setting (no cell phone conversations allowed); use of local seafood in Mexican dishes. [$] *Average main: $16* ✉ *Inn at Tamarind Court, Rte. 104, Cruz Bay* ☎ *340/776–6378* 🌐 *www.innattamarindcourt.com* ⏲ *No lunch.*

Lime Inn
$$$$ | **ECLECTIC** | The vacationers and mainland transplants who call St. John home like to flock to this cozy courtyard spot for the congenial hospitality and good food. There's still old favorites like clam chowder and key lime pie, but the second-generation owners have elevated the flavors with new Caribbean and Latin twists on the classics. **Known for:** fresh lobster; local crowd; Lime Out, a floating taco bar off Coral Bay. [$] *Average main: $32* ✉ *Lemon Tree Mall, King St., Cruz Bay* ☎ *340/776–6425* 🌐 *thelimeinn.com* ⏲ *Closed Sun. No lunch.*

★ **Morgan's Mango**
$$$$ | **CARIBBEAN** | Visiting this alfresco family-owned eatery requires climbing a long flight of stairs, but the food is well worth the effort. Although fish is the

Dine on fresh fish at Morgan's Mango.

specialty, try the coconut panko-crusted grouper topped with a white wine, coconut, and lemongrass reduction—the chef also creates a vegetarian platter with black beans, fried plantains, and a mound of truffled mashed sweet potatoes.
Known for: fresh fish; open-air garden setting; vegetarian dishes. $ *Average main: $39* ✉ *Across from V.I. National Park Visitors Center, North Shore Rd., Cruz Bay* ☎ *340/693-8141* ⊕ *morgansmango. com* ⊘ *No lunch.*

North Shore Deli
$ | ECLECTIC | At this air-conditioned (but no-frills) sandwich shop you place your order at the counter and wait for it to be delivered to your table or for takeout. The classic Reuben is a favorite, but other sandwiches, like the turkey pesto and vegan Greek flatbread pita with hummus and veggies, also get rave reviews.
Known for: hearty sandwiches; tropical fruit smoothies; grab-and-go menu makes great picnic fixings. $ *Average main: $10* ✉ *Mongoose Junction Shopping Center, North Shore Rd., Cruz Bay*

☎ *340/777-3061* ⊕ *www.northshoredelistjohn.com* ⊘ *No dinner.*

Sam and Jack's Deli
$$ | SANDWICHES | The sandwiches are scrumptious, but this deli also dishes up wonderful meals to-go that just need heating. There are a few seats inside, but most folks opt to eat at the tables in front of the deli. **Known for:** picnic-ready meals; The Wolf (crispy fried rock shrimp with Cajun remoulade); villa and yacht provisioning available. $ *Average main: $15* ✉ *Marketplace Shopping Center, Rte. 104, 3rd fl., Cruz Bay* ☎ *340/714-3354* ⊕ *www.samandjacksdeli.com* ⊘ *Closed Sun.*

Sun Dog Café
$$$ | ECLECTIC | There's an unusual assortment of dishes at this charming alfresco restaurant, which you'll find tucked into a courtyard in the upper reaches of the Mongoose Junction shopping center. The Jamaican jerk chicken salad and the black-bean quesadilla are good choices.
Known for: eclectic menu; white pizza with artichoke hearts; live music on weekends.

$ *Average main: $24* ✉ *Mongoose Junction Shopping Center, North Shore Rd., Hwy. 20, Cruz Bay* ☎ *340/693–8340* 🌐 *www.sundogcafe.com.*

The Tap Room Brew Pub
$$ | **AMERICAN** | More than a dozen house-brewed beers on tap, including the signature Tropical Mango Pale Ale, make dining at St. John Brewers' tap room special. The rich wood décor is the perfect place for a soft Bavarian-style pretzel, burgers, and build-your-own-pizzas. **Known for:** on-site microbrewery; lively atmosphere; local hangout. $ *Average main: $18* ✉ *Mongoose Junction Shopping Center, Rte. 104, Cruz Bay* ☎ *340/715–7775* 🌐 *stjohnbrewers.com.*

Uncle Joe's Barbecue
$$ | **AMERICAN** | **FAMILY** | Juicy ribs and tasty chicken legs dripping with house barbecue sauce make for one of St. John's best dining deals. An ear of corn, rice, and a generous scoop of macaroni salad, potato salad, or coleslaw round out the plate. **Known for:** casual sidewalk dining; good value; generous portions. $ *Average main: $15* ✉ *North Shore Rd., across from post office, Cruz Bay* ☎ *340/693–8806.*

Coffee and Quick Bites

St. John Scoops
$ | **ICE CREAM** | While you can get the usual chocolate and vanilla ice cream as well as smoothies at this tiny spot, owner Colette Rethage also dishes up frozen treats blended with alcoholic beverages. Try the Champagne sorbet, espresso martini, peach margarita, or that tropical favorite, the rum-laced Painkiller. **Known for:** boozy ice cream; house-made waffle cones; more than 20 flavors. $ *Average main: $6* ✉ *Mongoose Junction shopping center, North Shore Rd., Cruz Bay* 🌐 *www.StJohnScoops.com.*

Hotels

Coconut Coast Villas
$$$ | **HOTEL** | This small condominium complex with studio, two-, and three-bedroom apartments is a 10-minute walk from Cruz Bay, but it's insulated from the town's noise in a sleepy suburban neighborhood. **Pros:** good snorkeling; full kitchens; walk to Cruz Bay. **Cons:** small beach; some uphill walks; nearby utility plant can be noisy. $ *Rooms from: $389* ✉ *268 Estate Enighed, Near pond, Turner Bay, Cruz Bay* ☎ *340/693–9100, 800/858–7989* 🌐 *www.coconutcoast.com* 🛏 *9 units* 🍴 *No Meals.*

Estate Lindholm
$$$$ | **B&B/INN** | Built among 18th-century stone ruins on a lushly planted hill overlooking Cruz Bay, Estate Lindholm has an enchanting setting—you'll feel as if you're out of the fray, but still near enough to run into town when you want. **Pros:** lush landscaping; gracious host; pleasant décor. **Cons:** can be noisy; some uphill walks; on a busy road. $ *Rooms from: $510* ✉ *6B Estate Caneel Bay, Caneel Hill, Cruz Bay* ☎ *340/227–4724, 800/322–6335* 🌐 *www.estatelindholm.com* 🛏 *17 rooms* 🍴 *Free Breakfast.*

★ Gallows Point Resort
$$$$ | **RESORT** | You're a short walk from restaurants and shops at this waterfront location just outside Cruz Bay, but once you step into your condo, the hustle and bustle are left behind. **Pros:** walk to shopping; excellent restaurant; comfortably furnished rooms. **Cons:** some rooms can be noisy; mediocre beach; insufficient parking. $ *Rooms from: $795* ✉ *Bay St., 3AAA Estate Enighed, Cruz Bay* ☎ *340/776–6434, 800/323–7229* 🌐 *www.gallowspointresort.com* 🛏 *60 units* 🍴 *No Meals.*

Garden by the Sea Bed and Breakfast
$$ | **B&B/INN** | Located in a middle-class residential neighborhood, this adults-only, cozy bed-and-breakfast is an easy walk from Cruz Bay, and it's perfect for folks who enjoy peace and quiet: there are no

Local St. John Celebrations

Although the U.S. Virgin Islands mark all of the same federal holidays as the mainland, they have a few of their own. Transfer Day, on March 31, commemorates Denmark's sale of the territory to the United States in 1917. Emancipation Day, on July 3, marks the date slavery was abolished in the Danish West Indies in 1848. Liberty Day, on November 1, honors David Hamilton Jackson, who secured freedom of the press and assembly from King Christian X of Denmark.

While you're on St. John, don't hesitate to attend local events like the annual Memorial Day and Veterans Day celebrations and Fourth of July Festival Parade in Cruz Bay, complete with costumed troupes, steel pan bands, and stilt-walking Mocko Jumbies. These small parades give a poignant glimpse into island life. The St. Patrick's Day Parade is another blink-and-you'll-miss-it event. It's fun to join the islanders who come out decked in green. The annual Friends of Virgin Islands National Park meeting in January is another place to mix and mingle with the locals.

phones or TVs in the rooms. **Pros:** homey atmosphere; great breakfasts; breathtaking view from deck. **Cons:** noise from nearby power substation; some uphill walks; basic amenities. [$] *Rooms from: $372* ✉ *Near Small Pond by Frank Bay, Century St., 203 Contant and Enighed, Enighed* ☎ *340/779–4731* 🌐 *gardenbythesea.com* 🛏 *3 rooms* 🍴 *Free Breakfast.*

Inn at Tamarind Court
$ | **B&B/INN** | Good for travelers on a budget, the Inn at Tamarind Court has rooms with rather pedestrian décor, but they're clean, and you can't beat the location, a five-minute walk from the heart of Cruz Bay's action. **Pros:** walk to restaurants and shops; good breakfasts; convivial atmosphere. **Cons:** on a busy road; bland decor; need a car to get around. [$] *Rooms from: $228* ✉ *Rte. 104, Cruz Bay* ☎ *340/776-6378, 800/221–1637* 🌐 *www.innattamarindcourt.com* 🛏 *18 rooms* 🍴 *No Meals.*

Sea Shore Allure
$$$$ | **APARTMENT** | Located at the water's edge in a residential neighborhood, Sea Shore Allure combines attractive and modern décor with an easy, and safe, walk to Cruz Bay's restaurants and shops. **Pros:** lovely decor; waterfront location; close to town. **Cons:** no gym; need car or taxi to get to beach; road passes through modest (but safe) local neighborhood. [$] *Rooms from: $556* ✉ *271 and 272 Fish Fry Dr., Enighed* ☎ *340/779–2800, 855/779–2800* 🌐 *www.seashoreallure.com* 🛏 *8 units* 🍴 *No Meals.*

Serendip Vacation Condos
$$$ | **HOTEL** | This complex offers modern studio and 1-bedroom apartments on lush grounds with lovely views and makes a great pick for a budget stay in a residential locale. **Pros:** comfortable accommodations; good views; nice neighborhood. **Cons:** no beach; need car to get around; nearby construction. [$] *Rooms from: $399* ✉ *9-7 Serendip Rd., off Rte. 104, Enighed* ☎ *340/776–6646* 🌐 *www.serendipstjohn.com* 🛏 *8 condos* 🍴 *No Meals.*

🍸 Nightlife

The Beach Bar
LIVE MUSIC | There's live toe-tapping tunes—from rock and reggae to blues and jazz—almost every night of the week in season starting at 8 pm at this lively

venue. The beachfront stage, showing performances by local and visiting musicians, and the nearby bar serving burgers and frosty libations make this a perfect place to spend happy hour, watch the sunset, and jam into the night. ⊠ *4A Wharfside Village, Cruz Bay* ☎ *340/777–4220* ⊕ *www.beachbarstjohn.com.*

Woody's Seafood Saloon

BARS | Folks like to gather here, a short walk from the ferry dock, where the sidewalk tables provide a close-up view of Cruz Bay action. There's live entertainment on weekends. American country music star Kenny Chesney often stops here when on island and sings a song or two. ⊠ *Prince and King Sts., Cruz Bay* ✛ *2 blocks east of the ferry dock* ☎ *340/779–4625* ⊕ *www.woodysseafood.com.*

🛍 Shopping

Luxury goods and handicrafts abound on St. John. Most shops carry a little of this and a bit of that, so it pays to poke around. The main Cruz Bay shopping district runs from **Wharfside Village,** just around the corner from the ferry dock, to **Mongoose Junction,** an inviting shopping center on North Shore Road. (The name of this upscale shopping mall, by the way, is a holdover from a time when those furry island creatures gathered at a nearby garbage bin.) Out on Route 104, the **Marketplace** has the island's only pharmacy. It also has a good selection of kids' beach toys. On St. John, store hours run from 9 or 10 am to 5 or 6 pm. Wharfside Village and Mongoose Junction shops in Cruz Bay are often open into the evening.

ART GALLERIES

★ Bajo el Sol Gallery, Art Bar & Rum Room

ART GALLERIES | This gallery sells pieces from a roster of the island's best artists. You can shop for oils, pastels, watercolors, and turned-wood pieces as well as ceramic and metal works. Find potable art in the form of a full bar in the back. There's espresso, craft cocktails, and a good selection of aged rums, the latter of which you can sample in curated tasting flights. ⊠ *Mongoose Junction Shopping Center, North Shore Rd., Hwy. 20, Cruz Bay* ☎ *340/693–7070* ⊕ *www.bajo-el-sol-gallery.business.site.*

Caravan Gallery

JEWELRY & WATCHES | Caravan sells affordable jewelry, unique gifts, and artifacts that its owner, Radha Speer, has traveled the world to find. The more you look, the more you see—Caribbean larimar jewelry, unusual sterling pieces, and tribal art cover the walls and tables, making this a great place to browse. ⊠ *Mongoose Junction Shopping Center, North Shore Rd., Cruz Bay* ☎ *340/779–4566* ⊕ *www.caravangallery.com.*

Coconut Coast Studios

ART GALLERIES | This waterside shop, a five-minute walk from the center of Cruz Bay, showcases the work of Elaine Estern. She specializes in undersea scenes. ⊠ *Frank Bay, Tobacco Rd., Cruz Bay* ☎ *340/776–6944* ⊕ *www.coconut-coaststudios.com.*

BOOKS

★ Friends of the Park Store

BOOKS | Find books, maps, and beachwear—like tees printed with turtle and petroglyph designs—at this store run by the nonprofit group that raises money for Virgin Islands National Park. It's a great spot to buy educational materials for kids and books about the island. ⊠ *Mongoose Junction Shopping Center, North Shore Rd., Hwy 20., Cruz Bay* ☎ *340/779–4940* ⊕ *www.friendsvinp.org.*

National Park Headquarters Bookstore

BOOKS | FAMILY | The bookshop at Virgin Islands National Park Visitor Center sells several good histories of St. John. ⊠ *Visitor Center, North Shore Rd., Rte. 20, Cruz Bay* ☎ *340/776–6201* ⊕ *www.nps.gov/viis.*

CLOTHING

Big Planet Adventure Outfitters

MIXED CLOTHING | You knew when you arrived that someplace on St. John would cater to the outdoors enthusiasts who hike up and down the island's trails. This store sells flip-flops and Reef footwear, along with colorful and durable cotton clothing and accessories by Billabong. The store also sells children's clothes. ⊠ *Mongoose Junction Shopping Center, North Shore Rd., Hwy. 20, Cruz Bay* ☎ *340/776–6638* ⊕ *www.big-planet.com.*

FOOD

If you're renting a villa, condo, or cottage and doing your own cooking, there are several good places to shop for food in Cruz Bay; just be aware that prices are much higher than those at home.

Dolphin Market

FOOD | This small store in Cruz Bay is a good source for fresh produce, deli items, and all the basics. Two smaller branches are in Chocolate Hole, near Great Cruz Bay, and in Coral Bay. ⊠ *Boulon Center, Rte. 10, Cruz Bay* ☎ *340/776–5322* ⊕ *www.dolphinmarkets.com.*

Starfish Market

FOOD | The island's largest store usually has the best selection of meat, fish, and produce. ⊠ *The Marketplace, Rte. 104, Cruz Bay* ☎ *340/779–4949* ⊕ *www.starfishmarket.com.*

GIFTS

Bamboula

SOUVENIRS | This multicultural boutique carries unusual housewares, rugs, bedspreads, accessories, and men's and women's clothes and shoes that owner Jo Sterling has found on her world travels. ⊠ *Mongoose Junction Shopping Center, North Shore Rd., Cruz Bay* ☎ *340/693–8699* ⊕ *www.bamboulastjohn.com.*

Donald Schnell Studio

SOUVENIRS | You'll find distinctive clay pieces, unusual handblown glass, wind chimes, kaleidoscopes, fanciful fountains, and pottery bowls here. Your purchases can be shipped worldwide. ⊠ *Amore Center, 27 Southside Rd., near roundabout, Enighed* ☎ *340/776–6420, 800/253–7107* ⊕ *donaldschnell.com/the-studio.*

Gallows Point Resort Gift & Gourmet

SOUVENIRS | The gift shop at Gallows Point Resort has a bit of this and a bit of that. Shop for Caribbean books, picture frames decorated with shells, and T-shirts with tropical motifs. Residents and visitors also drop by for a cup of coffee or espresso. ⊠ *Gallows Point Resort, Bay St., Cruz Bay* ☎ *800/323–7229 ext. 608, 340/693–7730* ⊕ *www.gallowspointconcierge.com.*

Pink Papaya

SOUVENIRS | Head to this shop and art gallery for the work of longtime Virgin Islands resident Lisa Etre. There's also a huge collection of one-of-a-kind gifts, including bright tableware, trays, and tropical jewelry. ⊠ *Lemon Tree Mall, King St., Cruz Bay* ☎ *340/693–8535* ⊕ *www.pinkpapaya.com.*

JEWELRY

Freebird Creations

JEWELRY & WATCHES | This is your on-island destination for special handcrafted jewelry—earrings, bracelets, pendants, chains—as well as a good selection of water-resistant watches. ⊠ *Dockside Mall, next to ferry dock, Cruz Bay* ☎ *340/693–8625* ⊕ *www.freebirdcreations.com.*

Little Switzerland

JEWELRY & WATCHES | A branch of the St. Thomas store, Little Switzerland carries diamonds and other jewels in attractive

Sugar mill ruins at Annaberg Plantation

yellow- and white-gold settings, as well as strings of creamy pearls, watches, and other designer jewelry. ⊠ *Mongoose Junction Shopping Center, North Shore Rd., Cruz Bay* ☎ *248/809–5560, ext. 10040* ⊕ *www.littleswitzerland.com.*

Vibe Jewelry

JEWELRY & WATCHES | Handcrafted hook bracelets, carried here in sterling silver and 14k gold, are must-have statement pieces: wear the open side of the hook facing out and it means you're single; wear the hook facing your heart and it says you're taken. There are rings, earrings, and pendants too, including petroglyph designs that are a signature of St. John and its Amerindian past. There is another location in Mongoose Junction. ⊠ *Wharfside Landing #5, Cruz Bay* ☎ *340/643–1122* ⊕ *www.vibejewelry. com.*

North Shore

Sights

★ Annaberg Plantation

RUINS | In the 18th century, sugar plantations dotted the steep hills of this island. Enslaved people and free Danes and Dutchmen toiled to harvest the cane that was used to create sugar, molasses, and rum for export. Built in the 1780s, the partially restored plantation at Leinster Bay was once an important sugar mill. Although there are no official visiting hours, the National Park Service hosts tours, and some well-informed taxi drivers can show you around. Occasionally, you may see a living-history demonstration—someone making Johnny Cakes or weaving baskets. For information on tours and cultural events, contact the National Park Visitor Center or the Friends of the National Park. ⊠ *Leinster Bay Rd., Annaberg* ☎ *340/776–6201 National Park Visitor's Center, 340/779–4940 Friends*

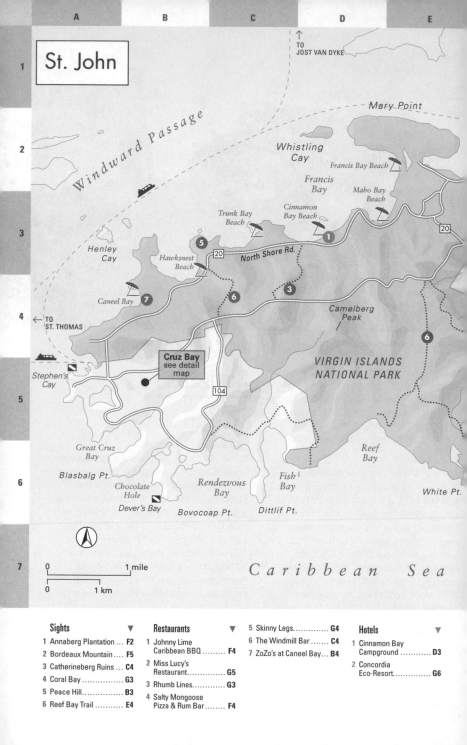

St. John

TO JOST VAN DYKE

Windward Passage

Mary Point

Whistling Cay

Francis Bay Beach

Francis Bay

Maho Bay Beach

Cinnamon Bay Beach

Trunk Bay Beach

20

Henley Cay

Hawksnest Beach

North Shore Rd.

Caneel Bay

Camelberg Peak

TO ST. THOMAS

Stephen's Cay

Cruz Bay
see detail map

104

VIRGIN ISLANDS NATIONAL PARK

Great Cruz Bay

Blasbalg Pt.

Chocolate Hole

Dever's Bay

Rendezvous Bay

Fish Bay

Reef Bay

White Pt.

Bovocoap Pt.

Dittlif Pt.

0   1 mile

0   1 km

Caribbean Sea

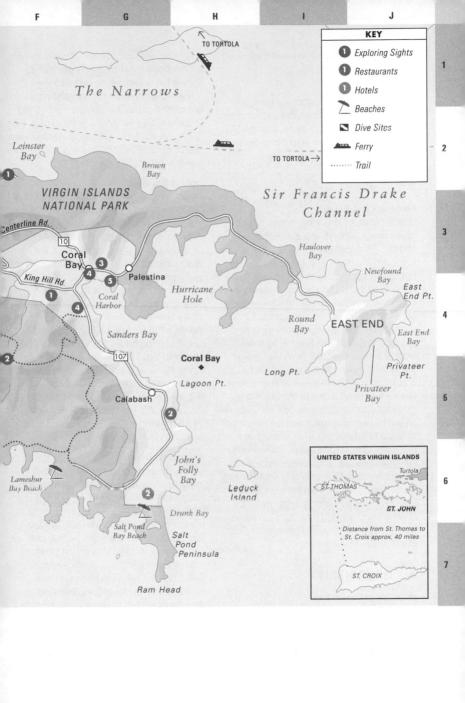

of the National Park 🌐 *www.nps.gov/viis; www.friendsvinp.org.*

Peace Hill

VIEWPOINT | It's worth stopping here, just past the Hawksnest Bay overlook, for great views of St. John, St. Thomas, and the BVI. On the flat promontory is an old sugar mill. ✉ *Off Hwy. 20, Estate Denis Bay.*

Beaches

Cinnamon Bay Beach

BEACH | **FAMILY** | This long, sandy beach faces beautiful cays and abuts the National Park campground. There's excellent snorkeling off the point to the right; look for the big angelfish and large schools of purple triggerfish. Afternoons on Cinnamon Bay can be windy—a boon for windsurfers but an annoyance for sunbathers—so arrive early to beat the gusts. The Cinnamon Bay hiking trail begins across the road from the beach parking lot; ruins mark the trailhead. There are actually two paths here: a level nature trail (with signs to identify flora) that loops through the woods and passes an old Danish cemetery and a steep trail that starts where the road bends past the ruins and heads straight up to Route 10. **Amenities:** parking; toilets; adjacent campground with restaurant, store, and water-sports rental. **Best for:** snorkeling; swimming; walking; windsurfing. ✉ *North Shore Rd., Hwy. 20, Cinnamon Bay* ✥ *About 4 miles (6 km) east of Cruz Bay* 🌐 *www.nps.gov/viis.*

Restaurants

★ ZoZo's at Caneel Bay

$$$$ | **MEDITERRANEAN** | Creative takes on true classics coupled with artfully presented plates draw crowds to this Mediterranean-inspired restaurant at Caneel Bay. The four-course menu starts with a selection of artisan-made antipasti, then moves to salads like the mango, feta, and prosciutto–topped frisee, followed by entrées such as butter-soft diver scallops and classic osso buco with a Caribbean twist of crispy plantains. **Known for:** breathtaking seaside views; romantic ambience; mango-and-coconut panna cotta. [$] *Average main: $140* ✉ *Caneel Bay, Northshore Rd., Hwy. 20, 1½ miles east of Cruz Bay, Estate Caneel Bay* ☎ *860/977–6323* 🌐 *www.zozosatcaneelbay.com* 🕓 *Closed Sat.*

Francis Bay Beach

BEACH | Because there's little shade, this beach gets toasty in the afternoon, when the sun comes around to the west, but the rest of the day it's a delightful stretch of white sand. The only facilities are a few picnic tables tucked among the trees and a portable restroom, but folks come here to watch the birds that live in the swampy area behind the beach. There's also a boardwalk here for bird-watching. In addition, the park offers weekly bird-watching hikes; sign up at the visitor center in Cruz Bay. To get here, turn left at the Annaberg intersection. **Amenities:** limited parking; toilets. **Best for:** snorkeling; swimming; walking. ✉ *North Shore Rd., Hwy. 20, Francis Bay* ✥ *¼ mile (½ km) from Annaberg intersection* 🌐 *www.nps.gov/viis.*

Hawksnest Beach

BEACH | Sea grapes and waving palm trees line this narrow beach, and there are portable toilets, cooking grills, picnic tables, and a covered shed for picnicking. It's the closest drivable beach to Cruz Bay, so it's often crowded with locals and visitors. A patchy reef just offshore means snorkeling is an easy swim away, but the best underwater views are reserved for ambitious snorkelers who head farther to the east along the bay's fringes. Watch out for boat traffic: although a channel of buoys marks where dinghies or other small vessels can come up onto the sand to drop off or pick up passengers, the occasional boater strays into the swim area. **Amenities:** parking; toilets. **Best for:** snorkeling; swimming. ✉ *North Shore Rd., Hwy 20,*

St. John Archaeology

Archaeologists continue to unravel St. John's past through excavations at Trunk Bay and Cinnamon Bay, both prime tourist destinations within Virgin Islands National Park.

Work began back in the early 1990s, when the park wanted to build new bathhouses at the popular Trunk Bay. In preparation for that project, the archaeologists began to dig, turning up artifacts and the remains of structures that date to AD 900. The site was once a village occupied by the Taíno, a peaceful group that lived in the area for many centuries. A similar but not quite as ancient village was discovered at Cinnamon Bay.

By the time the Taíno got to Cinnamon Bay—they lived in the area from about AD 1000 to 1500—their society had developed to include chiefs, commoners, workers, and slaves. The location of the national park's Cinnamon Bay campground was once a Taíno temple that belonged to a king or chief. When archaeologists began digging in 1998, they uncovered several dozen *zemis*, which are small clay gods used in ceremonial activities, as well as beads, pots, and many other artifacts.

Near the end of the Cinnamon Bay dig, archaeologists turned up another less ancient but still important discovery. A burned layer indicated that a plantation slave village had also stood near Cinnamon Bay campground; it was torched during the 1733 revolt because its inhabitants had been loyal to the planters. Since the 1970s, bones from slaves buried in the area have been uncovered at the water's edge by beach erosion.

Throughout the year, the nonprofit Friends of the National Park offers programs and seminars to the public that share the latest on the digs into the island's past. Check the organization's website (⊕ *www.friendsvinp.org*) for details.

4

St. John NORTH SHORE

Estate Hawksnest ⊕ *About 2 miles (3 km) east of Cruz Bay* ⊕ *www.nps.gov/viis.*

Maho Bay Beach

BEACH | This gorgeous strip of sand sits right along the North Shore Road. It's a popular place, particularly on weekends, when locals come out in droves to party at the picnic tables on the south end of the beach. The snorkeling along the rocky edges is good, but the center is mostly sea grass. If you're lucky, you'll cross paths with turtles. There are portable toilets at the end of the beach. Across the beach is Maho Crossroads, with food trucks, a bar, and a couple of shops. **Amenities:** food and drink; parking; toilets. **Best for:** snorkeling; swimming. ⊠ *North*

Shore Rd., Hwy. 20, Estate Maho Bay ⊕ *www.nps.gov/viis.*

★ Trunk Bay Beach

BEACH | FAMILY | St. John's most photographed beach is also the preferred spot for beginning snorkelers because of its underwater trail. (Cruise-ship passengers interested in snorkeling for a day flock here, so if you're looking for seclusion, arrive early or later in the day.) Crowded or not, this stunning beach is one of the island's most beautiful. There is a food concession, picnic tables, a gift shop, and lockers. The parking lot often overflows, but you can park along the road as long as the tires are off the pavement. **Amenities:** food and drink; lifeguards; parking; showers; toilets; water-sports rentals. **Best for:** snorkeling; swimming;

Camping in St. John

For those on a really tight budget, there is bare-bones camping at Camp St. John. Tents are $75 per night, while BYOT (bring your own tent) "bare sites" are $55. There are restrooms and showers on the property, and a bar and restaurant a two-minute walk down the hill. The mountainside views from Caneel Bay below and the Atlantic Ocean beyond are priceless. There are "bare sites" too, with and without tent rentals, at the Cinnamon Bay Campground, starting at $50 per night. Eco Tents at Cinnamon Bay, complete with bunks, basic cooking gear, and electricity, start at $190 per night or $245 for those right on the ocean. More comfy cottages, sturdily built on concrete pads, go for $280 and up a night. Past Coral Bay, there are "eco-cabanas" at Concordia Eco-Resort. Like at Cinnamon Bay, these appeal to those who don't mind bringing their own beach towels from home or busing their own tables at dinner. If you want your piña colada delivered beachside by a smiling waiter, you'd be better off elsewhere.

windsurfing. ✉ *North Shore Rd., Hwy. 20, Estate Trunk Bay* ✥ *About 2½ miles (4 km) east of Cruz Bay* 🌐 *www.nps.gov/viis* 🎟 *$5.*

Hotels

★ Cinnamon Bay Campground

$ | **RESORT** | **FAMILY** | Glamping is a good way to describe the vibe here, especially if you book an eco-tent, complete with bunks, basic cooking gear, and electricity, or a cottage, sturdily built on concrete pads with beds, ceiling fans, kitchen utensils, electricity, and outdoor picnic tables. **Pros:**. **Cons:**. [$] *Rooms from: $210* ✉ *U.S. National Park, Northshore Road, Rte 20, Cinnamon Bay Beach, Cinnamon Bay* ☎ *340/714–7144* 🌐 *www.cinnamonbayvi.com* 🛏 *40 cottage, 55 eco-tents, 31 bare sites* 🍴 *No Meals.*

Mid Island

Sights

Bordeaux Mountain

MOUNTAIN | St. John's highest peak rises to 1,277 feet. Route 10 passes near enough to the top to offer breathtaking vistas. Don't stray into the road here—cars whiz by at a good clip along this section. Instead, drive nearly to the end of the dirt road that heads off to Picture Point and the trailhead of the hike downhill to Lameshur. Get a trail map from the park service before you start. It's a relatively easy 2 miles (3 km) down, but the hike back up is strenuous due to the steep incline. ✉ *Rte. 10, Bordeaux.*

Catherineberg Ruins

RUINS | At this fine example of an 18th-century sugar and rum factory, there's a storage vault beneath the windmill. Across the road, look for the round mill, which was later used to hold water. In the 1733 slave revolt Catherineberg served as headquarters for the Amina

Waves crash against the rocky coastline near Lameshur Bay.

warriors, a tribe of Africans that had been captured into slavery. ✉ *Catherineberg Rd., off Rte. 10, St. John.*

★ Reef Bay Trail

TRAIL | This is one of the most interesting hikes on St. John, but the 1.5-mile return climb, rising 900 feet from sea level back to the trailhead, is a real workout. Along the way, one short side trail to the west takes you to a small pool where indigenous inhabitants carved petroglyphs into the rock. Another short side trail to the east leads to the plantation's great house, a gutted but mostly intact structure with vestiges of its former beauty. Down at sea level, walk around the sugar factory ruins or cool off at the beach before hiking back up. ✉ *Rte. 10, Reef Bay* ☎ *340/779–4940 Friends of the National Park, 340/776–6201 Virgin Islands National Park* 🌐 *www.nps.gov/viis, www.friendsvinp.org* 🎟 *Free to hike by yourself; $75 per person for a 5-hour Park Ranger guided trip with a boat ride back to Cruz Bay* ✍ *Reserve through Friends of the National Park, www.friendsvinp.org* ☞ *Mondays and Thursdays, 8:45 am to 3 pm.*

🍴 Restaurants

The Windmill Bar

$$ | AMERICAN | Come for the bird's-eye view over Hawksnest Bay and Pillsbury Sound, and stay to drink and dine. Rum-drenched libations are on special for happy hour between 3 pm to 5 pm. **Known for:** sunset views; live music; historic sugarmill ruin. [$] *Average main: $18* ✉ *17A Susannaberg, Susannaberg* ☎ *340/244–6002* 🌐 *windmillbar.com.*

Coral Bay and Environs

Sights

Coral Bay

TOWN | This laid-back community at the island's dry eastern end is named for its shape rather than for its underwater life—the word *coral* comes from *krawl*, Dutch for "corral." Coral Bay is growing fast, but it's still a small, neighborly place. You'll probably need a four-wheel-drive vehicle if you plan to stay at this end of the island, as some of the rental houses are up unpaved roads that wind around the mountain. If you come just for lunch, a regular car will be fine. ✉ *Coral Bay.*

Beaches

Lameshur Bay Beach

BEACH | This sea-grape-fringed beach is toward the end of a partially paved, rut-strewn road (don't attempt it without a four-wheel-drive vehicle) on the southeast coast. The reward for your bumpy drive is good snorkeling and a chance to spy on some pelicans. The beach has a couple of picnic tables, rusting barbecue grills, and a portable restroom. The ruins of the old plantation are a five-minute walk down the road past the beach. The area has good hiking trails, including a trek (nearly 2 miles [3 km]) up Bordeaux Mountain before an easy walk to Yawzi Point. **Amenities:** parking; toilets. **Best for:** snorkeling; swimming; walking. ✉ *Off Rte. 107, Lameshur Bay* ✥ *About 1½ miles (2½ km) from Salt Pond* ☎ *340/776–6201* 🌐 *www.nps.gov/viis.*

Salt Pond Bay Beach

BEACH | If you're adventurous, this rocky beach on the scenic southeastern coast—next to rugged Drunk Bay—is worth exploring. It's a short hike down a hill from the parking lot, and the only facilities are a portable toilet and a few picnic tables scattered about. Tide pools are filled with all sorts of marine creatures, and the snorkeling is good, particularly along the bay's edges. A short walk takes you to a pond where salt crystals collect around the edges. Hike farther uphill past cactus gardens to Ram Head for see-forever views. Leave nothing valuable in your car, as thefts are common. **Amenities:** parking; toilets. **Best for:** snorkeling; swimming; walking. ✉ *Rte. 107, about 3 miles (5 km) south of Coral Bay, Concordia* ☎ *340/776–6201* 🌐 *www.nps.gov/viis.*

Restaurants

Johnny Lime Caribbean BBQ

$$$ | **BARBECUE** | **FAMILY** | Good old-fashioned BBQ ribs and brisket, plus all the fixings like mac and cheese, cornbread, and okra are served from a bright yellow food truck. Dine outdoors on umbrella-covered picnic tables with a view of Coral Harbor. **Known for:** open air picnic table setting; locally sourced vegetables; on-site smoker for meats. [$] *Average main: $23* ✉ *Next to the Isola Shoppes, 10-41 Estate Carolina, Coral Bay* ☎ *340/513–0052* 🌐 *johnnylime.com* ⏲ *Closed Sun.*

Miss Lucy's Restaurant

$$$ | **CARIBBEAN** | Sitting seaside at remote Friis Bay, Miss Lucy's dishes up Caribbean food with a contemporary flair, like tender conch fritters, spicy callaloo stew, fried local fish, and a generous paella with seafood, sausage, and chicken. Sunday brunches are legendary, and if you're around at the time, stop by for the monthly full-moon parties. **Known for:** Sunday brunch; full-moon parties; outdoor dining. [$] *Average main: $28* ✉ *Rte. 107, Friis Bay* ☎ *340/693–5244* ⏲ *Closed Mon. No dinner Sun.*

Rhumb Lines

$$$ | **ASIAN FUSION** | Pacific-Rim-meets-Caribbean cooking in the cozy dining room of this open-air eatery, with bamboo furnishings and local flora providing a tropical backdrop. Thai crab cakes,

Cuban mojo pork, and sesame-encrusted Szechuan tuna are excellent choices. **Known for:** pupu platters; lively vibe; live music on weekends. [$] *Average main: $29* ✉ *3 Estate Emmaus, Rte. 10, Coral Bay* ☎ *340/776–0303* 🌐 *www.rhumblinesst-john.com.*

Salty Mongoose Pizza & Rum Bar
$$$ | PIZZA | Enjoy limin' (local speak for relaxing) at this open-air waterfront restaurant with views across Coral Bay. The bar is a big focal point, serving rum punch, Painkillers and frozen coladas, bushwackers, and margaritas. **Known for:** build-your-own-pizza; fresh herb toppings like basil sourced locally; casual waterfront setting. [$] *Average main: $24* ✉ *Isola Shoppes, 13A Carolina, Coral Bay* ☎ *340/643–8486* 🌐 *www.saltymon-goose.com* ⏲ *Closed Wed.*

★ Skinny Legs
$$ | AMERICAN | Sailors who live aboard boats anchored offshore and an eclectic coterie of residents and visitors gather for lunch and dinner at this funky spot in the middle of a boatyard and shopping complex. It's a great place for burgers (they're served with potato chips, not fries—there's no deep fryer), fish sandwiches, and whatever sports are on the satellite TV. **Known for:** people-watching; pub food; local flavor. [$] *Average main: $12* ✉ *9901 Estate Emmaus, Rte. 10, Coral Bay* ☎ *340/779–4982* 🌐 *www.skinnylegsvi.com* ⏲ *Closed Mon.*

Hotels

Concordia Eco-Resort
$ | RESORT | This off-the-beaten-path resort is on the remote Salt Pond peninsula with a back-to-nature bent and a decent level of comfort. **Pros:** good views; eco-friendly environment; beach nearby. **Cons:** need car to get around; lots of stairs. [$] *Rooms from: $275* ✉ *20 Concordia, Off Rte. 107, Concordia* ☎ *340/693–5855, 800/392-9004* 🌐 *www.concordiaecoresort.com* 🛏 *8 villas, 19 eco-cabanas* 🍴 *No Meals.*

Nightlife

Aqua Bistro
LIVE MUSIC | This open-air seafood, sandwich, and burger eatery is the perfect place to dine, drink, and listen to talented local and off-island musicians who play at happy hour and into the evenings, especially on the weekends. ✉ *Rte. 107, In the Cocolobo Complex, Coral Bay* ☎ *340/776–5336* 🌐 *www.aquabistrost-john.com* ⏲ *Closed Wed. and Thurs.*

Shopping

On the island's eastern side, there are a few stores here and there from the village of **Coral Bay** to the small complex at **Isola Shoppes** on the south side of Coral Harbor, selling clothes, jewelry, and artwork.

CLOTHING

Jolly Dog
MIXED CLOTHING | Head here for the stuff you forgot to pack. Sarongs in cotton and rayon, beach towels with tropical motifs, and hats and T-shirts sporting the "Jolly Dog" logo fill the shelves. ✉ *Isola Shoppes Complex, next to Coral Bay Caribbean Oasis, Rte. 107, Coral Bay* ☎ *340/690–2961* 🌐 *www.thejollydog.com.*

★ Sloop Jones
MIXED CLOTHING | This store's worth the trip all the way out to the island's East End to shop for made-on-the-premises clothing and pillows, in fabrics splashed with tropical colors. The clothes are made from cotton, gauze, and modal, and are supremely comfortable. Sloop also holds painting workshops. ✉ *Off Rte. 10, East End* ☎ *340/779–4001* 🌐 *www.sloopjones.com.*

Continued on page 128

BELOW THE WAVES By Lynda Lohr

Colorful reefs and wrecks rife with corals and tropical fish make the islands as interesting underwater as above. Brilliantly colored reef fish vie for your attention with corals in wondrous shapes. Scuba diving gets you up close and personal with the world below the waves.

Bright blue tangs and darting blue-headed wrasses. Corals in wondrous shapes— some look like brains, others like elk antlers. Colorful, bulbous sponges. All these and more can be spotted along the myriad reefs of the U.S. and British Virgin Islands. You might see a pink conch making its way along the ocean bottom in areas with seagrass beds. If you're really lucky, a turtle may swim into view, or a lobster may poke its antennae out of a hole in the reef or rocks. If you do a night dive, you might run into an octopus. But you may be surprised at how much you can see by simply hovering just below the surface, with nothing more than a mask and snorkel. It's a bird's-eye view, but an excellent one. Whether scuba diving or snorkeling, take along an underwater camera to capture memories of your exciting adventure. You can buy disposable ones at most dive shops or bring one from home.

DIVE AND SNORKELING SITES IN BRITISH VIRGIN ISLANDS

TORTOLA

Although a major base for dive operations in the BVI (due to its proximity to so many exceptional dive sites), Tortola itself doesn't have as much to offer divers. However, there are still some noteworthy destinations. The massive **Brewer's Bay Pinnacles** grow 70 feet high to within 30 feet of the surface; the rock mazes are only for advanced divers because of strong currents and they are not always acces-

sible. Abundant reefs close to shore make **Brewer's Bay** popular with snorkelers, as are **Frenchman's Cay** and **Long Bay Beef Island. Diamond Reef**, between Great Camanoe and Scrub Island, is a small wall about 200 yards long. **Shark Point**, off the northeast coast of Scrub Island, does have resident sharks. Though isolated in open ocean, the wreck of the *Chikuzen,* a Japanese refrigerator ship, is a popular site.

THE ISLANDS OF THE SIR FRANCIS DRAKE CHANNEL

Southeast of Tortola lie a string of islands with some of the BVI's finest dive sites, some world famous. The wreck of the royal mail ship *Rhone* is between Peter and Salt islands and is, perhaps, the most famous dive site in the BVI. **Wreck Alley,** consisting of three sunken modern ships, is between Salt and Cooper islands. At **Alice in Wonderland**, south of Ginger Island, giant,

mushroom-shaped corals shelter reef fish, moray eels, and crustaceans. **Alice's Backside**, off the northwestern tip of Ginger Island, is usually smooth enough for snorkeling and shallow enough so that beginner divers can get a good look at the myriad sealife and sponges.

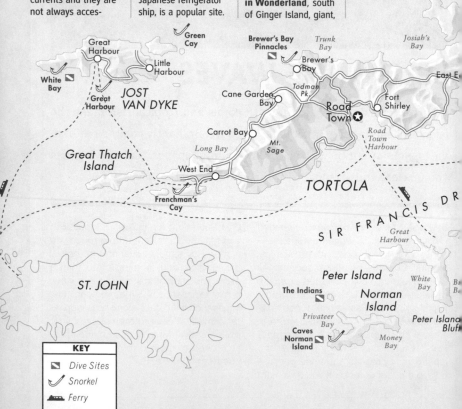

KEY

Dive Sites

Snorkel

Ferry

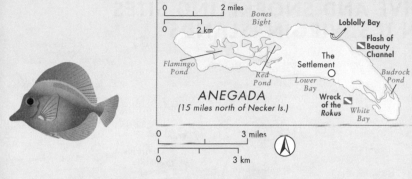

VIRGIN GORDA

The Baths, though busy, offers some of the best snorkeling in the Virgin Islands among giant boulders and the resulting grottoes. Nearby is **Spring Bay,** with fewer visitors and similar terrain. **The Aquarium,** close to Spanish Town and a good novice site, is so called because of the abundance of reef fish that swim around the submerged granite boulders that are similar to those of The Baths. Further west of Virgin Gorda, the Dog Islands have some in-

Sergeant major reef fish

teresting and popular sites, including **The Chimney,** a natural opening covered by sponges off Great Dog. South of Great Dog, **Coral Gardens** has a large coral reef with a submerged airplane wreck nearby. Fish are drawn to nearby **Cockroach Island.**

ANEGADA

Surrounded by the third-largest barrier reef in the world, Anegada has great snorkeling from virtu-ally any beach on the island. But there are also some notable dive sites as well. The **Flash of Beauty Channel** on the north shore is a great open-water dive, but only suitable for experienced divers. But even novices can enjoy diving at the **wreck of the Rokus,** a Greek cargo ship off the is-land's southern shore.

DIVE AND SNORKELING SITES IN U.S. VIRGIN ISLANDS

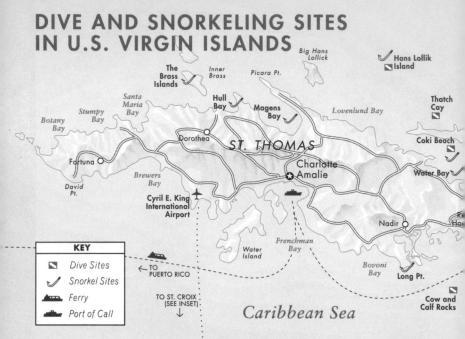

ST. THOMAS

St. Thomas has at least 40 popular dive sites, most shallow. Favorite reef dives off St. Thomas include **Cow and Calf Rocks**, which barely break water off the southeast coast of St. Thomas; the coral-covered pinnacles of **Frenchcap** south of St. Thomas; and tunnels where you can explore undersea from the Caribbean to the Atlantic at **Thatch Cay** (where the Coast Guard cutter *General Rogers* rests at 65 feet). **Grass Cay** and **Mingo Cay** between St. Thomas and St. John are also popular dive sites. **Coki Beach** offers the best off-the-beach snorkeling in St. Thomas. Nearby Coral World offers a dive-helmet walk for the untrained, and Snuba of St. Thomas has tethered shallow dives for non-certified divers. **Magens Bay**, the most popular beach on St. Thomas, provides lovely snorkeling if you head along the edges. You're likely to see some colorful sponges, darting fish, and maybe even a turtle if you're lucky. This is a stop on every island tour.

ST. JOHN

St. John is particularly known for its myriad good snorkeling spots—certainly more than for its diving opportunities, though there are many dive sites within easy reach of Cruz Bay. **Trunk Bay** often receives the most attention because of its underwater snorkeling trail created by the National Park Service; signs let you know what you're seeing in terms of coral and other underwater features. And the beach is easy to reach since taxis leave on demand from Cruz Bay. A patchy reef just offshore means good snorkeling at **Hawksnest Beach**. Additionally, **Cinnamon Bay** and **Leinster Bay** also get their fair share of praise as snorkeling spots. That's not to say that you can't find good dive sites near St. John. **Deaver's Bay** is a short boat ride around the point from Cruz Bay, where you can see angelfish, southern stingrays, and triggerfish feeding at 30 to 50 feet. **The Leaf** is a large coral reef off St. John's southern shore.

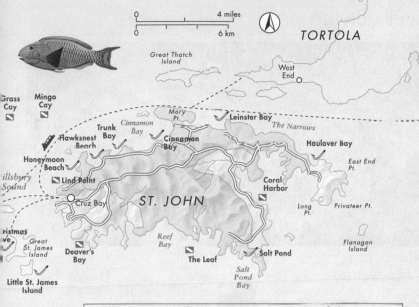

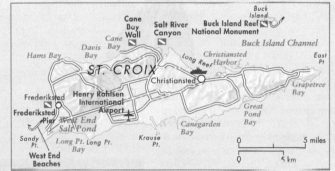

Coral near St. Croix

ST. CROIX

The largest of the U.S. Virgin Islands is a favorite of both divers and snorkelers and offers something for everyone. Snorkelers are often fascinated by the marked snorkeling trail at **Buck Island Reef**, which is a short boat ride from the island's east end; it's a U.S. national monument. Divers are drawn to the north shore, especially the **Cane Bay Wall**, a spectacular drop-off that's reachable from the beach, though usually reached by boat. Another north-shore site is the **Salt River Canyon**, where you can float downward through a canyon filled with colorful fish and coral. On the island's west end, **Frederiksted Pier** is home to a colony of sea horses, creatures seldom seen in the waters of the Virgin Islands. Casual snorkelers would also enjoy snorkeling at the **West End Beaches**.

SCUBA DIVING

St.Croix

If you've never been diving, start with an introductory lesson—often called a "resort course"—run by any one of the Virgin Islands' dive shops. All meet stringent safety standards. If they didn't, they'd soon be out of business. If you're staying at a hotel, you can often find the dive shop on-site; otherwise, your hotel probably has an arrangement with one nearby. If you're on a cruise, cruise-ship companies offer shore excursions that include transportation to and from the ship as well as the resort course. Certification requires much more study and practice, but it is required to rent air tanks, get air refills, and join others on guided dives virtually anywhere in the world.

The number one rule of diving is safety. The basic rules for safe diving are simple, and fools ignore them at their own peril. Serious diving accidents are becoming increasingly rare these days, thanks to the high level of diver training. However, they do still occur occasionally. Surfacing too rapidly without exhaling—or going too deep for too long—can result in an air embolism or a case of the bends.

Schneider Regional Medical Center in St. Thomas has a decompression chamber that serves all the Virgin Islands. If you get the bends, you'll be whisked to the hospital for this necessary treatment.

Fauna is another concern. Though sharks, barracuda, and moray eels are on the most-feared list, more often it's sea urchins and fire coral that cause pain when you accidentally bump them. Part of any scuba-training program is a review of sea life and the

Divers learn how to jump in from a boat

St.Croix

importance of respecting the new world you're exploring. Dive professionals recognize the value of protecting fragile reefs and ecosystems in tropical waters, and instructors emphasize look-don't-touch diving (the unofficial motto is: take only pictures, leave only bubbles). Government control and protection of dive sites is increasing, especially in such heavily used areas as the Virgin Islands.

While you can scuba dive off a beach—and you can find shops renting scuba equipment and providing airfills at the most popular beaches—a trip aboard a dive boat provides a more extensive glimpse into this wonderful undersea world. Since the dive shops can provide all equipment, there's no need to lug heavy weights and a bulky BC in your luggage. For the most comfort, you might want to bring your own regulator if you have one. The dive-boat captains and guides know the best dive locations, can find alternatives when the seas are rough, and will help you deal with heavy tanks and cumbersome equipment. Trips are easy to organize. Dive shops on all islands make frequent excursions to a wide variety of diving spots, and your

hotel, villa manager, or cruise-ship staff will help you make arrangements.

If you fly too soon after diving, you're at risk for decompression sickness, which occurs when nitrogen trapped in your bloodstream doesn't escape. This creates a painful and sometimes fatal condition called the bends, not a sickness you want to develop while you're winging your way home after a fun-filled beach vacation. Opinions vary, but as a rule of thumb, wait at least 12 hours after a single dive to fly. However, if you've made multiple dives or dived several days in a row, you should wait at least 18 hours. If you've made dives that required decompression stops, you should also wait at least 24 hours before flying. To be safe, consult with your physician.

The Virgin Islands offer a plethora of dive sites, and you'll be taken to some of the best if you sign on to a dive trip run by one of the many dive operations scattered around the islands.

DIVER TRAINING

(top) Underwater shot of tropical reef, (bottom) Diver silhouette, Cane Bay, St Croix

Good to know: Divers can become certified through PADI (⊕ www.padi.com), NAUI (⊕ www.naui.org), or SSI (⊕ www.divessi.com). The requirements for all three are similar, and if you do the classroom instruction and pool training with a dive shop associated with one organization, the referral for the open water dives will be honored by most dive shops. Note that you should not fly for at least 24 hours after a dive, because residual nitrogen in the body can pose health risks upon decompression. While there are no rigid rules on diving after flying, make sure you're well-hydrated before hitting the water.

NOT CERTIFIED?

Not sure if you want to commit the time and money to become certified? Not a problem. Most dive shops and many resorts will offer a discover scuba day-long course. In the morning, the instructor will teach you the basics of scuba diving: how to clear your mask, how to come to the surface in the unlikely event you lose your air supply, etc. In the afternoon, instructors will take you out for a dive in relatively shallow water—less than 30 feet. Be sure to ask where the dive will take place. Jumping into the water off a shallow beach may not be as fun as actually going out to the coral. If you decide that diving is something you want to pursue, the open dive may count toward your certification.

■ **TIP→** You can often book discover dives at the last minute. It may not be worth it to go out on a windy day when the currents are stronger. Also the underwater world looks a whole lot brighter on sunny days.

SNUBA

Beyond snorkeling or the requirements of scuba, you also have the option of "Snuba." The word is a trademarked portmanteau or combo of snorkel and scuba. Marketed as easy-to-learn family fun, Snuba lets you breathe underwater via tubes from an air-supplied vessel above, with no prior diving or snorkel experience required.

Sea urchin	Tiger grouper	Foureye butterflyfish
Parrotfish	Blue tang	Hogfish
Spottle eagle ray	Bonefish	Green sea turtle
Dolphin (mahi mahi)	Snook	French angelfish

REEF CREATURES IN THE VIRGIN ISLANDS

From the striped sergeant majors to bright blue tangs, the reefs of the Virgin Islands are teeming with life, though not nearly as many as in eons past. Warming waters and pollution have taken their toll on both coral and fish species. But many reefs in the Virgin Islands still thrive; you'll also see sponges, crustaceans, perhaps a sea turtle or two, and bigger game fish like grouper and barracuda; sharks are seen but are rarely a problem for divers. Beware of fire corals, which are not really corals but rather a relative of the jellyfish and have a painful sting; if you brush up against a fire coral, spread vinegar on the wound as soon as possible to minimize the pain.

FOOD
Calabash Market
FOOD | If you're renting a villa on the island's southeast end or headed to Salt Pond or Lameshur Bay for the day, provision at this small supermarket. The selection is quite good, including fresh steaks, seafood, and produce, and villa renters will find enough choices for simple meals and snacking. ⊠ *Rte. 107, Calabash Boom* ☎ *340/775–7172.*

GIFTS
Mumbo Jumbo
SOUVENIRS | With what may be the best prices in St. John, Mumbo Jumbo carries tropical clothing, stuffed sea creatures, local hot sauces, and other gifty items in a cozy little shop. ⊠ *Skinny Legs Shopping Complex, Rte. 10, Coral Bay* ☎ *340/779–4277.*

JEWELRY
ZEMI Island Designs
JEWELRY & WATCHES | The necklaces, bracelets, and rings sold at Zemi (the native Taíno term for spirit symbol) feature petroglyph designs as well as more contemporary hook bracelets, wreck coins, and gemstones. Its sister store, Jolly Dog, is next door. ⊠ *Isola Shoppes, Rte. 107, Coral Bay* ☎ *340/776–8355* ⊕ *www.zemistj.com.*

 Activities

BOATING AND SAILING
If you're staying at a hotel, your activities desk will usually be able to help you arrange a sailing excursion aboard a nearby boat. Most day sails leaving Cruz Bay head out along St. John's north coast. Those that depart from Coral Bay might drop anchor at some remote cay off the island's east end or even in the nearby British Virgin Islands. Your trip usually includes lunch, beverages, and at least one snorkeling stop. Keep in mind that inclement weather could interfere with your plans, though most boats will still go out if rain isn't too heavy.

Ocean Runner
BOATING | For a speedier trip to the cays and remote beaches off St. John, you can rent a powerboat with a captain from Ocean Runner. The company has everything from a 60-foot Sunseeker luxury yacht for up to 12 people for $4,500 to 15-foot runabouts for up to 4 people for $395 per day. Gas and oil will run you $100 to $300 a day extra, depending on how far you're going. ⊠ *Adjacent to Wharfside Village, Bay St., Waterfront, Cruz Bay* ☎ *340/693–8809* ⊕ *www. oceanrunnerusvi.com.*

St. John Concierge Service
BOATING | The capable staff can find a charter sail or powerboat that fits your style and budget. The company also books fishing and scuba trips. ⊠ *Henry Samuel St., booth across from post office, Cruz Bay* ☎ *340/514–5262* ⊕ *www.stjohnconciergeservice.com.*

DIVING AND SNORKELING
Although just about every beach has nice snorkeling—Trunk Bay, Cinnamon Bay, and Waterlemon Cay at Leinster Bay get the most praise—you need a boat to head out to the more remote snorkeling locations and the best scuba spots. Sign on with any of the island's water-sports operators to get to spots farther from St. John. Their boats will also take you to hot spots between St. John and St. Thomas, including the tunnels at **Thatch Cay,** the ledges at **Congo Cay,** and the wreck of the *General Rogers.* Dive off St. John at **Stephens Cay,** a short boat ride out of Cruz Bay, where fish swim around the reefs as you float downward. At **Devers Bay,** on St. John's south shore, fish dart about in colorful schools. **Carval Rock,** shaped like an old-time ship, has gorgeous rock formations, coral gardens, and lots of fish. It can be too rough here in winter, though. Count on paying $120 for a one-tank dive and $155 for a two-tank dive. Rates include equipment and a tour. If you've never dived before, try an introductory course called a resort course. Or

if certification is in your vacation plans, the island's dive shops can help you get your card.

Cruz Bay Watersports

SCUBA DIVING | Regular reef, wreck, and night dives, as well as USVI and BVI snorkel tours, are among this operator's offerings. There's a second location at the Ritz Carlton on St. Thomas. ⊠ *The Westin St. John, 300 Chocolate Hole, Cruz Bay* ☎ *340/776–6234, 844/359–5457* ⊕ *www. cruzbaywatersports.com.*

Low Key Watersports

SCUBA DIVING | This PADI Five Star training facility offers two-tank dives, night dives, and specialty courses. ⊠ *1 Bay St., Cruz Bay* ☎ *340/693–8999* ⊕ *www.divelowkey. com.*

FISHING

Well-kept charter boats—approved by the U.S. Coast Guard—head out to the north and south drops or troll along the inshore reefs, depending on the season and what's biting. The captains usually provide bait, drinks, and lunch, but you need to bring your own hat and sunscreen. Fishing charters start at about $1,300 for a full-day trip.

Offshore Adventures

FISHING | **FAMILY** | An excellent choice for fishing charters, Captain Rob Richards is patient with beginners—especially kids—but also enjoys going out with more experienced anglers. He runs the 32-foot and 40-foot center consoles, *Mixed Bag II and III*. ⊠ *The Westin St. John, 300A Chocolate Hole Rd., Estate Chocolate Hole and Great Cruz Bay* ☎ *340/513–0389* ⊕ *www.sportfishingstjohn.com.*

GUIDED TOURS

In St. John, taxi drivers provide tours of the island, making stops at various sites, including Trunk Bay and Annaberg Plantation. Prices run around $25 a person. The taxi drivers congregate near the ferry in Cruz Bay. The dispatcher will find you a driver for your tour. Along with providing trail maps and brochures about Virgin Islands National Park, the park service also gives several guided tours on- and offshore. Some are offered only during particular times of the year, and some require reservations.

Virgin Islands National Park Visitor Center.
⊠ *North Shore Rd., near creek, Cruz Bay* ☎ *340/776–6201* ⊕ *www.nps.gov/viis.*

HIKING

Although it's fun to go hiking with a Virgin Islands National Park guide, don't be afraid to head out on your own. To find a hike that suits your ability, stop by the park's Visitor Center in Cruz Bay and pick up the free trail guide; it details points of interest, trail lengths, and estimated hiking times, as well as any dangers you might encounter. Although the park staff recommends long pants to protect against thorns and insects, most people hike in shorts because it can get very hot. Wear sturdy shoes or hiking boots even if you're hiking to the beach. Don't forget to bring water and insect repellent.

HORSEBACK RIDING

Carolina Corral

HORSEBACK RIDING | **FAMILY** | Clip-clop along Coral Bay's shoreline and beaches for a slower-paced tour of St. John. Carolina Corral offers horseback trips and donkey wagon rides with its owner, Dana Bartlett. She has a way with animals and calms even novice riders. It's $85 for a two-hour ride; guided rides take place at 3 pm and 5 pm. ⊠ *Off Rte. 10, Coral Bay* ☎ *340/693–5778* ⊕ *www.horsesstjohn. com.*

SEA KAYAKING

Poke around crystal bays and explore undersea life from a sea kayak. Rates run about $70 for a full day in a double kayak. Tours start at $95 for a half day.

4

St. John CORAL BAY AND ENVIRONS

Arawak Expeditions

KAYAKING | This company uses traditional and sit-on-top kayaks for exploring the waters around St. John. They also rent stand-up paddleboards (SUP). Multiday kayak and SUP paddle and beach camping tours to neighboring deserted islands are also offered. ⊠ *Mongoose Junction Shopping Center, North Shore Rd., Cruz Bay* ☏ *340/693–8312, 800/238–8687* ⊕ *www.arawakexp.com.*

Cinnamon Bay Watersports

STAND UP PADDLEBOARDING | Rent stand-up paddleboards by the hour or longer. Kayaks, snorkel gear, and beach chairs are for rent here too. ⊠ *Rte. 20, Cinnamon Bay* ☏ *340/714–7144* ⊕ *www.cinnamonbayvi.com.*

Crabby's Water Sports

KAYAKING | Explore Coral Bay Harbor and Hurricane Hole on the eastern end of the island in a sea kayak or on a stand-up paddleboard from Crabby's, which also rents snorkel gear, beach chairs, umbrellas, coolers, and floats. ⊠ *Rte. 107, next to Cocoloba shopping center, Coral Bay* ☏ *340/626–1570* ⊕ *www.crabbyswatersports.com.*

ST. CROIX

Updated by
Anquanette Gaspard

👁 Sights	🍴 Restaurants	🛏 Hotels	🛍 Shopping	🍸 Nightlife
★★★★★	★★★★★	★★★★☆	★★★★☆	★★★☆☆

WELCOME TO ST. CROIX

TOP REASONS TO GO

★ **Sailing to Buck Island:** The beach at the western end of Buck Island is a great spot to relax after a snorkeling adventure or a hike up the hill to take in the stunning view.

★ **Diving the Wall:** Every dive boat in St. Croix makes a trip to the Cane Bay Wall, one of the Caribbean's best diving experiences, but you can also enjoy great shore diving from Cane Bay Beach.

★ **Exploring Fort Christiansvaern:** History buffs flock to Christiansted National Historic site. Head to the upper ramparts of Fort Christiansvaern to ponder how life was for early settlers.

★ **Fill up on flavor:** Savor the tastes of the island's cuisine by taking a walking food tour or visiting the Saturday farmer's market in Estate Lower Love.

★ **Sunrise at Point Udall:** Capture the sunrise at this easternmost point of the United States.

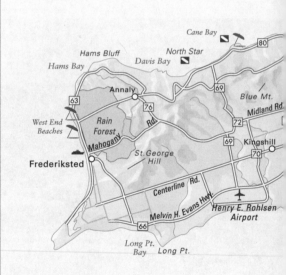

TO ↑
ST. THOMAS

Cane Bay
80
Hams Bluff   North Star
Davis Bay
Hams Bay
Annaly   69
63   76   Blue Mt.
Rd   Midland Rd.
West End   72
Beaches   Rain   69   Kingshill
Forest   70
Mahogany   St. George
Frederiksted   Hill
Centerline Rd.
Melvin H. Evans Hwy   Henry E. Rohlsen
66   Airport
Long Pt.
Bay   Long Pt.

0 ——————————— 2 miles
0 ——————————— 3 km

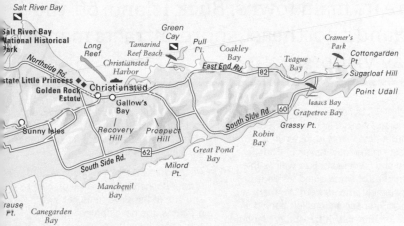

C a r i b b e a n   S e a

Buck Island

Buck Island Reef
National Monument

Salt River Bay

Salt River Bay
National Historical
Park

Long
Reef

Northside Rd.

Green
Cay

Tamarind
Reef Beach

Pull
Pt.

Christiansted
Harbor

Coakley
Bay

East End Rd.

82

Cramer's
Park

Cottongarden
Pt

Teague
Bay

Sugarloaf Hill

Point Udall

Estate Little Princess
Golden Rock
Estate

Christiansted

Gallow's
Bay

Isaacs Bay

Grapetree Bay

60

South Side Rd.

Grassy Pt.

Sunny Isles

Recovery
Hill

Prospect
Hill

Robin
Bay

Great Pond
Bay

South Side Rd.

62

Milord
Pt.

Manchenil
Bay

rause
Pt.

Canegarden
Bay

A T L A N T I C   O C E A N

The largest of the USVI, St. Croix is 40 miles (64 km) south of St. Thomas. Plantation ruins, reminders of the days when St. Croix was a big producer of sugar, dot the island. Its northwest is covered by a lush rainforest, its drier East End spotted with cacti. The restored Danish port of Christiansted and the more Victorian-looking Frederiksted are its main towns; Buck Island, off the island's northeast shore, attracts many day visitors.

Until 1917 Denmark owned St. Croix and her sister Virgin Islands, an aspect of the island's past that is reflected in street names in the main towns of Christiansted and Frederiksted, as well as the surnames of some island residents. Those early settlers from Denmark and other European nations left behind a slew of 18th- and 19th-century plantation ruins, all of them worked by enslaved people brought over on ships from Africa, their descendants, and white indentured servants lured to St. Croix to pay off their debt to society. Some of these ruins—such as the Christiansted National Historic site, Whim Plantation, the ruins at St. George Village Botanical Garden, and the ruins at Estate Mount Washington and Judith's Fancy—are open for easy exploration. Others are on private land, but a drive around the island passes the ruins of 100 plantations here and there on St. Croix's 84 square miles (218 square km). Their sugar mills, great houses, and factories are all that's left of the 224 plantations that once grew abundant sugarcane, tobacco, and other agricultural products.

An economic downturn began in 1801, further bolstered by a series of events. The end of the slave trade in 1803, droughts, the development of the sugar-beet industry in Europe, political upheaval, and a depression sent the island on a downward economic spiral.

Even though the slave trade ended in 1803, slavery continued here until 1848, when the enslaved people in St. Croix marched on Frederiksted to demand their freedom from the Danish government. The emancipation of enslaved people, followed by labor riots, fires, hurricanes, and an earthquake during the last half of the 19th century, brought what was left of the island's economy to its knees. The start of Prohibition in 1922 called a halt to the island's rum industry, further crippling the economy. The situation remained dire—so bad that President Herbert Hoover called the territory an "effective poorhouse" during a 1931 visit—until the rise of tourism in the late 1950s and 1960s. With tourism came economic improvements coupled with an influx of residents from other Caribbean islands and the mainland.

Today suburban subdivisions till the fields where sugarcane once waved in the tropical breeze. Condominium complexes line the beaches along the north coast outside Christiansted. Homes that are more elaborate dot the rolling hillsides. Modern strip malls and shopping centers sit along major roads. The island's robust culinary landscape offers a variety of local Caribbean eats, as well as American, Asian, Italian, and Mexican cuisines.

Although St. Croix sits firmly in the 21st century, with only a little effort you can easily step back into the island's past.

Planning

Getting Here and Around

AIR

You can fly nonstop to St. Croix from Atlanta (on Delta) or from Miami and Charlotte (on American Airlines). Spirit Airlines offers daily nonstop flights to St. Croix from Fort Lauderdale. You can also get connecting service through San Juan or St. Thomas via Cape Air, which offers code-share arrangements with all major airlines, ensuring a seamless transfer for all luggage to their final destination. Seaborne Airlines flies between St. Thomas, St. Croix, and San Juan.

BUS

Privately owned taxi vans crisscross St. Croix regularly, providing reliable service between Frederiksted and Christiansted along Route 70. This inexpensive ($2.50 one way) mode of transportation

is favored by locals, and though the many stops on the 20-mile (32-km) drive between the two main towns make the ride slow, it's never dull. Vitran public buses aren't the quickest way to get around the island, but they're comfortable and affordable. The fare is $1 between Christiansted and Frederiksted or to places in between.

CAR

You can certainly get by without a car, particularly if your hotel is close to Christiansted and offers a shuttle into town. However, having a car is a big advantage on St. Croix. With a wide assortment of celebrated restaurants and no large concentration of accommodations around either Christiansted or Frederiksted, a car can be beneficial regardless of where you are staying. Accommodations along the North Shore are even more isolated, making a car more of a necessity to travelers staying there. Even if you are staying in or near Christiansted, you will want to rent a car for a day or two to explore the island.

Although roads are not well signposted, there's a highway from the airport that travels to both east and west ends of the island that makes travel fairly easy. Street parking can be hard to find in Christiansted, but there are some paid lots. Be sure to remember that you drive on the *left* even though cars are U.S.–made with steering wheels on the left.

CAR RENTALS

Avis is at Henry Rohlsen Airport and at the cruise pier in Frederiksted. Budget has branches at the airport and near the seaplane terminal in Christiansted. Hertz is at the airport. Judi of Croix delivers vehicles to your hotel. Olympic is outside Christiansted, but will pick up at hotels.

CONTACTS Avis. ⊠ *Henry E. Rohlsen Airport* ☎ *340/778–9355, 800/352–7900* ⊕ *www.avis.com.* **Budget.** ⊠ *Henry E. Rohlsen Airport* ☎ *340/778–9636, 888/264–8894, 340/713–9289*

budgetstcroix.com. **Hertz.** ✉ *Henry
E. Rohlsen Airport* ☎ *340/778–1402,
888/248–4261, 340/778–9744* ⊕ *www.
rentacarstcroix.com.* **Judi of Croix.**
☎ *340/773–2123, 877/903–2123* ⊕ *www.
judiofcroix.com.* **Olympic.** ✉ *Rte. 70,
Christiansted* ☎ *340/718–3000* ⊕ *www.
olympicstcroix.com.* **Twin City Car Rental.**
✉ *The Village Mall, 113 Barren Spot, Suite
M3* ☎ *340/690–5043, 340/514–4136,
340/779–3564* ✎ *twincitycarrentalstx@
gmail.com* ⊕ *www.twincitycarrentalstx.
com.*

TAXI

Taxis are available in downtown Christiansted, at the Henry E. Rohlsen Airport, and at the Frederiksted pier during cruise-ship arrivals, or they can be called. In Frederiksted, all the shops are a short walk away, as is a great beach, so there's no need for a taxi if you are staying in town. Most cruise-ship passengers visit Christiansted on a tour since a taxi will cost $24 for one person plus $11 for each additional passenger (one way).

⚠ **There is no Uber or Lyft on St. Croix.**

CONTACTS St. Croix Taxi Association.
✉ *Henry E. Rohlsen Airport* ☎ *340/778–
1088.* **Native Son Taxi & Tours.** ☎ *340/626–
2767* ✎ *nativesonstx@yahoo.com.*

Beaches

St. Croix's beaches offer one-of-a-kind beauty with a level of tranquility and peace that you won't find in many places. One of the best beaches is on nearby Buck Island, a national monument where a marked snorkeling trail leads you through an extensive coral reef while a soft, sandy beach beckons a few yards away. Other great beaches are the West End beaches both south and north of Frederiksted, like Dorsch Beach and Rainbow Beach.

Hotels

You can find everything from plush resorts to simple beachfront digs in St. Croix. If you sleep in either the Christiansted or Frederiksted area, you'll be closest to shopping, restaurants, and nightlife. Most of the island's other hotels will put you just steps from the beach. St. Croix has several small but special properties that offer personalized service. If you like all the comforts of home, you may prefer to stay in a condominium or villa. Whether you stay in a hotel, a condominium, or a villa, you'll enjoy up-to-date amenities.

Although a stay right in historic Christiansted may mean putting up with a little urban noise, you probably won't have trouble sleeping. Christiansted rolls up the sidewalks fairly early, and humming air-conditioners drown out any noise. Solitude is guaranteed at hotels and inns outside Christiansted and on the outskirts of sleepy Frederiksted.

Families and groups may find more value in a condo that allows you to do a bit of cooking but still has access to a pool or a limited array of resort-style amenities. There are a lot of condos and apartment buildings on St. Croix, particularly along the North Shore and East End.

⇨ *Hotel prices are the lowest cost of a standard double room in high season.*

WHAT IT COSTS in U.S. Dollars

$	$$	$$$	$$$$
HOTELS			
under $276	$276–$375	$376–$475	over $475

PRIVATE CONDOS AND VILLAS

St. Croix has more than 350 private villas scattered all over the island, from modest two-bedroom houses with just the basics to lavish and luxurious five-bedroom compounds with every imaginable amenity. But most are located in the center or in the East End. Renting a villa gives you all the convenience of home as well as top-notch amenities. Many have pools, hot tubs, and deluxe furnishings. Most companies meet you at the airport, arrange for a rental car, and provide helpful information about the island.

If you want to be close to the island's restaurants and shopping, look for a condominium or villa in the hills above Christiansted or on either side of the town. An East End location gets you out of Christiansted's hustle and bustle, but you're still only 15 minutes from town. North Shore locations are lovely, with gorgeous sea views and lots of peace and quiet.

Nightlife

The island's nightlife is ever changing, and its arts scene is eclectic, ranging from holiday performances of *The Nutcracker* to locally organized shows. Folk-art traditions, such as quadrille dancers, are making a comeback. To find out what's happening, pick up the local newspapers—*V.I. Daily News* and *St. Croix Avis*—available at newsstands. Christiansted has a lively and eminently casual club scene near the waterfront. Frederiksted has a couple of restaurants and clubs offering weekend entertainment.

Restaurants

Seven flags have flown over St. Croix, and each has left its legacy in the island's cuisine. You can feast on Italian, French, and American dishes; there are even Chinese and Mexican restaurants in Christiansted. Fresh local seafood is plentiful and always good; wahoo, tuna, mahi mahi, and conch are most popular. Island chefs often add Caribbean twists to familiar dishes. For a true island experience, stop at a local restaurant for stew chicken, seasoned rice, kalalloo, or roast pork. Regardless of where you eat, your meal will be an informal affair. As is the case everywhere in the Caribbean, prices are higher than you'd pay on the mainland. Some restaurants may close for a week or two in September or October, so if you're traveling during these months it's best to call ahead.

St. Croix has restaurants scattered from one end to the other, so it's usually not hard to find a place to stop when you're exploring the island. Most travelers eat dinner near their hotel so as to avoid long drives on dark, unfamiliar roads. Christiansted has the island's widest selection of restaurants. Don't rule out Frederiksted, especially if you're out exploring the island. It has a handful of delightful restaurants.

⇨ *Restaurant prices are the average cost of a main course at dinner or, if dinner is not served, at lunch.*

WHAT IT COSTS in U.S. Dollars			
$	$$	$$$	$$$$
RESTAURANTS			
under $13	$13–$20	$21–$30	over $30

Safety

Don't wander the streets of Christiansted or Frederiksted alone at night. Don't leave valuables in your car, and keep it locked wherever you park. Don't leave cameras, purses, and other valuables lying on the beach while you snorkel for an hour (or even for a minute).

SCUBA DIVING EMERGENCIES
Roy L. Schneider Hospital on St. Thomas has the territory's only hyperbaric chamber.

Schneider Regional Medical Center. ⊠ *Roy L. Schneider Hospital, 9048 Sugar Estate, Charlotte Amalie* ☎ *340/776–8311* ⊕ *www.rlshospital.org.*

Shopping

When shopping on St. Croix, you're sure to uncover unique finds within the various small boutiques, gift emporiums, souvenir shops, and jewelry retailers found throughout the island. St. Croix shop hours are usually Monday through Saturday, from 9 am to 5 pm, but there are some shops in Christiansted open in the evening. Stores are often closed on Sunday.

If you've rented a condominium or a villa, you'll appreciate St. Croix's excellent stateside-style supermarkets (albeit with prices that are at least 30% higher than on the U.S. mainland). Fresh vegetables, fruits, and meats arrive from the mainland frequently and are always available. Try the open-air stands strung out along Route 70 for island produce.

In Christiansted the best shopping areas are the **Pan Am Pavilion** and **Caravelle Arcade,** off Strand Street, and along **King** and **Company Streets.** These streets give way to arcades filled with boutiques. **Gallows Bay** has a blossoming shopping area in a quiet neighborhood.

Tours

Sweeny's St. Croix Safari Tours offers van tours of St. Croix. Excursions depart from Christiansted and last about five hours starting at $70 per person. Walking tours of Christiansted's historic sites run $25. Virgin Islands Food Tours offers a guided food-tasting and cultural walking tour in downtown Christiansted with six authentic local food and drink tastings at $99 per person.

CONTACTS Sweeny's St. Croix Safari Tours. ⊠ *Christiansted* ☎ *340/773–6700* ⊕ *www.gotostcroix.com/guided-tours/sweenys-tours.* **Virgin Islands Food Tours.** ⊠ *Christiansted* ☎ *866/498–3684* ⊕ *www.vifoodtours.com.*

Visitor Information

If you want some friendly advice, pick up the *St. Croix This Week* magazine at airports, supermarkets, restaurants, and other locales within the island. This free publication has been around for 52 years offering a multitude of information for visitors ranging from events, attractions, and tours to restaurants, duty-free shopping, and much more. Check out ⊕ *gotostcroix.com* and ⊕ *visitusvi.com* for additional visitor information.

CONTACTS St. Croix Visitor Center. ⊠ *Frederiksted* ☎ *340/773–0357* ⊕ *www.visitusvi.com.* **USVI Department of Tourism.** ⊠ *321 King St., Frederiksted* ☎ *340/772–0357* ⊕ *www.visitusvi.com.* **St. Croix This Week.** ⊕ *virginislandsthisweek.com/st-croix.*

BANKS

St. Croix has branches of Banco Popular in the Orange Grove and Sunny Isles shopping centers. FirstBank is in Sunny Isles, Frederiksted, and Orange Grove. Oriental Bank (formerly Scotiabank), has a branch in Sunny Isles and ATMs in downtown Christiansted and Frederiksted. Bank of St. Croix has locations in Gallows Bay and Peters Rest.

Christiansted

Christiansted is a historic Danish-style town that has served as St. Croix's commercial center since the 1700s. Start off your day by checking out the historic sights when it's still cool. Break for lunch at an open-air restaurant before spending as much time as you like shopping.

Fort Christiansvaern, a National Historic site

In the 1700s and 1800s, Christiansted was a trading center for sugar, rum, and molasses. Today there are law offices, boutiques, duty-free shops, and restaurants lining the bustling streets within the downtown area. Many of the buildings, which start at the harbor and go up the gently sloped hillsides, still date from the 18th century. You can't get lost as all streets lead back downhill to the water.

◉ Sights

★ D. Hamilton Jackson Park
CITY PARK | When you need a break from sightseeing, stop at this shady park on the street side of Fort Christiansvaern for a rest. It's named for a famed labor leader, judge, and journalist who started the first newspaper not under the thumb of the Danish crown (his birthday, November 1, is a territorial holiday celebrated with much fanfare in St. Croix). Public restrooms are available. ⊠ *Between Fort Christiansvaern and Danish Customs House, Christiansted.*

★ Fort Christiansvaern
MILITARY SIGHT | **FAMILY** | The large yellow fortress dominates the waterfront. Because it's so easy to spot, it makes a good place to begin a walking tour. In 1749 the Danish built the fort to protect the harbor, but the structure was repeatedly damaged by hurricane-force winds and had to be partially rebuilt in 1771. It's now a National Historic Site, the best preserved of the few remaining Danish-built forts in the Virgin Islands. The park's visitor center is here, and rangers are on hand to answer questions. ⊠ *Hospital St., Christiansted* 🕾 *340/773–1460* ⊕ *www.nps.gov/chri* 🖃 *$7.*

Government House
GOVERNMENT BUILDING | One of the town's most elegant structures was built as a home for a Danish merchant in 1747. Today it houses offices and serves as the residence of the governor of the Virgin Islands. A sweeping staircase leads to a second-story ballroom, still used for official government functions. Out front, the traditional red Danish guard booth

Christiansted

Christiansted Harbor

Gallows Bay

D. Hamilton Jackson Park

KEY

- ① Exploring Sights
- ① Restaurants
- ① Quick Bites
- ① Hotels
- 🄸 Tourist Information

Sights ▶

1. D. Hamilton Jackson Park............**F1**
2. Fort Christiansvaern......**G1**
3. Government House......**F2**
4. Old Danish Customs House...........**F2**
5. Scale House............**F1**
6. Steeple Building.........**F2**

Restaurants ▶

1. Caroline's Breakfast & Brunch............**F1**
2. Coco Loco Tapas Bar & Grill...............**E1**
3. Hamilton's.................**F2**
4. Nate's Boathouse.......**D1**
5. Rum Runners...............**D1**
6. Savant...................**G2**
7. Too.Chez.................**E2**
8. Zeny's Restaurant........**D3**

Quick Bites ▶

1. Cafe 50.................**E3**
2. Grounded Cafe...........**E2**
3. Jump Up Deli.............**F2**
4. Twin City Coffee House and Gallery.........**F2**
5. What's Da Scoop?........**E2**

Hotels ▶

1. Club Comanche Hotel St. Croix............**E2**
2. Company House Hotel ...**F2**
3. Holger Danske Hotel.....**D2**
4. Hotel Caravelle............**D1**
5. Hotel on the Cay.........**F1**
6. King Christian Hotel **E1**
7. Sugar Apple Bed & Breakfast...........**D2**

with its pointed top used to be a popular photo op, but it's now inaccessible to the public for security reasons. ✉ *105 King St., Christiansted* ☎ *340/773–1404.*

Old Danish Customs House
HISTORIC SIGHT | FAMILY | Built in 1830 on foundations that date from a century earlier, the historic building, which is near Fort Christiansvaern, originally served as both a customs house and a post office. In 1926 it became the Christiansted Library, and it's been a national park facility since 1972. It's closed to the public, but the sweeping front steps make a nice place to take a break. ✉ *King St., Christiansted* ☎ *340/773–1460* 🌐 *www.nps.gov/chri.*

Scale House
HISTORIC SIGHT | FAMILY | This 1856 building on the Christiansted waterfront was once where goods passing through the port were weighed and inspected. Visitors can see an old Danish scale on the ground floor. ✉ *King St., Christiansted* ☎ *340/773–1460* 🌐 *www.nps.gov/chri.*

★ **Steeple Building**
HISTORY MUSEUM | The first Danish Lutheran church on the island when it was built in 1753, the Steeple Building has been given new life as a museum with archaeological artifacts and exhibits on plantation life, the architectural development of Christiansted, the island's native inhabitants, and one-time St. Croix resident Alexander Hamilton. As of this writing, however, the building was closed for roof repairs. Admission, when it's open, is included in the price of visiting Christiansted National Historic Site. ✉ *Church St., Christiansted* ☎ *340/773–1460* 🌐 *www.nps.gov/chri* 🎟 *$7.*

🍴 Restaurants

Caroline's Breakfast & Brunch
$ | AMERICAN | One of the newest eateries along the Christiansted Boardwalk, this tropical oceanfront restaurant overlooking historic Christiansted is one of the dining options provided by the newly renovated King Christian Hotel that features quality breakfast favorites and brunch cocktails. Try Caroline's Omelet, with roasted red pepper, balsamic caramelized onions, goat cheese, and baby spinach, paired with a passion fruit mimosa. **Known for:** unique brunch cocktails; quality breakfast dishes; stylish décor. [$] *Average main: $12* ✉ *Next to King Christian Hotel, 1102 King's Wharf Street, Christiansted* ☎ *340/773–6330* 🌐 *www.carolinesbreakfast.com.*

Big Event

St. Croix celebrates Carnival in late December with the Crucian Christmas Festival. If you don't book far enough in advance, it can be hard to find a room due to the influx of visitors from around the region and the world. 🌐 *www.vicarnivalschedule.com/stcroix.*

Coco Loco Tapas Bar & Grill
$$$ | SPANISH | This vibrant Spanish-inspired tapas bar and grill highlights the flavors of Latin cuisine by combining Spanish, Mexican, Cuban, Puerto Rican, and Peruvian cuisines with a Caribbean twist. Start off with a few tapas like the stuffed empanadas, bacon-wrapped maduros, and chicharron bites, followed by a main entrée like the seafood paella (made with the catch of the day) or the steak of the day. **Known for:** eclectic menu; cozy atmosphere; cocktails served in a coconut-shaped glass. [$] *Average main: $25* ✉ *Kings Alley Walkway, 57 Kings Wharf Street, Christiansted* ☎ *340/690–5626* 🌐 *cocolocostx.com* 🕒 *Closed Mon. and Tues.*

Hamilton's
$$$$ | AMERICAN | Named for the two Hamiltons of St. Croix—Alexander Hamilton and David Hamilton Jackson—this fine dining restaurant, with an extensive

wine list, prepares dishes with fresh ingredients and an abundance of flavor. The soup du jour and the fresh catch of the day—which might be a seafood chowder made with local conch and mahi mahi, and a pan-seared wahoo or wasabi-crusted tuna—are always a hit with guests. **Known for:** specialty curated wine list; house-made desserts; covered outdoor patio dining. [$] *Average main: $35* ⊠ *39 Queen Cross St, Christiansted* ☎ *340/773–5393* ⊕ *www.instagram.com/hamiltonsvi/* ⊘ *No lunch.*

Nate's Boathouse

$$$ | **ECLECTIC** | Serving breakfast, lunch, and dinner indoors and out, this dockside spot has something for everyone on its extensive menu. Dinner can be as fancy as tilapia and garlic shrimp with mushrooms, white wine, and garlic butter, or as basic as a burger or chicken sandwich. **Known for:** happy hour drinks specials; extensive menu; Sunday brunch. [$] *Average main: $26* ⊠ *1201 King Cross St., On the boardwalk, Christiansted* ☎ *340/692–6283* ⊕ *www.stxboathouse.com.*

★ Rum Runners

$$$ | **MODERN AMERICAN | FAMILY** | Sitting right on the Christiansted boardwalk behind Hotel Caravelle, Rum Runners serves a little bit of everything, including a to-die-for tropical salad topped with fresh local mango (in season) or pineapple. Heartier fare includes ribs and chili lime shrimp tossed with crab, bacon, and olive oil over a bed of spaghetti. **Known for:** stellar views; local hangout; boardwalk location. [$] *Average main: $30* ⊠ *Hotel Caravelle, 1044 Queen Cross St., Christiansted* ☎ *340/773–6585* ⊕ *www.rumrunnersstcroix.com* ⊘ *Closed Wed.*

★ Savant

$$$$ | **ECLECTIC** | One of those small but special spots that everyone loves, including critics who regularly rank it among the Caribbean's best restaurants, this lively spot relies on local ingredients in its fusion of Mexican, Thai, and Caribbean dishes that can include anything from Thai curry with chicken to a fillet of beef stuffed with portobello mushrooms and goat cheese. You can't go wrong with the daily egg roll special or the catch of the day. **Known for:** bustling atmosphere; creative fusion fare; courtyard dining. [$] *Average main: $35* ⊠ *4C Hospital St., Christiansted* ☎ *340/713–8666* ⊕ *www.savantstx.com* ⊘ *Closed Sun. No lunch.*

Too.Chez

$$$ | **FRENCH** | This beautiful courtyard restaurant serves French-inspired American cuisine; the barbecued ribs are excellent, and you can do a partially healthy offset by ordering the roasted Brussels sprouts dip and scooping it onto flatbread. Don't skip the desserts, particularly the apple crisp topped with house-made vanilla ice cream. **Known for:** mouthwatering desserts; courtyard dining; creative Caribbean cuisine. [$] *Average main: $28* ⊠ *53 King St., Christiansted* ☎ *340/713–8888* ⊕ *www.toochezstx.com* ⊘ *Closed Sun. and Mon.*

Zeny's Restaurant

$$ | **LATIN AMERICAN** | Serving local favorites for over 30 years, Zeny's Restaurant is open seven days a week whipping up mouthwatering dishes like stew chicken, seasoned rice, conch in butter sauce, and roast pork. The inconspicuous residential exterior transforms into a cozy, intimate restaurant inside. **Known for:** quick service; local cuisine; affordable prices. [$] *Average main: $15* ⊠ *15 King Street, Christiansted* ☎ *340/773–4393.*

☕ Coffee and Quick Bites

Cafe 50

$ | **CAFÉ** | This brand-new Internet café in Christiansted features coffee, lattes, and frappuccinos, plus delicious local pastries like coffee cakes, donuts, and muffins. Grab-and-go salads and sandwich wraps are a great lunch option when pressed for time. **Known for:** free Wi-Fi; cozy and intimate atmosphere; delicious pastries.

$ *Average main: $8* ⊠ *50 AB Company St., Christiansted* ⊘ *Closed Sun.*

Grounded Cafe

$ | **CAFÉ** | Choose from a wide variety of hot and cold beverages, signature sandwiches, specialty drinks, salads, soups, baked goods, and desserts. The locally made pates sell out quickly in the morning; get there early to grab one and pair with your favorite coffee or tea beverage. **Known for:** locally made pates; convenient location; fruit smoothies with whipped cream. $ *Average main: $7* ⊠ *1113 Strand St., Christiansted* ☎ *340/626–9993* ⊕ *www.groundedcafevi.com* ⊘ *Closed Sun.*

Jump Up Deli

$$ | **SANDWICHES** | This unique deli and gift boutique is the go-to spot for classic deli sandwiches and traditional meats, cheeses, soups, and salads. There are hot and cold sandwiches and other items to meet every dietary need. **Known for:** daily specials; cold cuts and cheeses sold by weight; hot and cold sandwiches. $ *Average main: $15* ⊠ *Inside Apothecary Hall, 6 Company Street, Christiansted* ☎ *340/712–0002* ⊕ *jumpupdeli.com* ⊘ *Closed Sun. and Mon.*

Twin City Coffee House and Gallery

$ | **CAFÉ** | This locally owned coffee shop uses local organic fruits and vegetables to prepare hearty breakfast and lunch dishes. Located steps from the Christiansted National Historic site, the covered sidewalk seating is great for people-watching and taking in the local scene while enjoying your favorite latte, breakfast platter, or salad. **Known for:** convenient location; specialty coffee drinks; filling lunch salads and wraps. $ *Average main: $12* ⊠ *2101 Company St., Christiansted* ☎ *340/773–9400* ⊕ *twincitycoffeehouse.myshopify.com* ⊘ *Closed Sun.*

What's Da Scoop

$ | **ICE CREAM** | **FAMILY** | Cool down with a scoop or two of local homemade ice cream from this family-run establishment. Popular flavors include Cruzan Rum Raisin, mango sorbet, Ponche Cuba with almonds, and vegan coconut. **Known for:** boozy milkshakes; house-made flavors; bright, colorful décor. $ *Average main: $8* ⊠ *1115 Strand St., Christiansted* ☎ *340/277–4673.*

Hotels

Club Comanche Hotel St. Croix

$ | **HOTEL** | This historic townhouse built in 1756 is located in the center of town within walking distance to art galleries, duty-free shops, custom jewelers, fine restaurants, waterfront bars, and the seaplane terminal. **Pros:** nearby beach; located near shopping and restaurants; friendly staff. **Cons:** no elevator; limited amenities; no close parking. $ *Rooms from: $199* ⊠ *1 Strand St., Christiansted* ☎ *340/773–0210, 888/406–8030* ⊕ *www.clubcomanche.com* ⇆ *23 rooms* ⦿ *No Meals.*

Company House Hotel

$ | **HOTEL** | With an elegant lobby, including a grand piano, and serviceable rooms, this hotel provides affordable accommodations in the heart of Christiansted. **Pros:** tastefully decorated rooms; convenient location; inexpensive. **Cons:** no parking; no beach; busy neighborhood. $ *Rooms from: $219* ⊠ *2 Company St., Christiansted* ☎ *340/773–1377* ⊕ *www.hotelcompanyhouse.com* ⇆ *33 rooms* ⦿ *No Meals.*

Holger Danske Hotel

$ | **HOTEL** | Old-world charm and old-world prices best describe this historic hotel on the Christiansted boardwalk. **Pros:** convenient location; friendly staff; freshwater pool. **Cons:** limited parking; no elevators on property; limited amenities. $ *Rooms from: $145* ⊠ *1200 King Cross St., Christiansted* ☎ *877/465–4375, 340/773–3600* ⊕ *holgerhotel.com* ⇆ *42 rooms* ⦿ *No Meals.*

Hotel Caravelle

$ | **HOTEL** | Located near the Christiansted harbor, Hotel Caravelle puts you at the waterfront end of a pleasant shopping arcade and steps from shops and restaurants. **Pros:** good restaurant; convenient location; parking on-site. **Cons:** no beach; pool closed for renovations as of this writing; busy neighborhood. [$] *Rooms from: $209* ✉ *44A Queen Cross St., Christiansted* ☎ *340/773–0687, 800/524–0410 Reservations* 🌐 *www.hotelcaravelle.com* 🛏 *43 rooms* 🍴 *No Meals.*

Hotel on the Cay

$ | **RESORT** | Hop on the $5 ferry to reach this peaceful time-share resort in the middle of Christiansted Harbor. **Pros:** quiet; convenient location; lovely beach. **Cons:** accessible only by a short ferry ride; limited food options; no parking. [$] *Rooms from: $169* ✉ *Protestant Cay, Christiansted* ☎ *340/773–2035, 855/654–0301* 🌐 *www.hotelonthecay.com* 🛏 *54 rooms* 🍴 *No Meals.*

King Christian Hotel

$$ | **HOTEL** | A stay at the King Christian puts you directly on the Christiansted waterfront next to the Christiansted National Historic Site. **Pros:** ocean views; fully remodeled rooms; convenient location. **Cons:** no beach; minimal furnishings in rooms; no parking lot. [$] *Rooms from: $299* ✉ *57 King St., Box 24467, Christiansted* ☎ *340/773–6330, 800/524–2012* 🌐 *www.kingchristianhotel.com* 🛏 *46 rooms* 🍴 *No Meals.*

Sugar Apple Bed & Breakfast

$ | **B&B/INN** | Formerly Pink Fancy Hotel, Sugar Apple Bed & Breakfast is one of the newest hotels on the island, though some of the property's old stone and coral structure date back to 1780. **Pros:** convenient location; kitchenette in each room; breakfast included. **Cons:** limited amenities; low water pressure at times; minimal staff. [$] *Rooms from: $159* ✉ *27 Prince St., Christiansted* ☎ *340/626–8141* 🌐 *www.sugarapplebnb.com* 🛏 *12 rooms* 🍴 *Free Breakfast.*

🍸 Nightlife

The Beach Bar at Hotel on the Cay

THEMED ENTERTAINMENT | For a mini adventure in downtown Christiansted, hop the two-minute ferry to this hotel bar on Protestant Cay for trivia Wednesdays, live music on weekends, and periodic Tiki Tuesday parties with a luau-style buffet, steel pan bands, fire dancers, and Mocko Jumbie performers. The beach bar is open until 10 pm, and the ferry from the Christiansted boardwalk—normally $5 per person for non–hotel guests—is free after 5 pm. ✉ *Protestant Cay, Christiansted* ☎ *340/773–2035* 🌐 *www.hotelonthecay.com.*

Breakers Roar Tiki Bar

BARS | Classic rum-based drinks in decorative tiki glasses (think: zombies, mai tais, and hurricanes) star at this dark, atmospheric bar with indoor and outdoor space. For something local, try the Iloilo, made with Mutiny vodka, or the Merciful Mistress, a tiki drink built around light Cruzan Diamond Estate rum. ✉ *The King Christian Hotel, 1102 King's Wharf, Christiansted* ☎ *340/773–6330* 🌐 *www.breakersroar.com.*

★ Brew STX

LIVE MUSIC | Locals and visitors come here to drink freshly brewed mango lager and listen to live music several nights a week. Oh, and there are crab races on Mondays. A nice selection of appetizers and sandwiches, plus shareable build-your-own salads make this waterfront microbrewery a fun place to nosh while you work your way through beer flights and people-watch on the boardwalk. ✉ *Boardwalk at King's Alley, 55 A&B King's Alley, Christiansted* ☎ *340/719–6339* 🌐 *www.brewstx.com.*

LEVELS

LIVE MUSIC | St. Croix's newest addition to the island's nightlife, LEVELS is a live music venue, bar, and creative space in downtown Christiansted where local and independent creatives go to showcase their music, performance, film, or mixed media. The venue hosts themed nights throughout the week including open mic nights, playlist Thursday, and live music performances featuring jazz, reggae, hip-hop, and R&B. Nightly drink specials are available at the fully stocked bar. ⊠ *54B Company St., Christiansted* ⊹ *Across from Luncheria* ⊕ *www.levelsvi.com* ♥ *Closed Sun., Mon., and Wed.*

Nirvana Bar & Lounge

COCKTAIL LOUNGES | Located right off the Christiansted Boardwalk, this upscale lounge offers a fun atmosphere for those looking for a lively night out. Try the Strawberry Moscow Mule or the Beach Bum for a delicious spin on classic drinks, while a DJ mixes reggae, soca, and calypso with a touch of Afrobeats, hip-hop, and R&B. Watch out for their themed events, which always draw a crowd. ⊠ *Pan Am Pavilion, 39 A Strand Street, Christiansted* ☎ *340/771–8423* ♥ *Closed Sun.–Wed.*

The Social Beer Garden

BEER GARDENS | At this open-air courtyard space, guests can enjoy handmade cocktails, wine, and beer while listening to smooth sounds of R&B, jazz, and Afrobeats. Weekly live music entertainment includes jazz bands, acoustic guitarists, saxophonists, and more. Enjoy happy hour every Tuesday and Wednesday with 50% off all cocktails and beers from 5 pm to 8 pm. ⊠ *50 AB Company St., Christiansted* ♥ *Closed Sun. and Mon.*

Velvet Haze Lounge

THEMED ENTERTAINMENT | Catch a vibe at St. Croix's premier hookah lounge, where funky iridescent lights, modern décor, and unique artworks create a relaxed and sophisticated atmosphere. Choose from a variety of shisha flavors, ranging from fruity and sweet to spicy and savory; you can even have a staff member create a personalized blend based on your preferences. The cocktail menu features classic cocktails like Long Island, Tequila Sunrise, and Midori Sour; with a full bar,

they can make almost anything your palate desires. Weekly events include cigar night, tequila Tuesdays, and karaoke night. ⊠ *1102 Strand St., Christiansted* ☎ *340/474–4328* ♥ *Closed Sun. and Mon.*

 Shopping

BOOKS
Undercover Books & Gifts

BOOKS | This well-stocked independent bookseller sells Caribbean-themed books as well as the latest good reads, like curated selections of books on Crucian history and culture. They have monthly book club meetups and frequent book-signing events that feature local authors, many of whom also participate in the annual St. Croix Literary Festival in April. ⊠ *5030 Anchor Way, Suite 11, Gallows Bay* ⊹ *Across from the post office* ☎ *340/719–1567* ⊕ *www.undercoverbooksstcroix.com* ♥ *Closed Sun.*

CLOTHING
Asha World Designs

MIXED CLOTHING | Climb the steps next to Common Cents Pub on Company Street to discover an eclectic assortment of adornments and attire from around the world. Open seasonally, Asha World Designs carries a signature clothing line that was handmade in India, Thailand, and Bali. Dive through the treasure trove of unique jewelry designs, accessories, gifts, textiles, and homewares to find that perfect item to accompany you back home. ⊠ *53B Company St., Christiansted* ⊹ *Upstairs next to Common Cents Pub* ☎ *340/690–6512* ⊕ *www.ashaworlddesigns.com* ♥ *Closed Sun.*

Belle Femme Boutique

WOMEN'S CLOTHING | For easy and beautiful clothing suitable for the island lifestyle, look no further than Belle Femme Boutique. Elegant evening wear and chic casual attire in a kaleidoscope of colors can be found here. Cool linen sets and comfy sandals are plentiful and the endless assortment of bags, accessories, and jewelry will have you wanting them all. They also carry quality business and casual shirts, shoes, belts, and slacks for men. ☒ *54 Kings Wharf St., Across from Government House on King Street, Christiansted* ☎ *340/773–2755* ◐ *Closed Sun.*

Envii Boutique

WOMEN'S CLOTHING | Find one-of-a-kind pieces designed to elevate your wardrobe and personal style at this upscale women's boutique, where you will discover chic dresses and tailored separates to statement jewelry and handbags that will have you looking and feeling your best. ☒ *2209 Queen Cross St., Christiansted* ✛ *Near intersection of Company & Queen Cross Streets* ☎ *340/227–3634* ◐ *Closed Sun.*

From the Gecko Boutique

MIXED CLOTHING | This store sells a variety of stylish men's and women's clothes on St. Croix, including a selection of fair trade and organic clothing, handbags, hats, swimwear, handmade ornaments, and jewelry. Bright, island-friendly colors rule the racks here. ☒ *55 Company St., Suite 1, Christiansted* ☎ *340/778–9433* ⊕ *fromthegecko.com* ◐ *Closed Sun.*

★ Hotheads Boutique

MIXED CLOTHING | As the name implies, this small store sells hats and more hats, but you will also find swimwear for all shapes and sizes, including hard-to-find separates, cup sizes, and eye-catching styles for full-figured women. Add one of their colorful sarongs or cover-ups to your on-island wardrobe or choose from one of their selection of bags, accessories, dressy clothing, and sandals. ☒ *1244 Queen Cross St., Christiansted* ☎ *340/773–7888* ◐ *Closed Sun. and Mon.*

KNG Men's Clothing & Accessories

MEN'S CLOTHING | The newest men's clothing store in downtown Christiansted is locally owned and operated, offering everything from casual wear like tees, polos, and hats to more formal options like jackets, bowties, and vests. Shop for accessories and fragrances as well as designer sneakers and slides. There are options for boys, too. ☒ *1114 King St., Suite 3, Christiansted* ◐ *Closed Sun.*

Southern Saint Boutique

MIXED CLOTHING | This luxury clothing and swimwear brand designs clothes ideal for island-living: boat wear made from natural fibers like bamboo, linen, and 100% organic cotton that are hand-dyed with natural ingredients. All Southern Saint merchandise is designed on St. Croix and manufactured around the world in countries like Guatemala, Honduras, and Bali. ☒ *1104 Strand St., Suite 101, Christiansted* ☎ *340/513–5695* ⊕ *southernsaintvi.com.*

Susan Mango

WOMEN'S CLOTHING | Austin native and fashion wholesaler Susan Connett brings her sense of style to St. Croix with a dazzling variety of resort wear, beachwear, and fabrics sourced from women producers in Bali, Africa, Guatemala, and elsewhere. ☒ *54 King St., Christiansted* ☎ *512/689–7049.*

GIFTS

Christa's Art Gallery

ART GALLERIES | At St. Croix's newest art gallery, you'll uncover artworks and products from artist Christa-Ann Davis Molloy that highlights the rich cross-cultural experience of the USVI and beyond. Get lost in the magic of paintings and sketches showcasing Mocko Jumbies, quadrille dancers, carnival masqueraders, steel pan drummers, and historic buildings, which are also captured on a host of houseware items including mugs, coasters, umbrellas, and bags. ☒ *57 Company St., Christiansted* ☎ *340/713–9959* ◐ *Closed Sun.*

★ Eden South

SOUVENIRS | An unexpected oasis of Crucian culture awaits at this locally owned gift shop. Check out their line of local preserves and syrups made using old-time recipes or pick up a book from a local author. They also carry colorful rainforest and recipe T-shirts as well as their famous Jack's Bay Pepper Sauce—your favorite foodie will thank you for this flavorful gift. ⊠ 3 Company St., Christiansted ☎ 340/713 1003 ☉ Closed Sun.

Many Hands

SOUVENIRS | This shop sells pottery in bright colors, paintings of St. Croix, and the Caribbean, prints, and maps. They are all made by local artists, and they all make for perfect take-home gifts. ■TIP→ The shop ships worldwide. ⊠ 6 Pan Am Pavilion, 1102 Strand St., Christiansted ☎ 340/773–1990.

Mitchell-Larsen Studio

SOUVENIRS | This glass gallery offers an interesting amalgam of carefully crafted glass plates, suncatchers, and more. The pieces, all made on-site by St. Croix glassmaker Jan Mitchell Larsen, are often whimsically adorned with tropical fish, flora, and fauna. Photography from Steffen Larsen is also on display and for sale. ⊠ 2000 Company St., Christiansted ☎ 340/719–1000 ⊕ www.mitchelllarsen-studio.com ☉ Closed Sun.

JEWELRY

★ Crucian Gold

JEWELRY & WATCHES | St. Croix native Brian Bishop's trademark piece is the Turk's Head ring (a knot of interwoven gold strands). The family tradition continues with his son, Nathan, and his wife, Therese, creating contemporary sterling and gold pendants, rings, earrings, necklaces, and pendants. Stop by to meet the Bishops, browse the jewelry, and "Feel the Love." ⊠ 1112 Strand St., Christiansted ☎ 340/244–2996, 877/773–5241 ⊕ www.cruciangold.com ☉ Closed Sun.

FantaSea Jewelry Studio & Gallery

JEWELRY & WATCHES | Precious metals and gemstones—like Caribbean larimar, blue topaz, and more—come together to highlight the beauty of island life at FantaSea

Jewelry. ⊠ 55 Company St., Christiansted ☎ 340/244–3110 ⊕ fantaseajewelry.com ☉ Closed Sun. and Mon.

★ ib designs

JEWELRY & WATCHES | This small shop showcases the handcrafted jewelry of local craftsman and "Island Boy" Whealan Massicott, including his signature, "infinity" style Crucian hook bracelet. Whether in silver or gold, the designs are simply elegant. ⊠ 2108 Company St., Christiansted ☎ 340/773–4322 ⊕ www.ibdesignsvi.com ☉ Closed Sun.

Joyia Inspirational Jewelry

JEWELRY & WATCHES | This family-operated studio creating handcrafted jewelry using silver, gold, and precious stones offers free engraving with each jewelry purchase, allowing you to set your intention with inspirational words, phrases, names, or special dates. Mix and match metals with their stackable rings and bangles. ⊠ 2220 Queen Cross St., #3A, Christiansted ☎ 340/713–4569 ⊕ joyiajewelry.com ☉ Closed Sun.

Oceanique Creations

JEWELRY & WATCHES | Chaney is jewelry made from shards of the antique Danish pottery that's found all over St. Croix; local residents find it in the ocean or buried in the ground and sell it to the owners of this Christiansted jewelry shop, who clean it, polish it, wrap it in silver wire, and sell it as earrings, necklaces, and bracelets. Seaglass jewelry is also sold here; like chaney, it's made in St. Croix. ⊠ 55 King Wharf St., Suite 1G, Christiansted ☎ 321/438–3012 ⊕ www.oceaniquecreations.com ☉ Closed Sun.

RJS Handmade Designs

JEWELRY & WATCHES | The handmade gold and silver jewelry created here is inspired by St. Croix's beauty and culture and designed to provoke intrigue. Each piece is unique thanks to the Lost Wax Casting Method used to make the jewelry. ⊠ 1104 Strand St., Suite 2, Christiansted

☎ 340/642–3291 ⊕ www.rjshandmad-edesigns.com ✆ Closed Sun.

Sonya Ltd.

JEWELRY & WATCHES | This boutique was founded by Crucian designer Sonya Hough, who invented the popular hook bracelet (wear the hook facing out if you're "available," inward if you're attached). Bracelets are priced from about $65 and up, depending on size and materials. In addition to the original silver and gold hooks in a variety of diameters, the shop sells variations that incorporate hurricane symbols, dolphins, hibiscus flowers, and infinity symbols. If you're going to splurge on one nice souvenir in St. Croix, make it a hook bracelet and you'll be recognized as an honorary Crucian whenever you wear it. ✉ 2101 Company St., Christiansted ☎ 340/773–8924 ⊕ www.sonyaltdstore.com ✆ Closed Sun.

LIQUOR AND TOBACCO
Baci Duty Free

DUTY-FREE | The walk-in humidor here has a good selection of Arturo Fuente, Partagas, Padron, and Macanudo cigars. Baci also carries high-end liquor; sleek watches from Tissot, Frederick Constance, Alpina, Mido, Luminox, Citizen, and Bering; Steiner binoculars from Germany; and fine jewelry. ✉ 1235 Queen Cross St., Christiansted ☎ 340/773–5040 ⊕ www.facebook.com/bacidutyfree ✆ Closed Sun.

PERFUMES
Belle Sorelle Beauty Bar

DUTY-FREE | Vintage designer handbags, totes, jewelry, imported designer cosmetics and fragrances, and accessories cover the assortment of duty-free finds found at Belle Sorelle Beauty Bar. There are options for both men and women. ✉ 55 A Kings Wharf St., Christiansted ☎ 340/773–2755.

Bougainvillea @ 41 King

COSMETICS | This locally owned and operated perfume and skin care boutique carries items by CHANEL, Lalique, Gucci, and many more. ✉ 41 King St., Christiansted ☎ 340/719–6020 ⊕ www.bougainvillea41king.com ✆ Closed Sun.

ROUGE Duty Free

DUTY-FREE | This luxury duty-free store carries a large selection of beauty, skincare and makeup, designer sunglasses, premium liquors, wines, and more. ✉ 52-B Company St., Christiansted ☎ 340/718–0054 ✆ Closed Sun.

West of Christiansted

Heading west from Christiansted, there are few sights worth seeing in this busy area. In Estate Golden Rock, you'll come across "Condo Row" where many vacation rentals are located, as well as a few notable restaurants and eateries in Estate Princesse.

🍴 Restaurants

Blues' Backyard BBQ & Grill

$$$ | **BARBECUE** | There's always something smokin' at Blues BBQ. Enjoy "succulicious" barbecue of brisket and ribs, burgers, and live music in a backyard atmosphere while sipping Cruzan Rum cocktails. **Known for:** live music; barbecue platters; juicy burgers. $ Average main: $22 ✉ 32K LaGrande Princesse, La Grande Princesse ☎ 340/514–2541 ✆ Closed Mon. and Tues.

Coral Sea Cafe & Restaurant

$$$ | **CARIBBEAN** | This oceanside eatery serves up a selection of Caribbean, American, and seafood dishes like fried snapper in a creole sauce with Johnny Cakes or Alfredo penne pasta topped with chicken, shrimp, or steak. Takeout is available. **Known for:** beachfront views;

great for seafood lovers; local cuisine. $ *Average main: $30* ⊠ *3220 Estate Golden Rock, Estate Golden Rock* ✥ *Located inside Mill Harbor Condominiums* ☎ *340/690–1974.*

Eden's Vegan Eatery
$$ | VEGETARIAN | This popular vegan restaurant prepares a variety of flavorful plant-based dishes, like vegan mac and cheese, BBQ tofu, and chickpea loaf. Try the crispy golden fried cauliflower, a perfect healthy alternative to French fries. **Known for:** daily changing menu; vegan desserts; local drinks. $ *Average main: $18* ⊠ *34D La Grande Princesse, La Grande Princesse* ✥ *Located across from St. Croix Avis building* ☎ *340/201–9225, 340/773–3367* ⊘ *Closed weekends.*

Le Cuisinier Restaurant & Bar
$$$ | CARIBBEAN | Formerly Breeze's Restaurant, Le Cuisinier offers a fusion of West Indian and American cuisine with themed offerings throughout the week like Taco Tuesday, Sushi Thursday, and Soul Food Saturday. Try the conch in butter sauce with seasoned rice and plantain or a surf-and-turf entrée of grilled rib eye steak and a half lobster. **Known for:** local cuisine; great location; spacious dining room. $ *Average main: $30* ⊠ *212 Estate Golden Rock, Estate Golden Rock* ☎ *340/713–2665.*

Two Plus Two Restaurant and Nightclub
$$ | CARIBBEAN | For a taste of local Crucian fare at an affordable price, head to Two Plus Two Restaurant. Fried chicken leg and French fries are consistently good; or try fish and fungi, the unofficial dish of the the Virgin Islands. **Known for:** fried chicken and fries; local cuisine; full bar service. $ *Average main: $18* ⊠ *17J La Grande Princesse, La Grande Princesse* ☎ *340/718–3710.*

 Hotels

Club St. Croix
$ | HOTEL | FAMILY | Sitting beachfront just outside Christiansted, this condominium complex faces a lovely stretch of sand and also has a pool. **Pros:** beachfront location; good restaurant; full kitchens. **Cons:** no meals included; need car to get around; sketchy neighborhood. $ *Rooms from: $215* ⊠ *3280 Golden Rock, Estate Golden Rock* ☎ *340/718–9150, 800/524–2025* ⊕ *www.antillesresorts.com* ⇆ *50 apartments* ⦿ *No Meals.*

Colony Cove
$ | HOTEL | FAMILY | In a string of condominium complexes, Colony Cove lets you experience comfortable beachfront living, offering large units that all have two bedrooms, two bathrooms, and washer–dryer combos—it's a good choice for families. **Pros:** beachfront location; swimming pool; good views. **Cons:** sketchy neighborhood; no meals included; need car to get around. $ *Rooms from: $240* ⊠ *3221 Golden Rock, Estate Golden Rock* ☎ *340/718–1965, 800/524–2025* ⊕ *www.antillesresorts.com* ⇆ *62 apartments* ⦿ *No Meals.*

The Palms at Pelican Cove
$ | RESORT | A 10-minute drive from downtown Christiansted, this adult-only resort sits on a gorgeous strip of white sand. **Pros:** nice beach; good restaurant; friendly staff. **Cons:** no meals included; need car to get out and about. $ *Rooms from: $225* ⊠ *4126 La Grande Princess, La Grande Princesse* ☎ *340/718–8920, 800/548–4460* ⊕ *www.palmspelican-cove.com* ⇆ *38 rooms* ⦿ *No Meals.*

Sugar Beach
$$$ | RESORT | FAMILY | With all the conveniences of home, Sugar Beach's apartments are immaculate and breezy. **Pros:** pleasant beach; full kitchens; space to spread out. **Cons:** sketchy neighborhood; no direct bookings; need car to get around. $ *Rooms from: $425* ⊠ *3245*

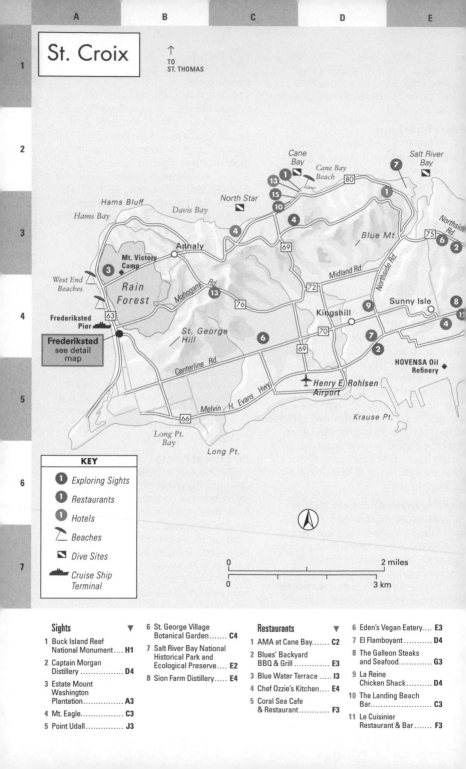

St. Croix

↑
TO
ST. THOMAS

Cane Bay
Cane Bay Beach
Salt River Bay
North Star
Hams Bluff
Davis Bay
Hams Bay
Annaly
Blue Mt.
Northside Rd.
Mt. Victory Camp
West End Beaches
Rain Forest
Midland Rd.
Sunny Isle
Frederiksted Pier
St. George Hill
Kingshill
HOVENSA Oil Refinery
Frederiksted see detail map
Centerline Rd.
Henry E. Rohlsen Airport
Melvin H. Evans Hwy.
Krause Pt.
Long Pt. Bay
Long Pt.

Mahogany Rd.

KEY

- ① Exploring Sights
- ① Restaurants
- ① Hotels
- ⌐ Beaches
- ◣ Dive Sites
- ⛴ Cruise Ship Terminal

0 — 2 miles
0 — 3 km

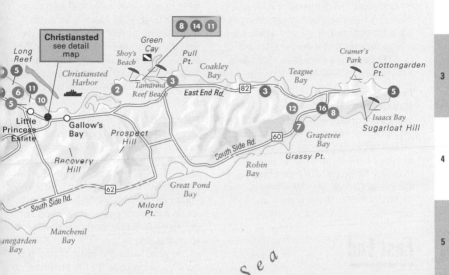

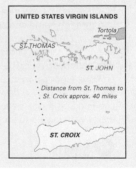

UNITED STATES VIRGIN ISLANDS

Tortola
ST. THOMAS
ST. JOHN

Distance from St. Thomas to St. Croix approx. 40 miles

ST. CROIX

Golden Rock, Estate Golden Rock
☎ *340/718–5345, 800/524–2049* ⇆ *46
apartments* ⦿ *No Meals.*

Shopping

Food Town Supermarket
SUPERMARKET | This neighborhood super-market has everything you're looking for, including fresh produce, meats and poul-try, a full-service bakery, and a deli, plus a large selection of wines and liquors. ⊠ *4037 LaGrande Princesse, Christian-sted* ☎ *340/718–9990* ⊕ *foodtownvi.com.*

Pueblo Supermarket
SUPERMARKET | This chain supermarket carries dry goods, fresh produce, meat, and seafood. There are two locations on the island—in Orange Grove, which is closer to downtown, and mid-island in Estate La Reine. ⊠ *Golden Rock Shopping Center, Rte. 75, Christiansted* ☎ *340/718–0118* ⊕ *www.wfmpueblo. com.*

East End

An easy drive (roads are flat and well marked) to St. Croix's eastern end takes you through some choice real estate. Ruins of old sugar estates dot the land-scape. You can make the entire loop on the road that circles the island in about an hour, a good way to end the day. If you want to spend a full day exploring, you can find some nice beaches and easy walks with places to stop for lunch.

Sights

★ Buck Island Reef National Monument
ISLAND | This national monument has pristine beaches that are just right for sunbathing, but there's also some shade for those who prefer to escape the heat of the sun. The snorkeling trail set in the reef allows close-up study of coral formations and tropical fish. Overly warm seawater temperatures have led to a

condition called coral bleaching that has killed some of the coral. The reefs are starting to recover, but how long it will take is anyone's guess. There's a hiking trail to the island's highest point (328 feet) and an overlook where you are rewarded for your efforts by spectacular views of St. John. Charter-boat trips leave daily from the Christiansted waterfront or from Green Cay Marina, about 2 miles (3 km) east of Christiansted. Big Beard's Adventure Tours, Caribbean Sea Adventures, and Llewellyn's Charter offer half- and full-day trips. ⊠ *Off East End of St. Croix* ☎ *340/773–1460* ⊕ *www.nps. gov/buis.*

Point Udall
VIEWPOINT | This rocky promontory, marked by a large stone sundial sculp-ture, is the easternmost point in the United States and about a half-hour drive from Christiansted. A paved road takes you to an overlook with glorious views; it's an especially popular gathering spot on New Year's Day for those who want to be the first to greet the first sunrise of the year. Make the most of your trip here by hiking down to the pristine beach below. The marked trail is easy to navigate for adults and children. ⊠ *Rte. 82, Whim.*

Beaches

★ Buck Island
BEACH | Part of Buck Island Reef National Monument, this is a must-see for anyone in St. Croix. The beach is beautiful, but its finest treasures are those you can see when you hop off the boat and adjust your mask, snorkel, and fins to swim over colorful coral and darting fish. Don't know how to snorkel? No problem—the boat crew will have you outfitted and in the water in no time. Take care not to step on those black-pointed spiny sea urchins or touch the mustard-color fire coral, which can cause a nasty burn. Most charter-boat trips start with a snorkel over the lovely reef before a stop

at the island's beach. A hike leads uphill to an overlook for a bird's-eye view of the reef below. **Amenities:** none. **Best for:** snorkeling; swimming. ☎ 340/773–1460 ⊕ www.nps.gov/buis.

Shoys Beach

BEACH | Located inside the entrance to The Buccaneer Hotel, Shoys Beach is a quiet and secluded beach on the island's east end. Enter the shaded entrance encircled by sea grape trees and go swimming in the calm waters, or bring your snorkel gear to catch a glimpse of lobster, small eels, and tropical fish. You're almost always likely to have the beach to yourself. **Amenities:** none. **Best for:** snorkeling; swimming; relaxing. ✉ Inside the entrance of Buccaneer Hotel, Shoys ✛ Enter the Buccaneer Hotel entrance and proceed to the guard gate to the right. Inform the guard you are going to Shoys Beach.

 Restaurants

Blue Water Terrace

$$$ | **CONTEMPORARY** | This family-owned restaurant has been serving the St. Croix community since 2010 with mouthwatering steaks and seafood. The Monday night all-you-can-eat crab legs and seafood bake is always a big hit; reservations are a must for this day. **Known for:** award-winning desserts; firestone pizza; great views. $ Average main: $30 ✉ 5261 Cotton Valley, Cotton Valley ☎ 340/692–2583 ⊕ bluewaterterracevi. com ⊘ Closed Tues. and Wed.

The Galleon Steaks and Seafood

$$$ | **ECLECTIC** | This popular dockside restaurant is the place to get off-the-boat seafood and Southern soul food in St. Croix—chef-owner Charles Mereday is a graduate of the South Carolina campus of Johnson and Wales University, after all. But you'll also find hand-cut steaks alongside crowd favorites like greenlip mussels, cauliflower wings, and mango mahi mahi. **Known for:** mango mahi mahi;

island classics; marina views. $ Average main: $30 ✉ Tamarind Reef Resort, 5000 Estate Southgate, Christiansted ☎ 340/244–6007 ⊕ www.thegalleon-stcroix.com ⊘ Closed Sun. and Mon. No lunch.

The New Deep End Bar & Grill

$$$ | **ECLECTIC** | A favorite with locals and vacationers, this poolside restaurant serves up salads, burgers, sandwiches, and seafood, as well as delicious pasta dishes and popular salads. Come for free salsa dance classes on Monday night, disco bingo on Thursday with dancing between games, the West Indian Caribbean Celebration on Fridays, Sunday brunch, and live music on weekends. **Known for:** lively atmosphere; beach setting; Sunday brunch. $ Average main: $23 ✉ Tamarind Reef Resort, 5001 Estate Southgate, Christiansted ☎ 340/718–7071 ⊕ www.newdeepend.com.

Sea Terrace Restaurant & Bar

$$ | **AMERICAN** | At this ocean-level restaurant located at the Grapetree Bay Hotel, you can dine on fish-and-chips, tacos, and Asian sticky pork ribs in a breezy open-air terrace. The all-you-can-eat brunch buffet on Sundays offers your typical breakfast fare like eggs, bacon, and pancakes, plus rotating lunch specials and a meat carving station. **Known for:** great views; house-made pizzas; Sunday Brunch buffet. $ Average main: $20 ✉ 5000 S Grapetree Bay Rd., Christiansted ☎ 340/249–0700 ⊕ grapetreebayho-tel.com.

Hotels

★ The Buccaneer

$$$$ | **RESORT** | **FAMILY** | Aimed at travelers who want everything at their fingertips, this family-friendly resort has sandy beaches, multiple restaurants, golf, tennis, a spa, and swimming pools. **Pros:** beachfront location; numerous activities; nice golf course. **Cons:** pricey; insular environment; need car to get around.

Family-friendly resort The Buccaneer sits on the grounds of a 300-acre former sugar plantation in St. Croix.

$ | *Rooms from: $480* ✉ *5007 Estate Shoys, Shoys* ☎ *340/712-2100, 800/255-3881* ⊕ *www.thebuccaneer.com* ⇥ *139 rooms* ❍ *Free Breakfast.*

Bungalows on the Bay

$ | **RESORT** | **FAMILY** | Bohemian meets island chic at this beachfront hotel known for its self-contained cottages. **Pros:** nightly entertainment; beachfront property; great location. **Cons:** under renovations; limited staff; limited menu at on-site restaurant. $ *Rooms from: $200* ✉ *5000 Estate Chenay Beach, Christiansted* ☎ *340/201-1309* ⊕ *bungalowsonthebay.com* ⇥ *35 rooms* ❍ *No Meals.*

Divi Carina Bay Resort & Casino

$$$$ | **RESORT** | An oceanfront location, one of the island's only casinos, and plenty of activities make this resort a reliable option for adults (guests must be 18 and over). **Pros:** spacious beach; good restaurant; on-site casino. **Cons:** need car to get around; many stairs to climb. $ *Rooms from: $525* ✉ *5025 Turner Hole Rd., Estate Turner Hole* ☎ *340/773-9700,*

800/367-3484 ⊕ *www.diviresorts.com* ⇥ *200 units* ❍ *All-Inclusive.*

Grapetree Bay Hotel and Villas

$$ | **HOTEL** | **FAMILY** | This newly renovated and restored boutique property offers family-friendly beachfront accommodations complete with a swimming pool, hiking trails, snorkeling, and more. The resort sits on 45 acres with charming views of the Caribbean Sea and boasts expansive outdoor lounge areas and three dining establishments. **Pros:** gorgeous views; chic accommodations; good restaurants. **Cons:** need a car to get around; limited food options; secluded location. $ *Rooms from: $315* ✉ *5000 S Grapetree Bay, Christiansted* ☎ *340/249-0700* ⊕ *grapetreebayhotel.com* ⇥ *18 rooms* ❍ *No Meals.*

Tamarind Reef Resort

$$ | **HOTEL** | Spread out along a sandy beach, these low-slung buildings offer casual comfort and appeal to independent travelers who want the option to eat in or out, as rooms have basic kitchenettes. **Pros:** good snorkeling; tasty

restaurant; rooms have kitchenettes. **Cons:** there's a walk to the restaurants; need car to get around; motel-style rooms. [$] *Rooms from: $308* ✉ *5001 Tamarind Reef, off Rte. 82, Cotton Valley* ☎ *340/718–4455, 800/619–0014* 🌐 *www.tamarindreefresort.com* 🛏 *40 rooms* 🍴 *No Meals.*

Villa Madeleine

$$ | **HOTEL** | If you like privacy and your own private pool, you'll like Villa Madeleine, where villas flow downhill from a West Indian plantation great house. **Pros:** pleasant décor; full kitchens; private pools. **Cons:** lower units sometimes lack views; need car to get around; no beachfront. [$] *Rooms from: $285* ✉ *Off Rte. 82, Teague's Bay* ☎ *340/690–3465* 🌐 *www.villamadeleine-stcroix.com* 🛏 *43 villas* 🍴 *No Meals.*

Nightlife

Divi Carina Bay Casino

GATHERING PLACES | The larger of St. Croix's two casinos (the other is in downtown Christiansted) is located across the street from the Divi Carina Bay Resort. For a night out on the island's East End, the casino has reel-type slot machines, video poker, and table games including blackjack, poker, roulette, and craps. Guests of the all-inclusive Divi Carina Bay eat and drink free at the Carina Cafe. ✉ *25 Rte. 60, Estate Turner Hole* ☎ *340/773–7529* 🌐 *www.divicarina.com.*

Shopping

Seaside Market and Deli

SUPERMARKET | This market, though on the smaller side, carries high-quality deli items, local produce, West Indian prepared foods, a florist, a bakery, and a pastry shop. ✉ *2001 Mount Welcome Rd., Christiansted* ☎ *340/719–9393* 🌐 *www.seasidemarketstx.com.*

Agrifest

Every year in February over President's Day weekend, St. Croix hosts one of the Caribbean's largest agricultural festivals. Agrifest, also known as Agriculture and Food Fair of the U.S. Virgin Islands, is a three-day event that attracts attendees from all across the world to highlight the importance of agriculture in the territory and across the Caribbean diaspora. Here you will see the best of the agriculture industry on St. Croix, ranging from locally grown fruits and vegetables to livestock, arts and crafts, informational exhibits, and local cuisine.

Mid Island

A drive through the rural areas between Christiansted and Frederiksted will take you past ruins of old plantations, many bearing the names bestowed by early owners (Morningstar, Solitude, Upper Love). The traffic moves quickly—by island standards—on the main roads, but you can pause and poke around if you head down some side lanes. It's easy to find your way west, but driving from north to south requires good navigation. Allow an entire day for this trip, so you'll have enough time for a swim at a North Shore beach. Although you can find lots of casual eateries on the main roads, pick up a picnic lunch if you plan to head off the beaten path.

Sights

Captain Morgan Distillery

DISTILLERY | The base for Captain Morgan-brand rum is made from molasses at this massive, industrial-scale distillery. The tour includes exhibits on island and rum history, a movie about the process, and a tram ride through the distillery. An extensive gift shop features a wide variety of branded clothing and keepsakes as well as rum for purchase. The tour ends with tastings of the many varieties of Captain Morgan rum (the original spiced, white, aged, dark, and fruit-flavored) plus two cocktails. ⊠ *1 Estate Annaberg & Shannon Grove, Annaberg and Shannon Grove* 🕾 *340/713–5654* ⊕ *www.captainmorganvisitorcenter.com* 🔯 *$15* 🕑 *Closed weekends.*

★ St. George Village Botanical Garden

GARDEN | At this 17-acre estate, fragrant flora grows amid the ruins of a 19th-century sugarcane plantation (the former overseer's house has been left open to the elements as a habitat for native fruit bats). There are miniature versions of each ecosystem on St. Croix, from a semiarid cactus grove to a verdant rainforest, along with walking trails, a small museum, and a collection of seashells. The garden's orchid and bromeliad blooms are impressive. ⊠ *127 Estate St. George, Estate Saint George* ✛ *Turn north at Estate Saint George sign* 🕾 *340/692–2874* ⊕ *www.sgvbg.org* 🔯 *$10.*

Sion Farm Distillery

DISTILLERY | Take a tour at this local distillery to learn about the Caribbean's original Island Vodka made from breadfruit, Mutiny Island Vodka. Try a flight tasting of the different Infusions like Ginger Lime, Smoked Hot Pepper, and the turmeric-ginger blend, or their best-selling Painkiller cocktail. The food menu features a wide variety of Caribbean-inspired options like guava roast pork, stuffed plantain, and coconut shrimp. Tours are provided to walk-in guests every hour on the half-hour, unless active distilling and bottling is taking place. ⊠ *4000 Sion Farm, Sion Farm* 🕾 *340/690–9322* ⊕ *www.sionfarmdistillery.com* 🕑 *Closed Sun.*

🍴 Restaurants

Chef Ozzie's Kitchen

$$ | CARIBBEAN | Dive into the best breakfast sandwiches on the island along with hearty Caribbean dishes like stew oxtail, veggie teriyaki stir fry, and curry chicken. The sandwiches are made with the local butter bread from Thomas Bakery and fresh local produce from island farmers. **Known for:** daily specials; tropical salmon salad; refreshing local drinks. 💲 *Average main: $18* ⊠ *Sunny Isles, 6089 Castle Coakley, Sunny Isle* ✛ *Inside Thomas Bakery* 🕾 *340/422–6382* 🕑 *Closed weekends.*

El Flamboyant

$$ | CARIBBEAN | This colorful family restaurant has been offering Caribbean-Latin cuisine to the local community for over 20 years. Fresh fish, lobster, and conch are almost always on the menu, as well as stew chicken, fried pork chops, and grilled steaks. **Known for:** seafood dishes; lively atmosphere; happy hour on Thursday and Friday nights. 💲 *Average main: $20* ⊠ *Mid-Island, Rt. 663, Estate Profit* ✛ *Between Centerline Road and the Melvin Evans Highway* 🕾 *340/779–3285* 🚫 *No credit cards.*

★ La Reine Chicken Shack

$$ | CARIBBEAN | This barn-like "Crucian-Rican" restaurant is often the first stop that locals make before heading to the airport and after arriving back home. Out back, dozens of chickens slowly rotate on a giant rotisserie; in front, regulars and a smattering of in-the-know visitors queue up for the juicy birds, traditional Johnny Cakes, and local food like stewed oxtail and conch in butter sauce. **Known for:** finger-licking rotisserie chicken; traditional Johnny Cakes; local vibe. 💲 *Average main: $15* ⊠ *24 Slob A-B Estate, La Reine* 🕾 *340/778–5717* 🕑 *Closed last Sun. of each month.*

Martha's Deli

$$ | **CARIBBEAN** | This modest storefront eatery fills up with locals getting to-go orders of the restaurant's traditional Crucian breakfast, including salt fish, Johnny Cake, boiled egg, cucumber salad, sautéed spinach, and—in a nod to the island's Danish heritage—smoked herring. Lunch options include chicken, shrimp, and fish roti, and a popular vegetable lentil soup. **Known for:** traditional Crucian breakfast; numerous roti options; delicious lentil soup. [$] *Average main: $13* ✉ *300 Peters Rest, Sion Farm* ✥ *Across from Plaza Extra East* ☎ *340/773–6054* ⏲ *Closed Sun. and Mon.*

Mt. Pellier Domino Club

$ | **CARIBBEAN** | You don't have to eat like a pig at this West End restaurant and bar in the rainforest, but you can feed a whole can of beer to one. The giant hogs residing here have developed a taste for the suds, and for $4 you can buy a nonalcoholic beer and offer it up to a pig who will crush the can in its powerful jaws, chug down the ingredients, and spit out the crushed aluminum when done. **Known for:** beer-drinking pigs; local daily specials; "mamajuana," a mix of Cruzan rum, honey, roots, leaves, and spices. [$] *Average main: $12* ✉ *Mahogany Rd., 42 Montpellier, Montpellier* ☎ *340/626–8116* ⏲ *Closed Mon.*

Nightlife

★ Leatherback Brewing

BREWPUBS | St. Croix's first large-scale brewing operation has a plant and tasting room near the oil refinery by the airport; drop by to try some of the more than two dozen beers produced here, including the popular Island Life lager and a saison inspired by local bush tea and flavored with basil, lemongrass, ginger, and sorrel. The kitchen serves appetizers, wraps, pizzas, and calzones. ■ **TIP→ You can find the beers at bars throughout the USVI and BVI, but they can't be shipped to the mainland.** ✉ *William Roebuck Industrial Park, 9902 Industrial Park, off Melvin H. Evans Hwy., Frederiksted* ☎ *340/277–2337* 🌐 *www.leatherbackbrewing.com.*

Shopping

FOOD

The Market St. Croix

SUPERMARKET | This is the largest full-service supermarket on the island featuring fresh local produce, imported cheeses, and fine cuts of meat prepared by their Master Butcher. You will find a good selection of Middle Eastern foods and island-sourced products, in addition to the typical grocery-store items. They also have a full service deli and bakery and an extensive assortment of wine and spirits. Hot foods and subs are served daily. ✉ *14 Plessen, Frederiksted* ☎ *340/719–1870* 🌐 *www.themarketstx.com.*

Plaza Extra East

SUPERMARKET | This full-service supermarket stocks both locally grown and imported produce as well as deli items, specialty foods, duty-free liquor, and pharmacy needs. Perky's Pizza is located here, too. ✉ *Rte. 70, 4200 United Shopping Plaza, Suite 1, Sion Farm* ☎ *340/778–6240* 🌐 *www.plazaextraeast.com.*

Pueblo Supermarket

SUPERMARKET | This chain supermarket carries dry goods, fresh produce, meat, and seafood. There are two locations on the island—in Orange Grove, which is closer to downtown, and mid-island in Estate La Reine. ✉ *Golden Rock Shopping Center, Rte. 75, Christiansted* ☎ *340/718–0118* 🌐 *www.wfmpueblo.com.*

Frederiksted

St. Croix's second-largest town, Frederiksted was founded in 1751. While Christiansted is noted for its Danish buildings, Frederiksted is better known for its Victorian architecture. One long cruise-ship

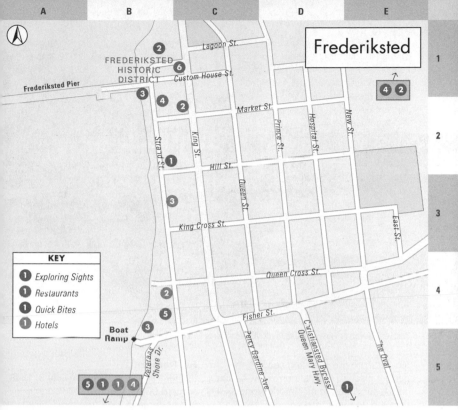

Frederiksted

FREDERIKSTED
HISTORIC
DISTRICT

Frederiksted Pier

Lagoon St.
Custom House St.
Market St.
Hill St.
King Cross St.
Queen Cross St.
Fisher St.

King St. · Strand St. · Queen St. · Prince St. · Hospital St. · New St. · East St.

Veterans Shore Dr. · Percy Gardine Ave. · Christiansted Bypass/Queen Mary Hwy. · The Oval

Boat
Ramp

KEY

- 1 Exploring Sights
- 1 Restaurants
- 1 Quick Bites
- 1 Hotels

Sights ▼

1 Caribbean Museum
  Center for the Arts...... **B2**
2 Fort Frederik............. **B1**
3 Frederiksted
  Welcome Center........ **B1**
4 Little La Grange
  Farm and Lawaetz
  Museum **E1**
5 Sandy Point National
  Wildlife Refuge.......... **B5**

Restaurants ▼

1 Beach Side Café........ **B5**
2 Ciboné..................... **C2**
3 Louie and Nachos
  Beach Bar.............. **B4**
4 Polly's at the Pier **B2**
5 Turtles Deli and
  BBQ **B4**
6 UCA House Kitchen
  & Rastafarian
  Cultural Center........... **C1**

Quick Bites ▼

1 Armstrong's
  Homemade
  Ice Cream............... **D5**
2 Nidulari
  Artisan Bakery........... **E1**

Hotels ▼

1 Cottages by the Sea.... **B5**
2 The Fred **B4**
3 The Frederiksted
  Hotel...................... **C3**
4 Sand Castle
  on the Beach............ **B5**

Just past the clear water lapping Frederiksted's pier is Fort Frederik.

pier juts into the sparkling sea. It's the perfect place to start a tour of this quaint city. A stroll around its historic sights will take you no more than an hour. Allow a little more time if you want to duck into the few small shops.

Sights

Caribbean Museum Center for the Arts

ART MUSEUM | Across from the waterfront in a historic building sits this small museum that hosts an always-changing roster of exhibits and also houses a bookstore and a gift shop. Some works are cutting-edge multimedia efforts that you might be surprised to find in such an out-of-the way location. Openings are popular events, as are the occasional jazz concerts presented in the upstairs galleries. The back courtyard is a peaceful space, where sculptures and statues are on display; free Wi-Fi is an added inducement to linger. ⊠ *10 Strand St., Frederiksted* ☎ *340/772–2622* ⊕ *www.cmcarts. org* 🖾 *Free* 🕙 *Closed Sun. and Mon.*

Fort Frederik

HISTORIC SIGHT | FAMILY | On July 3, 1848, some 8,000 slaves marched on this fort to demand their freedom. Danish governor Peter von Scholten, fearing they would burn the town to the ground, stood up in his carriage parked in front of the fort and granted their wish. The fort, completed in 1760, has walls constructed of coral and rubble bound together with molasses, a testament to the ingenuity and durability of 18th-century engineering. Climb the battlements for great views of the cruise dock and the Caribbean Sea. Inside, a museum includes exhibits on the slave trade, Mocko Jumbies, seashells and sea glass, indigenous artifacts from Salt River Bay, and local mahogany furniture. ⊠ *Waterfront, Frederiksted* ⊕ *www.nps.gov/ places/fort-frederiksted-usvi.htm* 🖾 *$7* 🕙 *Closed weekends.*

Frederiksted Welcome Center

VISITOR CENTER | Located on the pier, Frederiksted's welcome center has brochures from numerous St. Croix businesses, as

Marching on Frederiksted

On July 3, 1848, more than 8,000 enslaved people gathered on King Street in Frederiksted and marched towards Fort Frederik to demand their freedom. Their actions forever changed the course of history. Governor General Peter von Scholten stood up in his carriage in front of Fort Frederick to declare: "From this day onward, all unfree in the Danish West Indies are free."

Von Scholten was relieved of his position and charged with dereliction of duty by the Danish government. He departed from St. Croix on July 14, leaving behind his lover, a free black woman named Anna Heegaard. He never returned, and died in Denmark in 1852.

The revolt had its roots in the 1834 emancipation of enslaved people in Great Britain's Caribbean colonies, including what are now called the British Virgin Islands. The Danish government, sensing what was coming, began to "improve" the working conditions for its enslaved people. These efforts, however, failed, falling short of the demand for full freedom.

On July 28, 1847, Danish King Christian VIII ruled that slavery would continue a dozen more years, but those born during those 12 years would be free. This further angered the island's enslaved people. On July 3, 1848, a conch shell sounded, signifying that the enslaved people should start gathering. The die was cast, and the rest, as they say, is history.

After emancipation, the former enslaved people were forced to sign yearly contracts with plantation owners. Those contracts could only be renegotiated on October 1, still called Contract Day. This angered the planta tion workers and gave rise to other uprisings throughout the late 1800s.

---

well as a few exhibits about the island. It's only open when cruise ships are in port. When the welcome center is not open, visitors can check with the tourism office (open weekdays only) in the old Custom House at 321 King Street (Suite 7) ⊠ *Frederiksted Pier, Frederiksted* ☎ *340/772–0357.*

Little La Grange Farm and Lawaetz Museum
FARM/RANCH | For a trip back in time, tour this circa-1750 farm in a valley at La Grange. Tours include the lovely two-story house, aqueducts once used to transport water and cane juice, and the Little La Grange Farm, which produces organic crops for sale through the Ridge to Reef program. The great house includes the four-poster mahogany bed 19th-century owner Carl Lawaetz shared with his wife, Marie, the china

Marie painted, family portraits, and the fruit trees that fed the family for several generations. Initially a sugar plantation, the farm was subsequently used to raise cattle and grow produce. ⊠ *Rte. 76 (Mahogany Rd.), Estate Little La Grange* ☎ *340/473–1557* ⊕ *www.ridge2reef.org/little-lagrange-farm.html* ⊠ *$15* ⊗ *Closed Sun.–Tues., Thurs.–Fri.*

Sandy Point National Wildlife Refuge
WILDLIFE REFUGE | Located at the western tip of St. Croix, this 383-acre wildlife sanctuary provides critical habitat for leatherback, green, and hawksbill sea turtles, which nest on the refuge's long, sandy beaches. The beaches are open to visitors when not occupied by turtles. The mangrove-fringed West End Salt Pond, which lies partly within the refuge's boundaries, is a bird-watcher's delight.

Sea turtles nest in several places on St. Croix, including Sandy Point National Wildlife Refuge.

✉ *Veterans Shore Dr., Hesselberg* ☎ *340/773–4554* 🌐 *www.fws.gov/refuge/sandy_point* ⏲ *Closed weekdays and during turtle nesting season (Apr.–Aug.).*

Beaches

West End beaches

BEACH | There are several unnamed beaches along the coast road north of Frederiksted, but it's best if you don't stray too far from civilization. Most vacationers plop down their towel near one of the casual restaurants spread out along Route 63. Rainbow Beach, a five-minute drive outside Frederiksted, has the lively Rhythms at Rainbow Beach, a casual restaurant decorated with license plates from around the world. There you will also find West End Watersports renting jet skis, flyboards, and stand-up paddleboards by the half hour and beach chairs and umbrellas by the day. The beach is broad and sandy with clear, calm waters. If you want to be close to the cruise-ship pier, just stroll on over to the adjacent sandy beach in front of Fort Frederik. On the way south out of Frederiksted, the stretch near Sandcastle on the Beach hotel, known as Dorsch Beach, is also lovely. **Amenities:** food and drink; water sports. **Best for:** snorkeling; swimming; walking. ✉ *Rte. 63, north and south of Frederiksted, Frederiksted.*

Restaurants

Beach Side Café

$$$ | **ECLECTIC** | Sunday brunch is big here, but locals and visitors also flock to this oceanfront bistro at the Sand Castle on the Beach resort for lunch and dinner. Both menus include burgers and salads, but at dinner the daily pasta specials shine. **Known for:** oceanfront setting; seafood chowder; weekend brunch. [$] *Average main: $22* ✉ *Sand Castle on the Beach, 127 Smithfield, Frederiksted* ☎ *340/772–1266* 🌐 *www.sandcastleonthebeach.com.*

Turtles on St. Croix

Like creatures from the prehistoric past, green, leatherback, and hawksbill turtles crawl ashore during the annual April-to-November turtle nesting season to lay their eggs. They return from their life at sea every two to seven years to the beach where they were born. Since turtles can live for up to 100 years, they may return many times to nest in St. Croix.

The leatherbacks like Sandy Point National Wildlife Refuge and other spots on St. Croix's western end, but the hawksbills prefer Buck Island and the East End. Green turtles are also found primarily on the East End. Access to the pristine beach at Sandy Point is restricted during turtle nesting season.

All of these sea turtles are endangered species that face numerous predators, some natural, some the result of the human presence. Particularly in the Frederiksted area, dogs and cats prey on the nests and eat the hatchlings. Occasionally a dog will attack a turtle about to lay its eggs, and cats train their kittens to hunt at turtle nests, creating successive generations of turtle-egg hunters. In addition, turtles have often been hit by fast-moving boats, leaving large gashes in their shells if not killing them outright. The St. Croix Leatherback Project conducts an annual census of the Sandy Point sea turtles, and also runs a program that allows visitors to "adopt" turtles who are tagged and named each season.

Ciboné

$$$$ | **CONTEMPORARY** | Featuring an eclectic menu of French, Mediterranean, Crucian fusion, this intimate dining establishment in downtown Frederiksted uses wild-caught seafood and local farm-fresh ingredients. Try the Oysters Rockefeller to whet your appetite, followed by the poached whole snapper. **Known for:** intimate dining experience; eclectic menu; live music. Ⓢ *Average main: $32* ✉ *227 King St., Frederiksted* ☎ *340/719–2663* ◷ *Closed Sun.*

Louie and Nachos Beach Bar

$ | **MEXICAN** | The fare served here is the farthest thing from traditional Mexican food—in addition to the usual ingredients, you can get a taco stuffed with buffalo chicken, or jambalaya, and vegan options are available, too. The bar and restaurant are one story up, so the views of the beach and surf are nice. **Known for:** inventive tacos; Orange Crush cocktails; great ocean views. Ⓢ *Average main: $12* ✉ *37 Strand St., Frederiksted* ☎ *340/772–5151* ⊕ *www.louieandnachos.com.*

★ Polly's at the Pier

$$ | **ECLECTIC** | With an emphasis on fresh ingredients, this casual spot right on the waterfront serves delicious fare, starting with the BELT (bacon, egg, lettuce, and tomato) breakfast sandwich and continuing with gourmet grilled-cheese sandwiches with delicious additions like basil, Bosc pears, and avocado at lunch. Salads are a specialty, and many are made with local Bibb lettuce and organic mixed greens. **Known for:** local ingredients; waterfront location; neighborhood ambience. Ⓢ *Average main: $13* ✉ *3 Strand St., Frederiksted* ☎ *340/719–9434* ◷ *No dinner.*

Turtle's Deli and BBQ

$$ | **SANDWICHES** | **FAMILY** | Huge sandwiches at this tiny spot start with homemade bread and can be as basic as turkey and cheddar or as imaginative as the Beast, piled high with hot roast beef, raw onion, and melted Swiss cheese with horseradish and mayonnaise. Barbecue—including

Camping in St. Croix

Out on the West End, where few tourists stay, **Mount Victory Camp** (✉ *Creque Dam Rd., Frederiksted* ☎ *340/201–7983*) offers a remarkable quietude that distinguishes this out-of-the-way spread on 8 acres in the island's rainforest. If you really want to commune with nature, you'll be hard-pressed to find a better way to do it on St. Croix. Hosts Matt and Carmen are on hand to explain the environment. You sleep in a screened-in tent-cottage ($90) perched on a raised platform and covered by a roof. Each has electricity and a rudimentary outdoor kitchen. There is also an apartment built into the ruins of a historic schoolhouse ($110 per night) and some bare tent sites for $30 per night. The shared, spotlessly clean bathhouse is an easy stroll away. The location feels remote, but a lovely sand beach is a 2-mile (3-km) drive down the hill. In another 10 minutes you're in Frederiksted. Reservations are preferred.

pulled pork, chicken, and brisket plates—is another highlight. **Known for:** good-size portions; barbecue; ample shaded outdoor seating. [$] *Average main: $15* ✉ *625 Strand St., Frederiksted* ☎ *340/772–3676* ⏲ *No dinner.*

UCA House Kitchen & Rastafarian Cultural Center

$$ | **CARIBBEAN** | No two days are ever the same with daily vegan and vegetarian specials, veggie soups, stewed veggies, garden salads, and local drinks at this community favorite. Choose your plate size—small, medium, or large—and select from the list of proteins and sides that will leave you feeling nourished and satisfied. **Known for:** spicy popcorn snacks; unhurried service; healthy, consciously prepared foods. [$] *Average main: $20* ✉ *Customs House St., Frederiksted* ✥ *Behind the Oscar E. Henry Customs House* ☎ *340/772–5063* 💳 *No credit cards* ⏲ *Closed Mon. and Tues.*

☕ Coffee and Quick Bites

Armstrong's Homemade Ice Cream

$ | **ICE CREAM** | **FAMILY** | This family-run business has used the same Danish ice-cream recipe with local flavorings since 1900. Stop in for a sweet treat that includes a wide variety of tropically flavored homemade ice cream—almond, ginger, peanut, coconut, pumpkin—plus seasonal varieties like gooseberry, guava, mango, soursop, and passion fruit. **Known for:** house-made ice cream; interesting seasonal flavors; mouthwatering deli sandwiches. [$] *Average main: $5* ✉ *78-B Whim, Queen Mary Hwy., Whim* ☎ *340/772–1919* 🌐 *www.facebook.com/armstrongshomemadeicecream* ⏲ *Closed Mon.*

★ Nidulari Artisan Bakery

$$ | **BAKERY** | A distinctive gypsy cart on the side of Mahogany Road (Route 76) spills open with fresh baked breads, tarts, sandwiches, and toasties with unusual fillings like black bean hummus or homegrown banana. The farm-to-table menu, which changes daily to reflect what's available, includes local fare, Indian curries, British-influenced dishes, and Southern comfort food. **Known for:** goods baked in a traditional brick oven; chocolate made from local ingredients; everything is made from scratch. [$] *Average main: $18* ✉ *Little La Grange Village, 9 Little La Grange, Mahogany Rd., Frederiksted* ☎ *978/850–2924* 🌐 *www.nidulari.com* ⏲ *Closed Mon.–Wed.*

Hotels

Cottages by the Sea

$ | B&B/INN | Step out your door and onto a stunning stretch of white beach at this string of cottages beneath towering palm trees. **Pros:** beachfront location; delightful décor; friendly hosts. **Cons:** neighborhood sketchy at night; need car to get around; some rooms need freshening. $ *Rooms from: $220* ✉ *127A Smithfield Rd., Frederiksted* ☎ *340/772–0495, 800/323–7252* ⊕ *www.caribbeancottages.com* ⌁ *28 cottages* ❮❍❯ *No Meals.*

★ The Fred

$$ | HOTEL | This boutique hotel on the Frederiksted waterfront saucily beckons you to "Sleep with Fred" in one of a dozen bright and stylishly appointed guest rooms housed in a quartet of new and restored colonial buildings. **Pros:** spacious rooms; waterfront location; LGBTQ-friendly. **Cons:** adult-only resort; tiny spa; beach is a mix of sandy and rocky sections. $ *Rooms from: $340* ✉ *605 Strand St., Frederiksted* ☎ *340/777–3733* ⊕ *www.sleepwithfred. com* ⌁ *26 rooms* ❮❍❯ *No Meals.*

The Frederiksted Hotel

$ | HOTEL | If you want a laid-back atmosphere steps from interesting restaurants and shops, this is a decent choice offering basic but comfortable waterfront rooms for budget travelers. **Pros:** close to restaurants; walk to public beach; reasonable rates. **Cons:** neighborhood sketchy at night; limited amenities; need a car to get around. $ *Rooms from: $179* ✉ *21 Strand St., Frederiksted* ☎ *340/772–0500, 340/643–4939* ⊕ *thefrederikstedhotel. com* ⌁ *35 rooms* ❮❍❯ *No Meals.*

★ Sand Castle on the Beach

$$ | RESORT | Right on a gorgeous stretch of white beach, the adults-only Sand Castle has a tropical charm that harks back to a simpler time in the Caribbean; its nearness to Frederiksted's unique dining scene is also a plus. **Pros:** on the beach; good food; LGBTQ-friendly. **Cons:**

some rooms are small or lack views; no guests under age 18; small pool. $ *Rooms from: $280* ✉ *127 Smithfield, Frederiksted* ☎ *340/772–1205* ⊕ *www. sandcastleonthebeach.com* ⌁ *25 rooms* ❮❍❯ *Free Breakfast.*

North Shore

Sights

Estate Mount Washington Plantation

RUINS | Several years ago, the former owners of this property discovered the ruins of a circa-1750 sugar plantation beneath the rainforest brush. The grounds were cleared and opened to the public. The estate has since been sold and is now private property, but the new owners still allow visitors to take a self-guided walking tour of the mill, the rum distillery, and other ruins. An oversize wind chime ringing softly in the breeze and a stone-lined labyrinth create a sense of serenity. ✉ *Rte. 63, Estate Mount Washington and Washington Hill.*

Mt. Eagle

MOUNTAIN | At approximately 1,160 feet, this is St. Croix's highest peak. Determined hikers can follow a dirt path to the summit, or take a jeep tour with Tan Tan Tours. Route 78 (Scenic Road) climbs the shoulder of the mountain to the trailhead; use your GPS to locate the exact trailhead. ✉ *Rte. 69, Estate Fountain.*

Salt River Bay National Historical Park and Ecological Preserve

NATURE PRESERVE | If you want to learn more about St. Croix's indigenous Carib people while appreciating beautiful preserves that protect endangered species, head to this joint national and local park. Christopher Columbus's men skirmished with the Carib people here in 1493, on his second visit to what he deemed the New World. The peninsula on the bay's east side is named for the event: Cabo de las Flechas (Cape of the

Stroll the pristine waters of Cane Bay.

Arrows). A ball court, used by the Caribs in religious ceremonies, was discovered at the spot where the taxis park. Take a short hike up the dirt road to the ruins of an old earthen fort for great views of Salt River Bay. The area also encompasses a coastal estuary with the region's largest remaining mangrove forest, a submarine canyon, and several endangered species, including the hawksbill turtle and the roseate tern. The water at the beach can be on the rough side, but it's a nice place for sunning when the turtles aren't nesting. Local tour companies offer tours, including a visit to a pair of bioluminescent bays by kayak and pontoon boat. The park visitor center has been closed since Hurricane Maria damaged it in 2017. ⊠ *Rte. 75 to Rte. 80, Estate Salt River* ☏ *340/773–1460* ⊕ *www.nps.gov/sari.*

 Beaches

Cane Bay
BEACH | On the island's breezy North Shore, Cane Bay does not always have gentle waters but the scuba diving and snorkeling are wondrous. You can see elkhorn and brain corals, and less than 200 yards out is the drop-off called the Cane Bay Wall. Make Cane Bay an all-day destination by combining a dive with food and drinks at the casual bars and restaurants that line the waterfront, including the excellent AMA at Cane Bay. **Amenities:** food and drink. **Best for:** snorkeling; swimming. ⊠ *Rte. 80, Cane Bay* ⊹ *About 4 miles (6 km) west of Salt River.*

 Restaurants

★ **AMA at Cane Bay**
$$$ | **CARIBBEAN** | This waterfront restaurant on the back deck of the Waves at Cane Bay hotel serves sustainably sourced Caribbean-American food that pairs wonderfully with the creative craft cocktails, such as the Old Cuban made with 18-year-old Matusalem rum and Champagne. The dining room overlooks Cane Bay, a perfect backdrop to try the lobster pappardelle, local ceviche, or the catch of the day. **Known for:** location

overlooking Cane Bay; sustainable seafood from local purveyors; creative cocktails. $ *Average main: $30* ⊠ *Waves at Cane Bay, 112C Cane Bay, Cane Bay* ☎ *340/227–3432* ⊕ *www.amacanebay. com* ☽ *Closed Sun. and Mon.*

The Landing Beach Bar

$$ | **SEAFOOD** | Grilled mahi mahi sandwiches, falafel, tacos, and burgers are among the favorites at this open-air bar across the street from Cane Bay beach. Some dishes are prepared using local Leatherback beer, which is available behind the bar. **Known for:** fresh-off-the-boat seafood; live music; ocean views. $ *Average main: $15* ⊠ *110c Cane Bay, Cane Bay* ⊕ *Across the street from Cane Bay Beach* ☎ *340/718-0362* ⊕ *www. thelandingbeachbar.com* ☽ *Closed Tues.*

Off the Wall

$$ | **AMERICAN** | Divers fresh from a plunge at the North Shore's popular Cane Bay Wall gather at this breezy spot on the beach, where sunsets are celebrated with a toast at the bar and the winter months offer the possibility of whale sightings offshore. The menu includes deli sandwiches, burgers, and hot dogs, but the stars are the calzones and pizzas, which run the gamut from vegetarian to meat-lovers. **Known for:** friendly beach bar; amazing sunset views; pizza and calzones. $ *Average main: $20* ⊠ *Rte. 80, Cane Bay* ☎ *340/718-4771* ⊕ *www. otwstx.com* ☽ *Closed Fri.*

 Hotels

Arawak Bay: The Inn at Salt River

$ | **B&B/INN** | With stellar views of St. Croix's North Shore and an affable host, this 15-room hotel allows you to settle into island life at a price that doesn't break the bank. **Pros:** 20 minutes from Christiansted; stunning views; reasonable rates. **Cons:** no beach nearby; pool is small; can be some road noise. $ *Rooms from: $160* ⊠ *62 Salt River, Estate Salt River* ☎ *340/772–1684, 888/234–0416*

⊕ *www.arawakhotelstcroix.com* ☞ *14 rooms* ☽ *Free Breakfast.*

Carambola Beach Resort and Spa

$$ | **RESORT** | This expansive Marriott-branded resort has a stellar beach and peaceful ambience as well as standalone rooms with terra-cotta floors, ceramic lamps, mahogany ceilings and furnishings, and rocking chairs. **Pros:** lovely beach; relaxing atmosphere; close to golf. **Cons:** remote location; ongoing renovations as of this writing; limited amenities. $ *Rooms from: $350* ⊠ *Rte. 80, Estate Davis Bay, Estate Fountain* ☎ *340/778–3800, 888/236–2427, 800/228–9290* ⊕ *www.marriott.com* ☞ *151 rooms* ☽ *No Meals.*

Waves Cane Bay

$$ | **HOTEL** | The famed Cane Bay Wall is just offshore from this boutique hotel, giving it an enviable location. **Pros:** great diving; restaurants nearby; beaches nearby. **Cons:** need car to get around; on main road; bland décor. $ *Rooms from: $349* ⊠ *Rte. 80, 112C Cane Bay, Cane Bay* ☎ *340/718–1815* ⊕ *www.thewavescane-bay.com* ☞ *11 rooms* ☽ *No Meals.*

 Activities

BOAT TOURS

Your trip to St. Croix is incomplete without a day trip to Buck Island aboard a charter boat. Most leave from the Christiansted waterfront or from Green Cay Marina and stop for a snorkel at the island's eastern end before dropping anchor off a gorgeous sandy beach for a swim, a hike, and lunch. Sailboats can often stop right at the beach; a larger boat might have to anchor a bit farther offshore. A full-day sail runs about $110, with lunch included on most trips. A half-day sail costs about $85.

Big Beard's Adventure Tours

SAILING | Catamarans that depart from the Christiansted waterfront whisk you to Buck Island for half- and full-day snorkeling tours. The 42-foot *Adventure* has a glass viewing platform for those who want to see the fish but don't want to get in the water. The full-day tour on the *Renegade* concludes with dropping anchor at a private beach for an all-you-can-eat-and-drink barbecue. Sunset sails also are offered. ✉ *1247 Queen Cross St., Christiansted* ☎ *340/773–4482* ⊕ *www.bigbeards.com.*

Buck Island Charters

SAILING | Scheduled half-day trips to Buck Island on the trimaran *Teroro II* leave Green Cay Marina in the morning and afternoon. Bring your own lunch and drinks. Private charters for up to 10 passengers are also available on the 38-foot trimaran *Dragonfly.* ✉ *Green Cay Marina, Annas Hope* ☎ *340/718–3161* ⊕ *www.facebook.com/buckislandcharters* ▧ *$85.*

Caribbean Sea Adventures

SAILING | With boats leaving from the Christiansted waterfront, Caribbean Sea Adventures has both half- and full-day trips to Buck Island. Sunset sails, fishing excursions, and parasailing are also available. ✉ *Christiansted Boardwalk, 59 Kings Wharf, Christiansted* ☎ *340/773–2628* ⊕ *www.caribbeanseaadventures.com.*

Lyric Sails

BOAT TOURS | This sailing adventure on a 63-foot, custom-built catamaran called the *Jolly Mon* features live musical entertainment from local performers. Visitors can choose a private day sail or a sunset sail. ✉ *1D Strand St., Frederiksted* ☎ *340/201–5227* ⊕ *www.lyricsails.com.*

DIVING AND SNORKELING

At **Buck Island,** a short boat ride from Christiansted or Green Cay Marina, the reef is so nice that it's been named a national monument. You can dive right off the beach at **Cane Bay,** which has a spectacular drop-off called the Cane Bay Wall. Dive operators also do boat trips along the Wall, usually leaving from Salt River or Christiansted. **Frederiksted Pier** is home to a colony of seahorses, creatures seldom seen in the waters of the Virgin Islands. At **Green Cay,** just outside Green Cay Marina in the East End, you can see colorful fish swimming around the reefs and rocks. Two exceptional North Shore sites are **North Star** and **Salt River,** which you can reach only by boat. At Salt River you can float downward through a canyon filled with colorful fish and coral.

The island's dive shops take you out for one- or two-tank dives. Plan to pay about $110 for a one-tank dive and $140 for a two-tank dive, including equipment and an underwater tour. All companies offer certification and introductory courses called resort dives.

Which dive outfit you pick usually depends on where you're staying. Your hotel may have one on-site. If so, you're just a short stroll away from the dock. If not, other companies are close by. Where the dive boat goes on a particular day depends on the weather, but in any case, all St. Croix's dive sites are special. All shops are affiliated with PADI, the Professional Association of Diving Instructors.

★ Cane Bay Dive Shop

SCUBA DIVING | This Frederiksted shop is the place to go if you want to do a snorkel tour, shore dive, or boat dive along the North Shore, including the famous Cane Bay Wall, or to see the seahorses under the Frederiksted Pier. ✉ *2 Strand St., Frederiksted* ✛ *Across from cruise pier* ☎ *340/772–0715* ⊕ *www.canebay-scuba.com.*

Dive Experience

SCUBA DIVING | Convenient for those staying in Christiansted, Dive Experience runs trips to the North Shore walls and reefs, the Frederiksted Pier, and night dives, in addition to offering the usual certification and introductory classes. You also can help control the population of invasive lionfish by signing up for a spearfishing hunt. It's a PADI Five Star facility. ✉ *1000 King St., Suite 6, Christiansted* ☎ *340/773–3307, 800/235–9047* ⊕ *www.divexp.com.*

St. Croix Ultimate Bluewater Adventures

SCUBA DIVING | This company can take you to your choice of more than 75 dive sites; it also offers a variety of packages that include hotel stays, stylish and comfortable island wear, and dive gear available at the dive shop. Two locations—in downtown Christiansted and downtown Frederiksted—plus two dive boats make this one of the more versatile dive operations on the island. They offer a wide variety of dive training classes, too. ⊠ 81 Queen Cross St., Christiansted ✧ Next to Hotel Caravelle ☎ 340/773–5994 ⊕ www. stcroixscuba.com.

FISHING

Since the early 1980s, some 20 world records—many for blue marlin—have been set in these waters. Sailfish, skipjack, bonito, tuna (allison, blackfin, and yellowfin), and wahoo are abundant. A charter runs about $950 to $1,150 for a half day (for up to six people), with most boats going out for a four-, six-, or eight-hour trip.

Caribbean Sea Adventures

FISHING | This charter company can take your group out fishing for marlin, wahoo, tuna, and mahi mahi on the 42-foot Downeast Style Boat, Betty Ann. ⊠ 59 Kings Wharf, Christiansted ✧ Meeting point is at Green Cay Marina Slip A6, directly in front of the Galleon restaurant ☎ 340/773–2628 ⊕ www.caribbean-seaadventures.com.

Gone Ketchin'

FISHING | Captain Grizz, a true old salt, heads half- ($600), three-quarter ($800), and full-day ($1,000) fishing charter trips to troll for marlin, wahoo, mahi mahi, king mackerel, barracuda, and tuna. ⊠ Salt River Marina, Rte. 80, Estate Salt River ☎ 340/713–1175, 340/998–2055 ⊕ www. goneketchin.com.

GOLF

St. Croix's three courses welcome you with spectacular vistas. Check with your hotel or the tourism department to determine when major celebrity tournaments will be held. There's often an opportunity to play with the pros.

★ Buccaneer Golf Course

GOLF | The Buccaneer Resort 18-hole course, near Christiansted, mixes fun with risk. Some of the par fours are within reach of a long drive, making birdies possible. However, miscues on holes that run near the ocean or have ponds can be costly for those keeping score. Most golfers' memories are of the beautiful views, not the sand traps. The signature 3rd hole with the green sitting above a rocky coastline has some calling this course the Caribbean Pebble Beach. ⊠ 5007 Estate Shoys, Shoys ☎ 340/712–2144 ⊕ www.thebuccaneer.com 🏌 $115 ⚑ 18 holes, 5668 yards, par 70.

Carambola Golf Club

GOLF | Golfers will enjoy the exotic beauty of this difficult course in the Carambola Valley designed by Robert Trent Jones Sr., because they might not enjoy their score. An extra sleeve of balls might also be required. The long water holes never return splash balls, and the rough surrounding jungle seldom does. Most fairways are forgiving with ample landing area, but the length of many holes makes playing this par 72 course challenging. ⊠ 72 Estate River, Estate River ☎ 340/778–5638 ⊕ www.golfcarambola. com 🏌 $140 with cart ⚑ 18 holes, 5727 yards, par 72.

Reef Golf Course

GOLF | If you want to enjoy panoramic Caribbean views without paying big greens fees, the public, 9-hole Reef Golf Course on the island's East End is the place to go. The course design is basic, but the views from the hillside are spectacular. Trees on this course very seldom enter into play, and sand traps are absent. The 7th hole with its highly elevated tee is the most interesting. No good with a club in your hand? Try 18 holes of disc (Frisbee) golf, instead, or grab a racquet for a game of tennis or pickleball. ⊠ 5000

Did You Know?

You can join a horseback riding tour and ride along the beaches of St. Croix.

Teague Bay, Teague's Bay ☎ 340/773–8844 ⊕ www.reefgolfstcroixusvi.com ✉ $30 greens fee for nine holes, $10 for cart ⚑ 9 holes, 2,640 yards, par 35.

GUIDED TOURS

Joseph's VIP Taxi Tours

DRIVING TOURS | Guided island van tours are available with expert commentary on the sights, history, and culture of St. Croix. The cost is $250 for three hours or $350 for a full day with up to four passengers, plus $50 for each additional passenger. ✉ *Christiansted ☎ 340/277–6133.*

Sweeny's St. Croix Safari Tours

DRIVING TOURS | These open-air (but covered) safari truck tours of St. Croix depart from Christiansted and last about five hours. Costs run from $71 per person, plus admission to attractions like the St. George Village Botanical Garden and feeding beer to the pigs at the Mount Pellier Domino Club. A stop for lunch is included; be prepared to purchase your lunch or bring your own. ✉ *Christiansted ☎ 340/773–6700, 340/514–1594 ⊕ www.gotostcroix.com/guided-tours/sweenys-tours ✉ $71.*

Virgin Islands Food Tours

FOOD AND DRINK TOURS | **FAMILY** | This guided food tasting and cultural walking tour in downtown Christiansted offers guests a glimpse into St. Croix's vibrant food culture. Six tastings of local cuisine are offered on each tour with stops at locally owned and operated restaurants. While you satiate your appetite, you can learn about the island's dynamic connection to Puerto Rico, the preservation of Danish architecture throughout the island, and the importance of the renowned cultural figures known as Mocko Jumbies. ☎ *866/468–3984 ⊕ www.vifoodtours.com ✉ $99 ☾ Closed Sun.*

HIKING

Although you can set off by yourself on a hike through a rainforest or along a shore, having a guide will help elevate your overall experience as you discover the breathtaking views found on St. Croix's hiking trails.

Crucian Heritage And Nature Tourism (CHANT)

HIKING & WALKING | CHANT runs several educational tours focused on St. Croix's natural and cultural heritage, including 2½-hour historic walking tours of Frederiksted on Wednesdays, and a Christiansted tour on Tuesdays that focuses on Alexander Hamilton, who lived in St. Croix as a teenager. A half-day tour of Maroon Ridge, which explores hideouts used by escaped slaves, is offered by appointment. CHANT's cultural center in downtown Frederiksted has exhibits of local art. ✉ *217 Custom House St., Frederiksted ☎ 340/277–4834 ⊕ www.chantvi.org.*

HORSEBACK RIDING

Nick's Scenic Equine Tours

HORSEBACK RIDING | Saddle up for a unique horseback riding adventure into the rainforest and open pastures with this guided equestrian experience. Nick and Folksy will lead you on a scenic tour to discover local flora and fauna, diverse wildlife, and edible tropical fruits and plants, with a stop along the way at an old sugar mill for photos. ✉ *Estate River ☎ 340/513–9183 ✉ $160 ☾ Closed Tues. and Thurs.*

Paul and Jill's Equestrian Stables

HORSEBACK RIDING | From Sprat Hall, just north of Frederiksted, co-owner Jill Hurd will take you on a guided horseback ride through the rainforest, across the pastures, along the beaches, and through valleys—explaining the flora, fauna, and ruins on the way. A 1½-hour outing takes places in the morning or afternoon. ✉ *Sprat Hall, Rte. 58, Frederiksted ☎ 340/332–0417 ⊕ www.paulandjills.com ✉ $150 ☾ Closed weekends.*

KAYAKING

Sea Thru Kayak VI

KAYAKING | These tours of Salt River Bay use transparent kayaks so paddlers can see the marine life passing below their boat, including the tiny glowing dinoflagellates that light up St. Croix's bioluminescent bay. Stand-up paddleboard tours also are offered. ⊠ *Salt River Marina, Rte. 80, Estate Salt River* ☎ *340/244–8696* ⊕ *www.seathrukayaksvi.com.*

Virgin Kayak Tours

KAYAKING | Enjoy guided daytime, sunset, and evening kayak trips on Salt River Bay, including tours to see the bay light up with bioluminescent marine life on moonless nights. Other options include daytime ecological and history tours of the bay where Columbus landed and encountered indigenous Carib inhabitants, plus sunset and moonlight tours. The company also rents kayaks and SUPs so you can tour around by yourself for a half or full day. ⊠ *Rte. 80, Salt River Marina, Estate Salt River* ☎ *833/246–2291, 340/514–0062* ⊕ *www.virginkayaktours. com* 🖃 *$65.*

TENNIS

The public courts in Frederiksted (near the fort) and Christiansted (in Canegata Ball Park) are generally in good condition. You can also pay a fee and play at one of the hotel courts. Costs vary by resort, but count on paying anywhere between $10–25 an hour per person.

The Buccaneer

TENNIS | There are eight courts (two are lighted for night play), plus a full tennis shop. ⊠ *The Buccaneer, Rte. 82, Shoys* ☎ *340/773–3036* ⊕ *www.thebuccaneer. com.*

Club St. Croix

TENNIS | There are two turf tennis courts, one with lights. They are available only to resort guests. ⊠ *Club St. Croix, Rte. 752, Estate Golden Rock* ☎ *340/718–4800* ⊕ *www.antillesresorts.com.*

The Reef

TENNIS | There are two courts available including a fully stocked golf and tennis shop. ⊠ *The Reef Golf Course, 5000 Teague Bay, Christiansted* ☎ *340/773– 8844* ⊕ *www.reefgolfstcroixusvi.com* 🖃 *$10.*

WATER SPORTS

West End Water Sports

WATER SPORTS | Jet Skis, water scooters, kayaks, stand-up paddleboards, and snorkeling gear, as well as beach chairs, umbrellas, and sun ray floats are available here. ⊠ *Rainbow Beach, Frederiksted* ☎ *340/277–8295* ⊕ *wewatersports.com.*

ZIP-LINING

Carambola Zip-Line

ZIP-LINING | St. Croix's newest excursion combines exhilarating adventure with breathtaking views as you zip across the St. Croix Valley near the island's North Shore. Guests receive a land tour combined with a zip line tour for the price of one. Start with a 30-minute drive on the open-air safari bus with scenic views of neighboring islands and the North Shore coastline as you head to the first zip line platform. With close to 5,000 linear feet of zipping over three courses, this is one of the longest zip lines in the Caribbean. ⊠ *1-C Estate River, Estate River* ☎ *340/244–1464* ⊕ *www.carambolazipline.com* 🖃 *$108.*

Chapter 6

TORTOLA

Updated by
Claire Shefchik

⊙ Sights	🍴 Restaurants	🛏 Hotels	🛍 Shopping	🍸 Nightlife
★★★★☆	★★★★☆	★★★★☆	★★★☆☆	★★★★☆

WELCOME TO TORTOLA

TOP REASONS TO GO

★ **Charter a boat:** Tortola is the charter-yacht capital of the Caribbean and a popular destination for boaters.

★ **Hit the road:** You'll get the real flavor of the island by heading out in whatever direction you choose. The views are dramatic, and the traffic is light enough to allow for easy driving.

★ **Shop in Road Town:** The island's largest community is also home to an eclectic collection of stores.

★ **Hit the trail:** Tortola is home to Sage Mountain National Park, a small but quite nice nature reserve.

★ **Dive in:** Dive trips to spectacular locations leave from Tortola. If you're not certified to dive, an introductory course can teach you the basics and whet your appetite for more adventures under the sea.

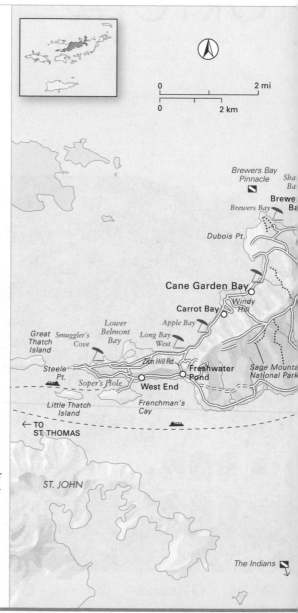

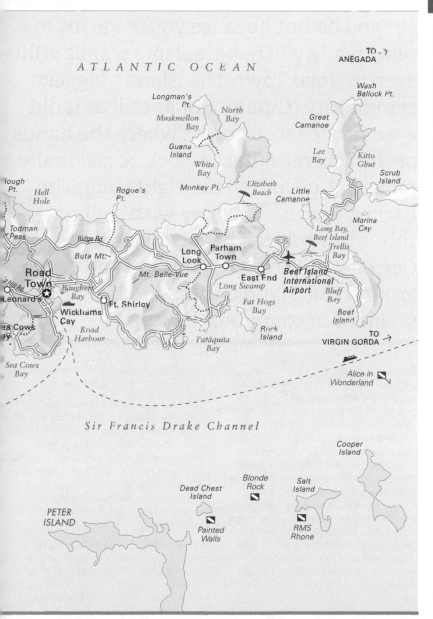

A day might not be enough to tour this island—all 21 square miles (56 square km) of it—not because there's so much to see and do but because you're meant to relax while you're here. Time stands still even in Road Town, the island's biggest community (though not as still as it did even in the recent past), where the hands of the central square's clock occasionally move but never tell the right time. The harbor, however, is busy with sailboats—this is the charter-boat capital of the Caribbean. Tortola's roads dip and curve around the island and lead to lovely, secluded accommodations.

Tortola is definitely busy these days, particularly when several cruise ships tie up at the Road Town dock. Passengers crowd the streets and shops, and open-air jitneys filled with them create bottlenecks on the island's byways. That said, most folks visit Tortola to relax on its deserted sands or linger over lunch at one of its many delightful restaurants. Beaches are never more than a few miles away, and the steep green hills that form Tortola's spine are fanned by gentle trade winds. The neighboring islands glimmer like emeralds in a sea of sapphire. It can be a world far removed from the hustle of modern life, but it simply doesn't compare to Virgin Gorda in terms of beautiful, secluded beaches—or even luxury resorts, for that matter.

Still a British colonial outpost, the island's economy depends on tourism and its offshore financial-services businesses. With a population of around 24,000, most people work in those industries or for the local government. You'll hear lots of crisp British accents thanks to a large number of expats who call the island home, but the melodic West Indian accent still predominates.

Initially settled by the indigenous Taíno people, Tortola saw a string of visitors over the years. Christopher Columbus sailed by in 1493 on his second voyage to the New World, and Spain, Holland,

and France made periodic visits about a century later. Sir Francis Drake arrived in 1595, leaving his name on the channel between Tortola and sister islands like Norman Island, Cooper Island, and Virgin Gorda. Pirates and buccaneers followed, the British finally laying claim to the island in the late 1600s. In 1741, John Pickering became the first lieutenant governor of Tortola, and the seat of the British government moved from Virgin Gorda to Tortola. As the agrarian economy continued to grow, enslaved people were imported from Africa. The slave trade was abolished in 1807, but enslaved people in Tortola and the rest of the BVI did not gain their freedom until August 1, 1834, when the Emancipation Act was read at Sunday Morning Well in Road Town. That date is celebrated every year as part of the island's annual Emancipation Festival.

Planning

Getting Here and Around

AIR

There's no nonstop air service from the continental United States to Tortola; connections are usually made through San Juan, Puerto Rico, or St. Thomas, USVI.

CAR

You might get by with taxis, especially if you are staying in Road Town, but if you are in a villa or an isolated resort, a car is a necessity here. Remember that driving is on the *left* even though cars are generally American-made. Tortola's main roads are well paved for the most part, but there are exceptionally steep hills and sharp curves; driving demands your complete attention. A main road circles the island, and several roads cross it, mostly through mountainous terrain.

Road Town's traffic and parking can be horrific, so avoid driving along Waterfront

Drive during morning and afternoon rush hours.

■ TIP➜ It's longer—but often quicker—to drive through the hills above Road Town. (And the views are great as well.)

Parking can also be very difficult in Road Town, particularly during high season. There's parking along the waterfront and on the inland side on the eastern end of downtown, but if you're planning a day of shopping, go early to make sure you snag a space. Or, take a taxi.

CAR RENTALS

Only Hertz and National have offices at the airport, but most companies will pick you up. It's usually best to reserve a car in advance.

CONTACTS Avis. ✉ *Tortola Pier Park, Wickham's Cay, Road Town* ☎ *284/495–4973 West End, at Road Town cruise pier, 284/495–0110 airport branch* ⊕ *www.avis. com.* **Denzil Clyne Jeep Rentals.** ✉ *West End Rd.* ☎ *284/495–4900* ⊕ *denzilclyne-rentals.com.* **Itgo Car Rental.** ✉ *Mill Mall, Wickham's Cay I, Road Town* ☎ *284/494–5150, 284/494–2639* ⊕ *www.itgobvi. com.* **National.** ✉ *Terrance B Lettsome International Airport* ☎ *284/495–2626, 284/494–3197 Road Town (Maria's Hotel by the Sea)* ⊕ *www.nationalcar.com.*

FERRY

Frequent daily ferries connect Tortola with St. Thomas, which many vacationers decide to use as their main air gateway. Ferries go to and from both Charlotte Amalie and Red Hook. There's huge competition between the Tortola-based ferry companies on the St. Thomas–Tortola runs, with boats leaving close together. As you enter the ferry terminal to buy your ticket, crews may try to convince you to take their ferry. Ferries also link Tortola to St. John, where all Red Hook–bound ferries stop in Cruz Bay to clear customs and immigration. Ferries also link Tortola with Jost Van Dyke, Norman Island, Peter Island, and Virgin Gorda. You can also connect to Anegada from Road

Town and Trellis Bay on Beef Island. Tortola has two ferry terminals—one at West End and one in Road Town—and a jetty at Beef Island where ferries depart for Virgin Gorda, so make sure you hop a ferry that disembarks closest to where you want to go. Ferry schedules vary, and not all companies make daily trips. Departures can be suddenly canceled, particularly in the summer. The BVI Tourist Board website has links to all the ferry companies.

TAXI

Taxi rates are set on Tortola, but you should still check with your driver before you start your trip. Fares are per destination, not per person here, so it's cheaper to travel in groups, because the fare will be the same whether you have one, two, or three passengers. On Tortola the BVI Taxi Association has stands in Road Town near Wickham's Cay I. The Waterfront Taxi Association picks up passengers from the Road Town ferry dock. The Airport Taxi Association operates at the Terrance B. Lettsome Airport on Beef Island. You can also usually find a West End Taxi Association taxi at the West End ferry dock.

CONTACTS Beef Island Taxi Association.
☎ 284/495–1982.

Beaches

Beaches in the BVI are less developed than those on St. Thomas or St. Croix, but they are also less inviting. The best BVI beaches are on deserted islands reachable only by boat, so take a snorkeling or sailing trip at least once. Tortola's north side has several palm-fringed, white-sand beaches that curl around turquoise bays and coves, but none really achieves greatness. Nearly all are accessible by car (preferably a four-wheel-drive vehicle), albeit down bumpy roads that corkscrew precipitously. Some of these beaches, like Cane Garden Bay, are lined with bars and restaurants as well as water-sports equipment stalls; others have absolutely nothing.

Hotels

Tortola resorts are intimate—only a handful have more than 50 rooms. Guests are treated as more than just room numbers, and many return year after year. This can make booking a room at popular resorts difficult, even off-season, despite the fact that more than half the island's visitors stay aboard their own or chartered boats. Hotels in Road Town don't have beaches, but they do have pools and are within walking distance of restaurants, bars, and shops. Accommodations outside Road Town are relatively isolated, but most face the ocean. Some places close during the peak of hurricane season—August through October—to give their owners a much-needed break.

Luxury on Tortola is more about a certain state of mind—serenity, seclusion, gentility, and a bit of Britain in the Caribbean—than about state-of-the-art amenities and fabulous facilities. Some properties, especially the vacation villas, are catching up with current trends, but others seem stuck in the 1980s. But don't let a bit of rust on the screen door or a chip in the paint on the balcony railing mar your appreciation of the ambience. You will likely spend most of your time outside, so the location, size, or price of a hotel should be more of a deciding factor than the décor.

A stay at any one of the hotels and guesthouses on Tortola's north side will put you closer to the beach, but not to worry: it doesn't take that long to get from one side of the island to the other. Visitors who want to be closer to Road Town's restaurants and shops can find a handful of places in and around the island's main town.

⇨ *Hotel prices are the lowest cost of a standard double room in high season.*

WHAT IT COSTS in U.S. Dollars			
$	$$	$$$	$$$$
HOTELS			
under $276	$276–$375	$376–$475	over $475

PRIVATE VILLAS

Renting a villa is growing in popularity. Vacationers like the privacy, the space to spread out, and the opportunity to cook meals. As is true everywhere, the most important thing is location. If you want to be close to the beach, opt for a villa on the North Shore. If you want to dine out in Road Town every night, a villa closer to town may be a better bet. Prices per week during the winter season run from around $2,000 for a one- or two-bedroom villa up to $10,000 for a five-room beachfront villa. Rates in summer are substantially less. Most, but not all, villas accept credit cards.

Smiths Gore

TRAVEL AGENCIES | Smiths Gore has properties all over the island available as long-term (a month or more) rentals as well as vacation villas for shorter term stays. They range from two to four bedrooms: expect stellar views, lovely furnishings, and lush landscaping. ⊠ *Brittanic Hall, Main St., Road Town* ☎ *284/494–2446* ⊕ *villavacationsbvi.com.*

Nightlife

Like any other good sailing destination, Tortola has watering holes that are popular with salty and not-so-salty dogs. Many offer entertainment; check the weekly *Limin' Times* for schedules and up-to-date information. The local beverage is the Painkiller, an innocent-tasting mixture of fruit juices and rums. It goes down smoothly but packs quite a punch, so give yourself time to recover before you order another. Road Town and Cane Garden Bay are your best bets for nightlife that goes later than 10 pm.

Restaurants

Local seafood is plentiful on Tortola, and although other fresh ingredients are scarce, the island's chefs are a creative lot who apply their skills to whatever the boat delivers. Contemporary American dishes with Caribbean influences are very popular, but you can find French and Italian fare as well. The more expensive restaurants have dress codes: long pants and collared shirts for men and elegant but casual resort wear for women. Prices are often a bit higher than you'd expect to pay back home, and the service can sometimes be a tad slow, but enjoy the chance to linger over the view.

Restaurants are scattered from one end of the island to the other, so you're never far from a good meal. Cane Garden Bay, with a handful of restaurants along the beach, is a popular dining destination. Eateries in Road Town are a short stroll from each other, making it easy to find a place that pleases everyone. Most hotels have restaurants that welcome nonguests.

⇨ *Restaurant prices are the average cost of a main course at dinner or, if dinner is not served, at lunch.*

WHAT IT COSTS in U.S. Dollars			
$	$$	$$$	$$$$
RESTAURANTS			
under $13	$13–$20	$21–$30	over $30

Safety

Although crime is rare, use the same common sense you would on any vacation. Don't leave your camera on the beach while you take a dip, for example.

Sights

Tortola doesn't have an abundance of historic sights, but it does have lots of spectacular natural scenery and beautiful beaches. Although you could explore the island's 21 square miles (56 square km) in a few hours, opting for such a whirl-wind tour would be a mistake. There's no need to live in the fast lane when you're surrounded by some of the Caribbean's most breathtaking panoramas. In any event, you come to Tortola to relax, read in the hammock, and spend hours at dinner, not to dash madly around the island ticking yet another sight off your list. Most island sights are best seen when you stumble upon them on your round-the-island drive.

Tours

Romney Associates/Travel Plan Tours can arrange island tours, boat tours, snorkeling and scuba-diving trips, dolphin swims, and yacht charters from its Tortola base. Tours can also be booked directly with operators including taxis, scuba diving operators, and power- and sail-charter boats. Their contacts can be found at the BVI Tourism Board website and on the BVI Now mobile app.

CONTACTS Romney Associates/Travel Plan Tours. ⊠ *Road Town* ☎ *284/494–4000* ⊕ *romascogroup.com.*

Visitor Information

CONTACTS BVI Tourist Board. ☎ *212/563– 3117, 800/835–8530 in the U.S.* ⊕ *www. bvitourism.com.*

BANKS
On Tortola, banks are near the waterfront at Wickham's Cay I. All have ATMs. Look for Banco Popular, First Caribbean International Bank, First Bank, and Scotiabank, among others.

Road Town

The bustling capital of the BVI looks out over Road Harbour. It takes only an hour or so to stroll down Main Street and along the waterfront, checking out the traditional West Indian buildings painted in pastel colors and with corrugated-tin roofs, bright shutters, and delicate fretwork trim. For sightseeing brochures and the latest information on everything from taxi rates to ferry schedules, stop in the BVI Tourist Board booth near the ferry dock. Or just choose a seat on one of the benches in Sir Olva Georges Plaza, on Waterfront Drive, and watch the people come and go from the ferry dock and customs office across the street.

⊙ Sights

Cyril B. Romney Tortola Pier Park
PEDESTRIAN MALL | The Cyril B. Romney Tortola Pier Park is the point of disembarkation for cruise ship passengers visiting the island. This Road Town development has a cigar bar, pizza joint, Caribbean fusion restaurant, an outpost of Myett's bar, and an ice cream parlor. Diverse shopping options include jewelry stores, art galleries, and clothing boutiques. You can rent a car here or join in one of the frequent festivals and special events held at the complex. Public restrooms are available as well. ⊠ *Wickhams Cay I, Road Town* ☎ *284/494–8775* ⊕ *www. tortolapier.com.*

Fort Burt
HISTORIC SIGHT | The most intact historic fort on Tortola (that's not saying much, however) was raised by the Dutch in the early 17th century to safeguard Road Harbour, then rebuilt by the British. It sits on a hill at the western edge of Road Town and is now the site of a small hotel (also named Fort Burt). The foundations and magazine remain, and the structure offers a commanding view of the harbor. ⊠ *Waterfront Dr., Road Town* 🎫 *Free.*

A scenic view of the Tortola Pier Park and the surrounding landscape.

H.M. Prison Museum

JAIL/PRISON | Road Town's formidable prison was constructed in the mid-19th century and went on to hold prisoners in relatively primitive conditions for more than a century before closing in 1997. The prisoners confined to the humid barred cells were lucky compared to those who were hung in a creepy chamber, where the gallows claimed its last victim in the 1970s. Informative, docent-led tours offer insights into island history and the administration of justice from the colonial period into the early 21st century. ⊠ *Main St., Road Town* ☎ *284/468–2151* 🎫 *$5* 🕐 *Closed weekends.*

J.R. O'Neal Botanical Gardens

GARDEN | This 3-acre showcase of plant life has sections devoted to prickly cacti and succulents, hothouses for ferns and orchids, gardens of medicinal herbs, and plants and trees indigenous to the seashore. A boulevard of royal palms was previously one of the most prominent features, but a number of these were felled in the 2017 hurricane. Otherwise, the gardens have recovered quite nicely. ⊠ *Botanic Station, Road Town* ☎ *284/393–9284* ⊕ *www.bvinpt. org/jr-o-neal-botanical* 🎫 *$3* 🕐 *Closed weekends.*

★ Old Government House Museum

HISTORIC HOME | The official government residence until 1997, this gracious building now displays a nice collection of artifacts from Tortola's past. The rooms are filled with period furniture, hand-painted china, books signed by Queen Elizabeth II on her 1966 and 1977 visits, and numerous items reflecting Tortola's seafaring legacy. ⊠ *Waterfront Dr., Road Town* ☎ *284/468–3505* ⊕ *www.oghm.org* 🎫 *$5* 🕐 *Closed weekends.*

🍴 Restaurants

Bamboushay Restaurant and Lounge

$$$ | ECLECTIC | Watch the world go by with a passion-fruit mojito and a platter of coconut shrimp or crispy tamarind wings as you mingle with locals and visitors in a social environment and the friendliest

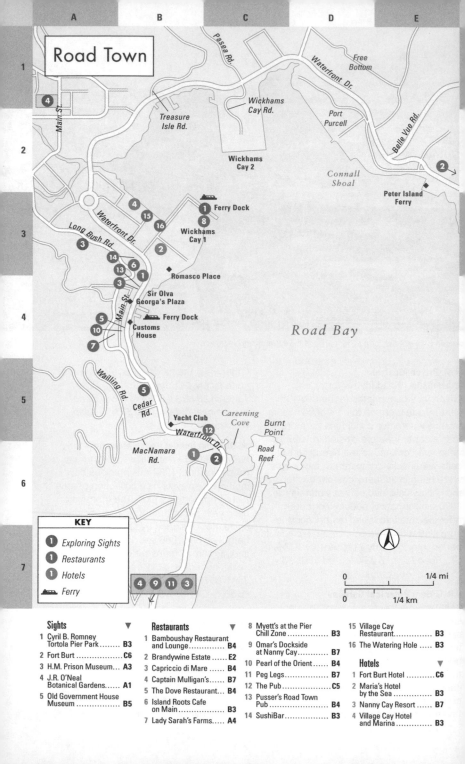

Road Town

A **B** **C** **D** **E**

Passea Rd.

Free Bottom

Waterfront Dr.

Main St.

Treasure Isle Rd.

Wickhams Cay Rd.

Port Purcell

Belle Vue Rd.

Wickhams Cay 2

Connall Shoal

Peter Island Ferry

④ Waterfront Dr.

Long Bush Rd.

④ ⑮ ⑯ ② ③

Ferry Dock ①
⑧
Wickhams Cay 1

⑭ ⑥ ⑬ ① ③

Romasco Place

Sir Olva Georga's Plaza

Ferry Dock

⑤ ⑩ ⑦

Customs House

Road Bay

Wailling Rd.

Main St.

Cedar Rd.

⑤

Yacht Club

Careening Cove

Burnt Point

Waterfront Dr. ⑫

MacNamara Rd.

① ②

Road Reef

KEY

- ① *Exploring Sights*
- ① *Restaurants*
- ① *Hotels*
- 🚢 *Ferry*

④ ⑨ ⑪ ③

0   1/4 mi
0   1/4 km

Sights ▼

1 Cyril B. Romney Tortola Pier Park **B3**
2 Fort Burt **C6**
3 H.M. Prison Museum... **A3**
4 J.R. O'Neal Botanical Gardens...... **A1**
5 Old Government House Museum **B5**

Restaurants ▼

1 Bamboushay Restaurant and Lounge.............. **B4**
2 Brandywine Estate **E2**
3 Capriccio di Mare **B4**
4 Captain Mulligan's..... **B7**
5 The Dove Restaurant... **B4**
6 Island Roots Cafe on Main **B3**
7 Lady Sarah's Farms..... **A4**

8 Myett's at the Pier Chill Zone **B3**
9 Omar's Dockside at Nanny Cay............. **B7**
10 Pearl of the Orient **B4**
11 Peg Legs................. **B7**
12 The Pub **C5**
13 Pusser's Road Town Pub **B4**
14 SushiBar................. **B3**

15 Village Cay Restaurant................. **B3**
16 The Watering Hole **B3**

Hotels ▼

1 Fort Burt Hotel **C6**
2 Maria's Hotel by the Sea **B3**
3 Nanny Cay Resort **B7**
4 Village Cay Hotel and Marina.............. **B3**

American or British?

Yes, the Union Jack flutters overhead in the tropical breeze, schools operate on the British system, place-names have British spellings, King Charles III appoints the governor—and the king's picture hangs on many walls. Indeed, residents celebrate the monarch's birthday every June with a public ceremony. You can overhear that charming English accent from a good handful of expats when you're lunching at Road Town restaurants, and you can buy British biscuits—which Americans call cookies—in the supermarkets.

But you can pay for your lunch and the biscuits with American money because the U.S. dollar is legal tender here. The unusual circumstance is a matter of geography. The practice started in the mid-20th century, when BVI residents went to work in the nearby USVI. On trips home, they brought their U.S. dollars with them. Soon they abandoned the exchange system, and in 1959 the U.S. dollar became the official currency. Interestingly, the government sells stamps for use only in the BVI that often carry pictures of the king and other royalty with the monetary value in U.S. dollars and cents.

The American influence continued to grow when Americans began to open businesses in the BVI because they preferred its quieter ambience to the hustle and bustle of St. Thomas. Inevitably, cable and satellite TV's U.S.-based programming, along with Hollywood-made movies, further influenced life in the BVI. And most goods are shipped from St. Thomas in the USVI, meaning you can find more American-made Oreos than British-produced Peek Freans on supermarket shelves.

service in town. The menu offers something for everyone, with lobster and daily fresh fish specials, as well as standard pub fare like shepherd's pie and fish-and-chips. **Known for:** eclectic menu; live music; local bar scene. [$] *Average main: $23* ✉ *Waterfront Dr., Road Town* ☎ *284/494–7752* 🌐 *bamboushaylounge.business.site.*

★ Brandywine Estate

$$$$ | **MEDITERRANEAN** | At this Brandywine Bay restaurant, candlelit outdoor tables have sweeping views of nearby islands. The menu has a Mediterranean bistro flair but changes often; you might find grilled local kingfish or a classic paella. **Known for:** gardenlike atmosphere; stunning Caribbean views; extensive Mediterranean tapas selection. [$] *Average main: $36* ✉ *Sir Francis Drake Hwy., east of Road Town, Brandywine Bay* ☎ *284/495–2301* 🌐 *www.brandywine.vg* 🕑 *Closed Mon. and Tues.*

★ Capriccio di Mare

$$$ | **ITALIAN** | Stop by this casual, authentic Italian outdoor café—look for the turquoise Vespa out front—for an espresso, gelato, a fresh pastry, a bowl of perfectly cooked pasta, or a crispy tomato-and-mozzarella pizza. **Known for:** authentic Italian fare; lively street setting; Neapolitan-style pizza. [$] *Average main: $27* ✉ *196 Waterfront Dr., Road Town* ☎ *284/494–5369* 🌐 *www.capricciobvi.com* 🕑 *Closed Sun. and Mon.*

Captain Mulligan's

$$ | **BURGER** | **FAMILY** | Located at the entrance to Nanny Cay, this sports bar attracts expats, locals, and sailors with its promise to have "the second-best burger on the island," underlining the eatery's irreverent tone (we never found out who has the best!). Hot wings, pizza, ribs, and burgers are on the menu, and most people come to watch the game on the big-screen TVs. **Known for:** sports bar scene; family- and pet-friendly atmosphere; BBQ ribs. $ *Average main: $18* ✉ *Sir Francis Drake Hwy., Nanny Cay* ☎ *284/494–0602.*

The Dove Restaurant

$$$$ | **ECLECTIC** | This reopened Road Town institution is a restaurant and lounge where you will find Asian fusion and gastropub fare and craft cocktails with local ingredients. Get comfy in the romantic dark wood dining room downstairs and start out with the mushroom Wellington, then move onto the pan-fried duck breast before finishing with British sticky toffee pudding with ginger ice cream. **Known for:** hip cocktail lounge; pub specials; Asian fusion dining. $ *Average main: $32* ✉ *67 Main St., Road Town* ✥ *Front entrance on Waterfront Dr.* ☎ *284/494–0313* 🌐 *www.thedovebvi.com* 🕓 *Closed Sun. and Mon.*

Island Roots Cafe on Main

$ | **ECLECTIC** | Located in the historic Customs House, Island Roots is part café, part bookstore, and part art gallery. You can order sandwiches, salads, espresso, or smoothies from the counter and browse unique artwork and historic prints while waiting for your meal. **Known for:** breakfast all day on Saturdays; historic setting; rotating daily soup specials. $ *Average main: $12* ✉ *15 Main St., Road Town* ☎ *284/494–8985* 🌐 *www.islandrootsbvi.com* 🕓 *Closed Sun. No dinner.*

Lady Sarah's Farms

$$ | **ECLECTIC** | Put on your biggest floppy hat and join the lunching ladies at this airy restaurant and coffee shop, where hyper-local, farm-to-table ingredients take center stage. The standouts from the rotating menu—prepared by chef-owner Portia Harrigan—include velvety pumpkin soup, fish croquettes, gourmet burgers, an elevated grilled cheese with aged cheddar, and sun-dried-tomato pesto, or build-your-own Caribbean jasmine rice bowls with calypso or chimichurri sauces. **Known for:** breakfast and lunch; espresso drinks; eclectic rotating menu with organic ingredients. $ *Average main: $18* ✉ *60 Main St.* ☎ *284/541–8011* 🌐 *www.ladysarahsfarms.com* 🕓 *Closed Sun.–Tues. No dinner.*

Myett's at the Pier Chill Zone

$$ | **ECLECTIC** | When the cruise ships are in, this comfortable, breezy space just off the cruise pier—bearing little resemblance to its sister establishment on Tortola's North Shore—gets high-spirited with tourists drinking Painkillers; without the ships, it's a calm, chill oasis in the pier park where locals congregate for happy hour on weeknights after shopping near the pier. Expect a surprising menu featuring burgers, tacos, and the only authentic Buffalo wings in the BVI. **Known for:** tacos and wings; harbor views; lively cruise ship crowd during the day. $ *Average main: $18* ✉ *Cyril B. Romney Tortola Pier Park, Road Town* ☎ *284/346–9458* 🕓 *Closed weekends when no ships are in.*

Omar's Dockside at Nanny Cay

$$$ | **ECLECTIC** | The central gathering space for Nanny Cay's fresh-off-the-yacht crowd is now a day-to-night fusion of Omar's first two locations in West End, from its lavish breakfast offerings in the morning—omelets, pancakes, eggs Benedict, and chicken and waffles—to authentic Indian curries and sophisticated specialty cocktails at night. Friday happy hour features $5 rum punches and Painkillers. **Known for:** Indian dinner offerings; decadent breakfast; lively sailing crowd. $ *Average main: $21* ✉ *Nanny Cay, Nanny Cay* ☎ *284/440–7172.*

Pearl of the Orient

$$ | **SUSHI** | This friendly, unassuming spot is one of the oldest and best sushi joints still open in the BVI, with competitive prices. Make sure to start with one of the luscious appetizers like chicken gyoza and veggie spring rolls, followed by rolls

ike the Mango Dragon (with prawn tempura, cucumber, and mayo topped with mango) or the Jazz Maki (with prawn tempura, avocado, and mango rolled in crunchy tanuki); or opt for the seared tuna with seaweed salad or the spicy sashimi platter. **Known for:** sushi; good prices; casual atmosphere. $ *Average main: $17* ✉ *Waterfront Dr., Road Town* ☎ *284/543-4118* ☉ *Closed Sun.*

Peg Legs

$$$ | **ECLECTIC** | Take in views of Sir Francis Drake Channel and sidle up to the outdoor beach bar to hear yachties swap sea stories at this mariner-friendly eatery, or snag a table on the sand for dinner. Two separate menus are available, one with burgers and pizzas and another with pasta dishes and daily fresh seafood entrées. **Known for:** people-watching; great views; Spring Regatta after-parties. $ *Average main: $29* ✉ *Nanny Cay, Nanny Cay* ☎ *284/394-2518* ⊕ *nannycay.com.*

The Pub

$$$ | **ECLECTIC** | Hamburgers, salads, and sandwiches are typical lunch offerings at this Road Town eatery with a harbor view, along with classic British fare such as shepherd's pie and fish-and-chips. In the evening you can get your Anegada lobster grilled or jerked, and choose from entrées like Cajun lamb chops or fried grouper. **Known for:** billiards and bar games; tasty pub classics; jerk seafood. $ *Average main: $21* ✉ *Waterfront Dr., Road Town* ☎ *284/494-2608.*

Pusser's Road Town Pub

$$$ | **ECLECTIC** | **FAMILY** | Almost everyone who visits Tortola stops here at least once to have a bite and to sample the famous Painkiller, made with Pusser's Royal Navy rum, pineapple and orange juices, and cream of coconut. The predictable menu includes pizza, shepherd's pie, fish-and-chips, burgers, and occasional seafood specials. **Known for:** pub-like interior; Pusser's rum; reliably

good comfort fare. $ *Average main: $22* ✉ *Waterfront Dr., Road Town* ☎ *284/494-3897* ⊕ *www.pussers.com.*

SushiBar

$$ | **SUSHI** | An oasis of calm awaits you in SushiBar's lush, enchantingly landscaped outdoor patio area—it's the place to go in the busy heart of Road Town for sushi, sashimi, ramen, and other Asian-inspired offerings. Signature rolls include a lobster roll and a hurricane roll with salmon, tuna, and crab. **Known for:** outdoor dining in a lovely garden setting; signature sushi rolls; cocktails. $ *Average main: $18* ✉ *Waterfront Dr., Road Town* ☎ *284/495-1122* ⊕ *sushibarbvi.com* ☉ *Closed Sun.*

Village Cay Restaurant

$$$ | **ECLECTIC** | Docked sailboats stretch nearly as far as the eye can see at this busy Road Town marina restaurant. The alfresco dining and convivial atmosphere make it popular with both locals and visitors. **Known for:** lunch buffet; happy hour; outdoor dining. $ *Average main: $28* ✉ *Wickham's Cay I, Road Town* ☎ *284/494-2771* ⊕ *www.villagecaybvi. com.*

The Watering Hole

$$ | **ECLECTIC** | Quietly tucked into a corner on Road Town's waterfront, the Watering Hole is an oasis amidst the jungle of concrete government buildings and banks in downtown Road Town. South African wine and local and imported beer—along with espresso, Wi-Fi, and light fare like pizza, sandwiches, wraps, tacos, and a new tapas menu—make this a popular lunch spot for Road Town professionals and charter-yacht crews. **Known for:** South African wines; breakfast; good nightly specials. $ *Average main: $18* ✉ *Wickham's Cay, Road Town* ✛ *Wickham's Cay* ☎ *284/346-5950* ⊕ *www.facebook.com/ wateringholebvi* ☉ *Closed Sun.*

Hotels

Fort Burt Hotel
$ | **HOTEL** | The Fort Burt Hotel surrounds the ruins of an old Dutch fort, giving you a sense of history along with a night's sleep. **Pros:** nice views; historic site; inexpensive. **Cons:** little parking; long walk to Road Town; need car to get around. [$] *Rooms from: $110* ✉ *Waterfront Dr., Road Town* ☎ *284/494–2587* 🌐 *www.fortburt.com* 🛏 *18 rooms* 🍴 *No Meals.*

Maria's Hotel by the Sea
$ | **HOTEL** | Sitting near the water in busy Road Town, Maria's Hotel by the Sea is perfect for budget travelers who want to be near shops and restaurants but who don't need many frills. **Pros:** good location; spacious rooms; walk to shops and restaurants. **Cons:** busy street; little parking; need car to get around. [$] *Rooms from: $170* ✉ *Waterfront Dr., Road Town* ☎ *284/494–2595* 🌐 *www.mariasbythesea.com* 🛏 *67 rooms* 🍴 *No Meals.*

Nanny Cay Resort
$ | **HOTEL** | This quiet oasis is far enough from Road Town to give it a secluded feel but close enough to make shops and restaurants convenient. **Pros:** nearby shops and restaurants; pleasant rooms; marina atmosphere. **Cons:** not a lot of frills in the rooms; busy location; need a car to get around. [$] *Rooms from: $185* ✉ *Waterfront Dr., Nanny Cay* ☎ *284/394–2512* 🌐 *www.nannycay.com* 🛏 *52 rooms* 🍴 *No Meals.*

Village Cay Hotel and Marina
$ | **HOTEL** | If you want to be able to walk to restaurants and shops, you simply can't beat Village Cay's prime location in the heart of Road Town. **Pros:** prime location; restaurant on-site; nautical ambience. **Cons:** little parking; busy street; need a car to get to the beach. [$] *Rooms from: $185* ✉ *Wickham's Cay I, Road Town* ☎ *284/494–2771* 🌐 *www.villagecaybvi.com* 🛏 *22 rooms* 🍴 *No Meals.*

Big Event

Tortola celebrates its annual carnival, known as the August Emancipation Festival, on and around August 1 to mark the anniversary of the end of slavery in 1834. A slew of Festival activities, culminating with a parade through the streets, take place in Road Town. You can also catch localized festivities in Carrot Bay and East End. Hotels fill up fast, so make sure to reserve your room and rental car well in advance.

Nightlife

Tola Beverage Company
BREWPUBS | The island's first microbrewery and taproom is worth a visit for its friendly service, free samples, and pints of the BVI's own take on the Caribbean-style lager, IPA, stout, and other rotating offerings. There's no on-site kitchen, but the non-beer drinkers will find a full bar. The space, located in a warehouse just outside of town on the Road Harbour waterfront, has a pubby, social atmosphere. ✉ *Burt Point, Road Town* ☎ *284/541–8088* 🌐 *www.tolabeverage.com* 🕒 *Closed Sun.*

Shopping

Many shops and boutiques are clustered along and just off Road Town's **Main Street.** You can find higher-end offerings in the Cyril B. Romney Tortola Pier Park, off the cruise pier. The **Crafts Alive Market** on the Road Town waterfront is a collection of colorful West Indian–style buildings with shops that carry items made in the BVI. You might find pretty baskets or interesting pottery or perhaps a bottle of home-brewed hot sauce.

Streetscape of Road Town

ART
Nutmeg & Co.
SOUVENIRS | The shelves of this Waterfront Drive shop are chock-a-block with colorful paintings by local artists like Aileen Malcolm, Jinx Morgan, and Jill Tattersall. You'll also find soap, jewelry, home goods, crafts, hot sauce and spices, and even recycled tote bags courtesy of co-owner Annie MacPhail. They also offer custom framing and regularly host gallery openings and meet-and-greets with local artists. ⊠ *Waterfront Dr., Road Town* ☎ *284/494–1426* ⊕ *nutmeg-and-co. shoplightspeed.com* ⊗ *Closed Sun.*

CLOTHES AND TEXTILES
Arawak
MIXED CLOTHING | This boutique carries batik sundresses, sportswear, swimwear, jewelry, and resort wear for men and women. There's also a selection of Indonesian teak furniture and children's clothing and books. Look for brands like Reef and Havaianas for sandals, Maui Jim sunglasses, and Hurley and Quicksilver for clothes. Other locations include a furniture shop on Waterfront Drive in Road Town and at Soper's Hole in West End. There are also two locations in Virgin Gorda. ⊠ *Nanny Cay Marina, Nanny Cay* ☎ *284/494–5240* ⊕ *www.arawakvi.com.*

Latitude 18°
MIXED CLOTHING | This store sells Maui Jim, Ray-Ban, and Oakley sunglasses; Freestyle watches; and a fine collection of beach towels, sandals, Crocs, sundresses, and sarongs. Find a second location next to Myett's in Cane Garden Bay. ⊠ *Waterfront Dr., Road Town* ☎ *284/494–7807* ⊕ *www.latitude18.com* ⊗ *Closed Sun.*

Pusser's Company Store
MIXED CLOTHING | The Road Town Pusser's sells its nautical memorabilia, clothing for both men and women, handsome decorative bottles of Pusser's rum, and gift items—including its iconic tin cup—bearing Pusser's classic logo. Other locations are at Soper's Hole in Tortola's West End and at Leverick Bay in Virgin Gorda's North Sound. ⊠ *Main St., Road Town* ☎ *284/494–3897* ⊕ *www.pussers.com.*

FOODSTUFFS
Grape Expectations
FOOD | These provisioners and wholesalers operate a small retail location six days a week from their warehouse in Road Reef, where you'll find meats, seafood, and gourmet items unavailable at the local supermarkets. Visit for grass-fed beef, all-natural chicken, artisan cheeses, and specialty condiments, including an extensive selection of Asian foodstuffs. They'll also deliver to your villa or boat. ⊠ *Burt Point, Road Town* ✛ *Across from Virgin Islands Search and Rescue, next to Tola Brewery* ☎ *284/346–9463* ☉ *Closed Sat. afternoon and Sun.*

RiteWay
SUPERMARKET | This supermarket has fresh produce, deli, prepared foods, meats, bakery, and all the grocery items you'll need for your villa or yacht. You can shop for yourself or set up a provisioning order. You'll find RiteWay locations all over Tortola, and there's also one on Virgin Gorda. ⊠ *Waterfront Dr. at Pasea Estate, Road Town* ☎ *384/347–1188* ⊕ *www.rtwbvi.com.*

GIFTS
Crafts Alive Village
CRAFTS | The collection of colorful West Indian cottages offering handicrafts, cloths, and souvenirs at the Crafts Alive Village makes for excellent one-stop souvenir shopping. ⊠ *Waterfront Dr., Road Town.*

West End

Sights

Fort Recovery
MILITARY SIGHT | An unrestored but largely intact 17th-century Dutch fort sits amid a profusion of tropical greenery on the grounds of the Fort Recovery Beachfront Villas and Suites. The most interesting thing to see here are the remains of a martello tower, a type of fortification used to make up for the site's lack of elevation; it's rarely found in the Caribbean. There are no guided tours, but you're welcome to stop by and poke around. ⊠ *Sir Francis Drake Hwy., Freshwater Pond, Road Town* ☎ *284/541–0955, 518/435–5436* ⊕ *www.fortrecovery.com* ☜ *Free.*

Soper's Hole
TOWN | On this little island connected by a causeway to Tortola's western end, you can find a marina and a captivating complex of pastel West Indian–style buildings with shady balconies, shuttered windows, and gingerbread trim that house art galleries, boutiques, and restaurants, including the popular Pusser's Landing West End and two Omar's restaurants (Omar's Cafe and Fusion and Omar's Coffee House). ⊠ *Soper's Hole.*

Beaches

Long Bay Beach
BEACH | This beach is a stunning, mile-long stretch of white sand; have your camera ready to snap the breathtaking approach. The entire beach is open to the public and is often used by people staying in villas in the Long Bay/Belmont area and at the Long Bay Beach Resort. The water isn't as calm here as at Cane Garden or Brewers Bay, but it's still swimmable. If you're coming from the southern part of the island, turn left at Zion Hill Road, then travel about half a mile. **Amenities:** none. **Best for:** swimming. ⊠ *Long Bay Rd., Long Bay.*

Smuggler's Cove Beach
BEACH | A beautiful, palm-fringed beach, Smuggler's Cove is down a pothole-filled dirt road. After bouncing your way down (a four-wheel-drive rental is highly recommended), you'll feel as if you've found a hidden piece of the island. You probably won't be alone on weekends, though, when the beach attracts snorkelers and sunbathers. There's a fine view of Jost Van Dyke. The popular Nigel's Boom

Boom Beach Bar has grilled food and the requisite Painkillers; the extremely informal Patricia's beach bar is next door. Follow Long Bay Road past Long Bay Beach Club, keeping to the roads nearest the water until you reach the beach. It's about a mile past the resort. **Amenities:** food and drink; parking. **Best for:** snorkeling; swimming. ⊠ *Long Bay.*

Restaurants

The Admiral Pub
$$$ | PIZZA | Crispy thin-crust pizza with specialty toppings—the burrata with prosciutto, tomatoes, arugula, and balsamic reduction is a can't-miss—is the star at this hidden gem tucked in Soper's Hole Marina. There's also a bar with live music on weekends, a lively, nautical crowd, and outdoor seating with an up-close view of the megayachts. **Known for:** marina view; sailing crowd; specialty pizzas. $ *Average main: $22* ⊠ *Soper's Hole, Soper's Hole* ☎ *284/340–1716* ⊘ *Closed Sun. and Mon. Dinner only.*

Omar's Cafe and Fusion
$$$ | ECLECTIC | Omar's Cafe has joined forces with Omar's Fusion in the Fusion location, offering some of Tortola's best omelets, French toast, and waffles for breakfast and the best of Indian and West Indies cooking for lunch and dinner. You can find innovative curry and masala dishes alongside steaks, burgers, pizza, and local fish and lobster dishes. **Known for:** East-West fusion cuisine; breakfast; curry and masala dishes. $ *Average main: $24* ⊠ *Soper's Hole Marina* ☎ *284/345–4771* ⊕ *omarfusion.com, omarscafebvi.com.*

★ Omar's Coffee House
$$ | ECLECTIC | This pretty pastel Soper's Hole eatery has reinvented itself as a coffeehouse, but you can still get "Sunday" brunch every day until mid-afternoon or sip your prosecco or cappuccino during "Mimosa Mondays" with live music. Omelets, crepes, high-protein breakfast bowls (with vegetarian and vegan options), and even the "full English" breakfast are served at a breezy counter–dining room combo, but the best seats are out back by the marina. ■**TIP→ The same owners operate Omar's Cafe and Fusion, which serves delicious West and East Indian cuisine just down the street.** **Known for:** espresso; brunch every day; friendly crowd. $ *Average main: $14* ⊠ *Soper's Hole Marina, Soper's Hole* ☎ *284/344–0514* ⊘ *No dinner.*

Pusser's Landing West End
$$ | ECLECTIC | Yachties navigate their way to the Soper's Hole boardwalk location of this locally renowned restaurant chainlet, guided by the big red Pusser's sign facing the water. From late morning to well into the evening, you can belly up to the outdoor mahogany bar or sit downstairs for sandwiches, fish-and-chips, and wings. **Known for:** Painkillers; pub fare; outdoor deck. $ *Average main: $19* ⊠ *Soper's Hole* ☎ *284/495–4554* ⊕ *www. pussers.com.*

Shopping

There's an ever-growing number of art and clothing stores at **Soper's Hole** in West End.

ART
Allamanda Gallery
ART GALLERIES | Photography by the gallery's owner, Amanda Baker, as well as books, gifts, and cards are on display and available to purchase at this shop in Soper's Hole in Tortola's West End. ⊠ *Moorings Marina, Wickham's Cay II, Road Town* ☎ *284/494–6680* ⊕ *www. theallamandagallery.com* ⊘ *Closed Sun.*

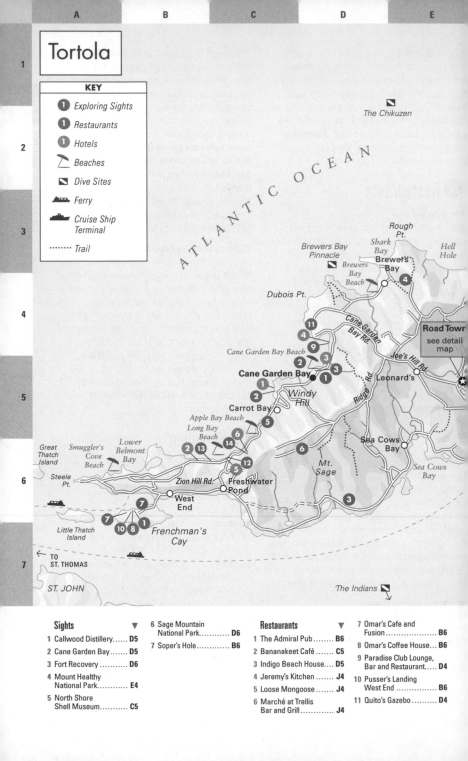

Tortola

KEY

- ❶ Exploring Sights
- ❶ Restaurants
- ❶ Hotels
- 🏖 Beaches
- 🔻 Dive Sites
- ⛴ Ferry
- 🚢 Cruise Ship Terminal
- ⋯⋯ Trail

ATLANTIC OCEAN

The Chikuzen

Rough Pt.

Brewers Bay Pinnacle

Shark Bay

Hell Hole

Brewers Bay Beach

Brewer's Bay

Dubois Pt.

Road Town
see detail map

Cane Garden Bay Rd.

Cane Garden Bay Beach

Cane Garden Bay

Joe's Hill Rd.

Leonard's

Windy Hill

Ridge Rd.

Carrot Bay

Apple Bay Beach

Long Bay Beach

Sea Cows Bay

Mt. Sage

Sea Cows Bay

Great Thatch Island

Smuggler's Cove Beach

Lower Belmont Bay

Steele Pt.

Zion Hill Rd.

Freshwater Pond

West End

Little Thatch Island

Frenchman's Cay

← TO ST. THOMAS

ST. JOHN

The Indians 🔻

Sights ▼

1 Callwood Distillery...... **D5**
2 Cane Garden Bay....... **D5**
3 Fort Recovery **D6**
4 Mount Healthy National Park........... **E4**
5 North Shore Shell Museum........... **C5**
6 Sage Mountain National Park........... **D6**
7 Soper's Hole............. **B6**

Restaurants ▼

1 The Admiral Pub **B6**
2 Bananakeet Café **C5**
3 Indigo Beach House.... **D5**
4 Jeremy's Kitchen **J4**
5 Loose Mongoose **J4**
6 Marché at Trellis Bar and Grill **J4**
7 Omar's Cafe and Fusion **B6**
8 Omar's Coffee House... **B6**
9 Paradise Club Lounge, Bar and Restaurant..... **D4**
10 Pusser's Landing West End **B6**
11 Quito's Gazebo **D4**

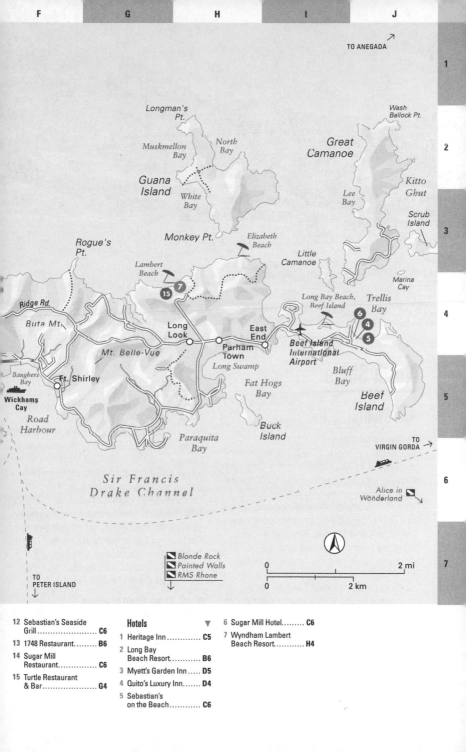

TO ANEGADA

Longman's Pt.

Muskmellon Bay

North Bay

Guana Island

White Bay

Wash Ballock Pt.

Great Camanoe

Kitto Ghut

Lee Bay

Scrub Island

Monkey Pt.

Elizabeth Beach

Little Camanoe

Marina Cay

Rogue's Pt.

Lambert Beach

15   7

Long Bay Beach, Beef Island

Trellis Bay

6
4
5

Ridge Rd.

Buta Mt.

Long Look

East End

Beef Island International Airport

Parham Town

Long Swamp

Bluff Bay

Beef Island

Mt. Belle-Vue

Baughers Bay

Ft. Shirley

Wickhams Cay

Road Harbour

Fat Hogs Bay

Buck Island

Paraquita Bay

TO VIRGIN GORDA

Sir Francis Drake Channel

Alice in Wonderland

TO PETER ISLAND

Blonde Rock
Painted Walls
RMS Rhone

0   2 mi

0   2 km

Cane Garden Bay has a popular beach lined with bars and restaurants.

North Shore

 Sights

Callwood Distillery

DISTILLERY | Nobody is really sure how long rum has been made at the Callwood Distillery, but it's been at least 200 years, and one thing is certain: it houses the longest continuously operated copper pot still in the Caribbean. Located on a side street in Cane Garden Bay, the ancient distillery offers tours and tastings of its uniquely flavored rums, made directly from the juice of pressed sugar cane, not molasses or refined sugar. For a true taste of the BVI, it doesn't get more authentic than Callwood's barrel-aged spirits. ⊠ *Cane Garden Bay, Cane Garden Bay* ☎ *284/495–9383* ⊕ *www.callwood-cane-rum.myshopify.com* ⊠ *Tours $5, tastings $1* ⊘ *Closed Sun. except when cruise ships are in port.*

★ Cane Garden Bay

TOWN | Once a sleepy village, Cane Garden Bay has become one of Tortola's most popular destinations. Stay at a small hotel or guesthouse here, or stop by for lunch, dinner, or drinks at a seaside restaurant, or popular nightspots like Quito's and Paradise Club. You can find a few small shops selling clothing and basics such as sunscreen, and one of Tortola's most popular beaches is at your feet. Myett's offers hotel rooms almost directly on the beach, while the newer Quito's Inn has smartly appointed rooms. The roads in and out of this area are dauntingly steep, so use caution when driving. ⊠ *Cane Garden Bay.*

North Shore Shell Museum

OTHER ATTRACTION | Egbert Donovan, the "shell man" of Carrot Bay, entertains passing buses full of tourists with tunes on his guitar and welcomes those who tarry longer to visit his museum crammed with thousands of sea shells, gathered over the course of almost 30 years from the nearby waters and shoreline. Donovan's shell-gathering boat was a victim of Hurricane Irma, so now he spends more time showing off his shells and serving bush tea and turtle soup to visitors. ✉ *Carrot Bay, Cane Garden Bay* ☎ *284/343–7581* 🎫 *Free.*

Beaches

Apple Bay Beach

BEACH | Along with nearby Little Apple Bay and Capoon's Bay, this is your spot if you want to surf—although the white, sandy beach itself is narrow. Sebastian's, a casual hotel, caters to those in search of the perfect wave. Otherwise, there's nothing else in the way of amenities. Good waves are never a sure thing, but you're more apt to find them in January and February. If you're swimming and the waves are up, take care not to get dashed on the rocks. **Amenities:** none. **Best for:** surfing; swimming. ✉ *North Shore Rd. at Zion Hill Rd., Apple Bay.*

Brewers Bay Beach

BEACH | This beach is easy to find, but the steep, twisting roads leading down to it can be a bit daunting. Normally, the beach is calm and suitable for children, but beware when a north swell comes in. An old sugar mill and the ruins of a rum distillery are off the beach along the road. Nicole's Beach Bar provides the strongest rum cocktails—filled right up to the top—to thirsty sunbathers. It also hosts the only walk-in scuba dive site in the BVI, with a reef home to a rich variety of marine life. You can reach the beach from either Brewers Bay Road East or Brewers Bay Road West. **Amenities:** drinks. **Best for:** snorkeling; swimming; diving. ✉ *Brewers Bay Rd. E, off Cane Garden Bay Rd., Brewers Bay.*

★ Cane Garden Bay Beach

BEACH | This silky stretch of sand boasts exceptionally calm crystalline waters—except when storms at sea turn the water murky. Snorkeling is good along the edges. Casual guesthouses, restaurants, bars, and shops are steps from the beach in the village of the same name. The beach is a laid-back, even somewhat funky place to put down your towel. It's the closest beach to Road Town and one of the BVI's best-known anchorages. Unfortunately, it can be very crowded with day-trippers when cruise ships dock in Road Town. Water-sports shops rent equipment. **Amenities:** food and drink; toilets; water sports. **Best for:** snorkeling; swimming; partiers. ✉ *Cane Garden Bay Rd., Cane Garden Bay.*

Restaurants

★ Bananakeet Café

$$$$ | **ECLECTIC** | The sunset sea-and-mountain views are stunning at this poolside restaurant at the Heritage Inn, so arrive early for the predinner happy hour. Caribbean fusion best describes the fare, with an emphasis on steaks, seafood, and pasta, including shrimp swimming in ginger butter sauce and pork tenderloin marinated in rum. **Known for:** sunset happy hour; panoramic views; good wine and cocktail list. [$] *Average main: $36* ✉ *Heritage Inn, North Coast Rd., Great Carrot Bay* ☎ *284/494–5842* 🕒 *No lunch.*

Indigo Beach House

$$ | **ECLECTIC** | This unique and welcome addition to Cane Garden Bay's western beachfront is located in the owners' revamped former residence, where you'll find tacos, burgers, roti, and an eclectic collection of small plates filling enough for a meal, such as crispy Asian cauliflower and steak kebabs. Owner and bartender Vishaal Mohabir keeps the wine and conversation flowing behind an elegant bar you'd never know was made of reclaimed wood from Hurricane Irma. **Known for:** small plates; intimate beachfront dining; lively atmosphere. [$] *Average main: $16* ✉ *North Coast Rd., Cane Garden Bay* ☎ *284/343–5503* 🕒 *Closed Mon.*

Rocking the Bay

Cane Garden Bay is the place to go for live music, with Quito Rymer frequently delighting the crowds at his Quito's Gazebo. Myett's is also a happening place and has live music nightly in season, while Paradise Club and the Elm Beach Bar host lively local music some nights.

There are no chain hotels or sprawling resorts here—all the places to stay are small and locally owned, even the new high-rise Quito's Luxury Inn. In addition to the handful of properties on the beach, there are plenty of others up on the hillsides that have eye-popping views. The area has plenty of places to eat, with lobster the specialty on many a menu. A Painkiller, a rum punch, or a bushwhacker is a common alcoholic accompaniment.

The area fairly bustles on cruise-ship days as busload after busload of round-the-island tour groups disembark to snap a few pictures. Don't be surprised to be asked to pay for a lounge chair on the most packed days. Once the cruise shippers are gone, however, a modicum of peace returns to the village.

Paradise Club Lounge, Bar and Restaurant
$$ | PIZZA | Find this Cane Garden Bay eatery and bar on the beach by the "I Love BVI" sign—it's known for its traditional Caribbean breakfast, brick-oven pizza, lamb and chicken shawarma, and daily drink specials. DJs get a good beach jam going at night, including monthly full-moon parties and themed events. **Known for:** Caribbean breakfast; pizza; beach parties. Ⓢ *Average main: $15* ⊠ *Cane Garden Bay* ☎ *284/345–2541.*

★ **Quito's Gazebo**
$$$ | CARIBBEAN | This beachside bar and restaurant is owned and operated by island native Quito Rymer, a multitalented recording star, which explains why there's live music nearly every night of the week. The menu is Caribbean, with an emphasis on fresh fish—try the conch fritters or the jerk chicken. **Known for:** live music; lighter options like burgers and fish tacos; casual picnic table dining. Ⓢ *Average main: $21* ⊠ *Cane Garden Bay* ☎ *284/495–4837* ⊕ *www.quitosbvi.com.*

Sebastian's Seaside Grill
$$$ | ECLECTIC | The waves practically lap at your feet at this friendly beachfront restaurant on Tortola's North Shore, a perfect spot to stop for lunch on your around-the-island tour. The dinner menu emphasizes seafood—especially lobster and local fish—but you can also find barbecued chicken, burgers, ribs, and New York strip steak. **Known for:** surfer vibe; live entertainment at night; weekend brunch. Ⓢ *Average main: $29* ⊠ *Sebastian's on the Beach, North Coast Rd., Apple Bay* ☎ *284/544–4212* ⊕ *www. sebastiansbvi.com.*

1748 Restaurant
$$$$ | INTERNATIONAL | Relax over dinner in this open-air eatery at Long Bay Beach Resort. Expect to find starters like carrot hummus served with house-made focaccia or Vietnamese fish cakes, and entrées like fresh-caught seafood, tenderloin filet steak with truffle demi-glace, and Thai coconut green curry with your choice of protein. **Known for:** airy beach setting; sophisticated Caribbean fusion cuisine; breakfast. Ⓢ *Average main: $36* ⊠ *Long Bay Beach Resort, Long Bay Rd., Long Bay* ☎ *284/495–4252* ⊕ *www.longbay.com.*

The hiking trails in Sage Mountain National Park lead to panoramic views.

★ Sugar Mill Restaurant
$$$$ | **CONTEMPORARY** | Candles gleam and the background music is peaceful in this romantic restaurant inside a 17th-century sugar mill. Well-prepared selections on the à la carte menu, which changes nightly, include pasta and vegetarian entrées, but the best deal is the three-course prix-fixe menu. **Known for:** memorable historic setting; banana flambé; inventive Caribbean cuisine. [$] *Average main: $49* ✉ *Sugar Mill Hotel, North Coast Rd., Apple Bay* ☎ *284/344–8612* 🌐 *www.sugarmillhotel.com* 🕒 *No lunch.*

Hotels

Heritage Inn
$ | **B&B/INN** | The gorgeous sea and mountain views are the stars at this small hotel perched on the edge of Windy Hill, offering modest but pleasant rooms with splashes of turquoise accenting a white background. **Pros:** stunning views; fun vibe; room has kitchenette, but there's also a great restaurant. **Cons:** need car to get around; close to road; not on beach. [$] *Rooms from: $175* ✉ *North Coast Rd., Great Carrot Bay* ☎ *284/494–5842* 🌐 *www.heritageinn.vg* 🛏 *7 rooms* 🍴 *No Meals.*

Long Bay Beach Resort
$$$$ | **RESORT** | Reopened and completely reinvented in 2022 by its new owners, this chic and ultra-posh resort on one of the island's most gorgeous stretches of beach features airy accommodations with private verandas, urbane design-driven décor, stylish 1748 Restaurant and Johnny's Beach Bar, and a slew of pleasurable amenities, from massages on the beach to cabanas and daybeds. **Pros:** stunning location; sleek, urbane décor; numerous activities. **Cons:** need car to get around; no meals included; on the spendy side. [$] *Rooms from: $489* ✉ *Long Bay, Long Bay* ☎ *284/345–3773* 🌐 *www.longbay.com* 🛏 *37 rooms* 🍴 *No Meals.*

Myett's Garden Inn
$$ | **HOTEL** | Tucked away in a beachfront garden, this tiny treehouse-style hotel puts you right in the middle of Cane

Garden Bay's hustle and bustle, and its adjacent restaurant is one of the area's hot spots. **Pros:** beautiful beach; good restaurant; shops nearby. **Cons:** busy location; need a car to venture out; few common amenities. [$] *Rooms from: $175* ✉ *Cane Garden Bay* ☎ *284/495–9649* 🌐 *www.myetts.com* 🛏 *11 units* 🍴 *No Meals.*

Quito's Luxury Inn

$$$$ | HOTEL | The tireless Quito Rymer, one of the island's most popular musicians, opened this high-rise hotel in 2019 across the street from the beach and his eponymous restaurant-bar (where he still performs). **Pros:** near bars and restaurants; pool and spa on-site; good restaurant. **Cons:** busy location; not on beach; need car to venture further. [$] *Rooms from: $492* ✉ *Cane Garden Bay* ☎ *284/495–4837* 🌐 *quitosbvi.com* 🛏 *21 rooms* 🍴 *No Meals.*

Sebastian's on the Beach

$ | HOTEL | Sitting on the island's north coast, Sebastian's has a casual beach vibe and rooms that vary in amenities and price, all of them attractively remodeled following Hurricane Irma, with the 12 oceanfront rooms a bit more up-to-date than those that the hotel calls "tropical." These less expensive rooms are across the street from the ocean and lack views. **Pros:** nice beach; good restaurants; beachfront rooms. **Cons:** on busy road; some rooms nicer than others; need car to get around. [$] *Rooms from: $160* ✉ *North Coast Rd., Apple Bay* ☎ *284/544–4212, 284/495–4206* 🌐 *www.sebastiansbvi.com* 🛏 *42 units* 🍴 *No Meals.*

★ Sugar Mill Hotel

$$$ | RESORT | Though it's not a sprawling resort, this renowned historic property has a Caribbean cachet that's hard to beat, thanks to its lovely gardens, prime North Shore location just across from the sand, and its iconic restaurants, which are set in a 400-year-old sugar mill and on the beach, respectively. **Pros:** lovely rooms; outstanding restaurants; blissful views. **Cons:** on busy road; small beach; need car to get around. [$] *Rooms from: $399* ✉ *North Coast Rd., Apple Bay* ☎ *284/344–8612* 🌐 *www.sugarmillhotel.com* 🛏 *22 units* 🍴 *Free Breakfast.*

Nightlife

★ Myett's Garden & Grille Restaurant

BARS | Local bands play at this popular spot on the beach, which has live music several nights a week and a popular happy hour. ✉ *Cane Garden Bay* ☎ *284/495–9649* 🌐 *www.myetts.com.*

Quito's Gazebo

LIVE MUSIC | BVI recording star Quito Rhymer sings island ballads and love songs at his rustic beachside bar–restaurant. Quito usually performs on Thursday or Friday night. Check the restaurant's social media pages for details. ✉ *North Coast Rd., Cane Garden Bay* ☎ *284/495–4837* 🌐 *quitosbvi.com.*

Sebastian's

BARS | There's often live music at Sebastian's on Sunday and Wednesday evenings in season, and you can dance under the stars (but call ahead for the schedule). ✉ *North Coast Rd., Apple Bay* ☎ *284/495–4212* 🌐 *www.sebastiansbvi.com.*

Stoutt's Lookout

BARS | Long-distance views are on the menu in the reggae-colored Stoutt's Lookout, the domain of gregarious owner Prince Stoutt, who serves a punch made with local Callwood rum and pineapple, guava, and orange juice. Free Wi-Fi encourages you to linger in seats along a railing overlooking Cane Garden Bay. ✉ *Cane Garden Bay, Cane Garden Bay* ✥ *At the intersection of Windy Hill and Ridge Rd.* ☎ *284/442–0432.*

Mid Island

Sights

Mount Healthy National Park
RUINS | The remains of an 18th-century sugar plantation can be seen here. The windmill structure, the last one standing in the BVI, has been restored, and you can also see the ruins of a factory with boiling houses, storage areas, stables, a hospital, and many dwellings. It's a nice place to picnic and reflect on the island's history. ✉ *Ridge Rd., Todman Peak* ☎ *284/393–9284* 🎟 *Free.*

Sage Mountain National Park
NATIONAL PARK | At 1,716 feet, Sage Mountain is the highest peak in the BVI. From the parking area, a trail leads you in a loop not only to the peak itself (and extraordinary views) but also to a small rainforest that is sometimes shrouded in mist. There are a dozen hiking trails in the park. Most of the forest was cut down over the centuries for timber, to create pastureland, or for growing sugarcane, cotton, and other crops. In 1964, this 127-acre park was established to preserve what remained. Up here you can see mahogany trees, white cedars, mountain guavas, elephant-ear vines, mamey trees, and giant bullet woods, plus birds like mountain doves and thrushes. Take a taxi from Road Town or drive up Joe's Hill Road and make a left onto Ridge Road toward Chalwell and Doty villages. The road dead-ends at the park. ✉ *Ridge Rd., Sage Mountain* ☎ *284/393–9284.*

East End

Beaches

Lambert Beach
BEACH | Home to a Wyndham resort, Lambert Beach is a palm-lined, wide, sandy beach with parking along its steep downhill access road. The road to the resort is gated, but the beach is free to all. The main attraction here is peace and quiet, but there is a bar and restaurant at the hotel. Turn at the sign for the Wyndham Lambert resort. **Amenities:** food and drink; parking; toilets. **Best for:** solitude; swimming. ✉ *Lambert Rd., off Ridge Rd., East End.*

Long Bay Beach, Beef Island
BEACH | If this beach wasn't located right next to the airport, it probably would show up on lists of the Caribbean's most beautiful strands. Long Bay on Beef Island has superlative scenery: the beach stretches seemingly forever, and you can catch a glimpse of Little Camanoe and Great Camanoe islands. Just keep your eyes out to sea and not on the runway behind you. If you walk around the bend to the right, you can see little Marina Cay and Scrub Island. Swim out to wherever you see a dark patch for some nice snorkeling. Turn left shortly after crossing the bridge to Beef Island. **Amenities:** food and drink; toilets. **Best for:** snorkeling; swimming. ✉ *Beef Island Rd.*

Restaurants

Jeremy's Kitchen
$$ | **AMERICAN** | Situated on Trellis Bay's beachfront, brightly painted Jeremy's Kitchen is the ideal spot to enjoy a leisurely breakfast or lunch while people-watching. Omelets, croque madame and monsieur sandwiches, and eggs Benedict are breakfast favorites, while pasta, curries, roti, and quesadillas round out the lunch and dinner options. "Jeremy's Awesome Sandwich" fits a choice of meats and seafood between slices of seven-grain bread with grilled cheese, vegetables, and mango relish. **Known for:** "Jeremy's Awesome Sandwich"; laid-back island vibes; beachfront dining. [$] *Average main: $13* ✉ *Trellis Bay* ☎ *284/345–5177* 🌐 *www.jeremyskitchen.com.*

Continued on page 208

TRY A YACHT CHARTER

IT'S SURPRISINGLY AFFORDABLE

Savoring a freshly brewed mug of coffee, I sat on the front deck of our chartered 43-foot catamaran and watched the morning show. Laserlike rays of sunlight streamed through a cottony cloud bank, bringing life to the emerald islands and turquoise seas. What would it have been like to sail with Columbus and chart these waters for the first time? How would it feel to cast about the deserted beaches for the perfect place to bury plundered treasure? The aroma of freshly made banana pancakes roused me from my reverie.

Once considered an outward-bound adventure or exclusive domain of the rich and famous, chartering a boat can be a surprisingly affordable and attractive vacation alternative. Perhaps you're already a sailor and want to explore beyond your own lake, river, or bay. Or maybe your idea of sailing has always been on a cruise ship, and now you're ready for a more intimate voyage. Or perhaps you've never sailed before, but you are now curious to cast off and explore a whole new world.

By Carol M. Bareuther

CREWED CHARTER

Family sailing in the British Virgin Islands

On a crewed charter, you sit back and relax while the crew provides for your every want and need. Captains are licensed by the U.S. Coast Guard or the equivalent in the British maritime system. Chefs have skills that go far beyond peanut butter and jelly sandwiches. There are four meals a day, and many chefs boast certificates from culinary schools ranging from the Culinary Institute of America in New York to the Cordon Bleu in Paris.

The advantage of a yacht chartered crewed by captain and chef is that it takes every bit of stress out of the vacation. With a captain who knows the local waters, you get to see some of the coves and anchorages that are not necessarily in the guidebooks. Your meals are prepared, cabins cleaned, beds made up every day—and turned down at night, too. Plus, you can sail and take the helm as often as you like. But at the end of the day, the captain is the one who will take responsibility for anchoring safely for the night while the chef goes below and whips up a gourmet meal.

APPROXIMATE COSTS	PROS	CONS
From $4,800 for 2 people for 5 days	■ Passengers just have to lay back and relax (unless they want to help sail)	■ More expensive than a bareboat, especially if you get a catamaran
From $5,500 for 2 people for 7 days	■ Most are catamarans, offering more space than monohulls	■ Less privacy for your group than on a bareboat
From $12,000 for 6 people for 5 days	■ You have an experienced, local hand on board if something goes wrong	■ Captain makes ultimate decisions about the course
From $15,000 for 6 people for 7 days	■ Water toys and other extras are often included	■ Chance for personality conflicts: you have to get along with the captain and chef. This is where a charter yacht broker is helpful in determining what yachts and crews might be a good fit.
Prices are all-inclusive for a 50- to 55-foot catamaran yacht in high season except for 15%–20% gratuity.	■ Competively priced within an all-inclusive resort	

BAREBOAT

If you'd like to bareboat, don't be intimidated. It's a myth that you must be a graduate of a sailing school in order to pilot your own charter boat. A bareboat company will ask you to fill out a resume. The company checks for prior boat-handling experience, the type of craft you've sailed (whether powerboat or sailboat), and in what type of waters. Real-life experience, meaning all those day and weekend trips close to home, count as valuable know-how. If you've done a bit of boating, you may be more qualified than you think to take out a bareboat.

Costs can be very similar for a bareboat and crewed charter, depending on the time of year and size of the boat. You'll pay the highest rates between Christmas and New Year's, when you may not be allowed to do a charter of less than a week. But there are more than 800 bareboats between the USVI and BVI, so regardless of your budget, you should be able to find something in your price range. Plus, you might save a bit by chartering an older boat from a smaller company instead of the most state-of-the-art yacht from a larger company.

APPROXIMATE COSTS	PROS	CONS
From $3,800 for a small monohull (2–3 cabins)	■ The ultimate freedom to set the yacht's course	■ Must be able to pass a sailing test
From $6,300 for a large monohull (4–5 cabins)	■ A chance to test your sailing skills	■ Those unfamiliar with the region may not find the best anchorages
From $6,500 for a small catamaran (2 cabins)	■ Usually a broader range of boats and prices to choose from	■ You have to cook for and clean up after yourself
From $8,900 for a large catamaran (4 cabins)	■ More flexibility for meals (you can always go ashore if you don't feel like cooking)	■ You have to do your own provisioning and planning for meals
Prices exclude food, beverages, fuel, and other supplies. Most bareboat rates do not include water toys, taxes, insurance, and permits.	■ You can always hire a captain for a few days	■ If something goes wrong, there isn't an experienced hand onboard

WHAT TO CONSIDER

Whether bareboat or a crewed yacht, there are a few points to ponder when selecting your boat.

HOW BIG IS YOUR GROUP?

As a general rule, count on one cabin for every two people. Most people also prefer to have one head (bathroom) per cabin. A multihull, also called a catamaran, offers more space and more equal-size cabins than a monohull sailboat.

WHAT TYPE OF BOAT?

If you want to do some good old traditional sailing, where you're heeling over with the seas at your rails, monohulls are a good option. On the other hand, multihulls are more stable, easier to board, and have a big salon for families. They're also ideal if some people get seasick or aren't as gung-ho for the more traditional sailing experience. If you'd like to cover more ground, choose a motor yacht.

DO YOU HAVE A SPECIAL INTEREST?

Some crewed charter boats specialize in certain types of charters. Among these are learn-to-sail excursions, honeymoon cruises, scuba-diving adventures, and family-friendly trips. Your broker can steer you to the boats that fit your specific needs.

WHAT KIND OF EQUIPMENT DO YOU WANT ONBOARD?

Most charter boats have satellite navigation systems and autopilots, as well as regulation safety gear, dinghies with motors, and even stereos and entertainment systems. But do you want a generator or battery-drive refrigeration system? How about air-conditioning? Do you want a satellite phone? Do you want water toys like kayaks, boogie boards, and Windsurfers?

Now that you've decided on bareboat versus crewed charter and selected your craft, all you need to do is confirm the availability of the date with the company or broker and pay a nonrefundable deposit equal to 50% of the charter price.

TO SAIL OR NOT TO SAIL?

If you're not sure whether a charter yacht vacation is right for you, consider this: Would you enjoy a floating hotel room where the scenery outside your window changed according to your desires? A "yes" may entice wary companions to try chartering. A single one-week trip will have them hooked.

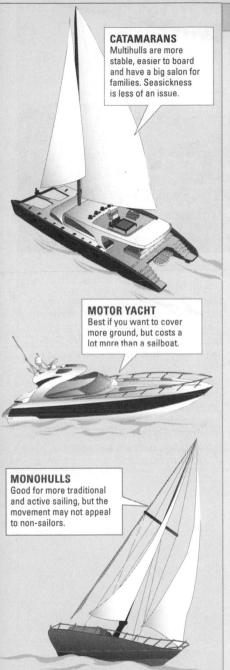

CATAMARANS
Multihulls are more stable, easier to board and have a big salon for families. Seasickness is less of an issue.

MOTOR YACHT
Best if you want to cover more ground, but costs a lot more than a sailboat.

MONOHULLS
Good for more traditional and active sailing, but the movement may not appeal to non-sailors.

CHOOSING A CHARTER

Information on charters is much easier to find now than even a decade ago. Websites for bareboat companies show photos of different types of boats—both interiors and exteriors—as well as layout schematics, lists of equipment and amenities, and sample itineraries. Many sites will allow you to book a charter directly, while others give you the option of calling a toll-free number to speak with an agent first.

There are two types of websites for crewed charters. If you just want some information, the **Virgin Islands Professional Charter Association** (⊕ www.vipca.org) and the **Charter Yacht Society of the British Virgin Islands** (⊕ www.bvicrewedyachts.com) both help you understand what to look for in a crewed charter, from the size of the boat to the amenities. You can't reserve on these sites, but they link to the sites of brokers, who are the sales force for the charter yacht industry. Most brokers, whether they're based in the Caribbean, the United States, or Europe, attend annual charter yacht shows in St. Thomas, Tortola, and Antigua. At these shows, brokers visit the boats and meet the crews. This is what gives brokers their depth of knowledge for "matchmaking," or linking you with a boat that will meet your personality and preferences.

The charter companies also maintain websites. About 30% of the crewed charter yachts based out of the U.S. and British Virgin Islands can be booked directly. This saves the commission an owner has to pay to the broker. But while "going direct" might seem advantageous, there is usually little difference in pricing, and if you use a broker, he or she can help troubleshoot if something goes wrong or find a replacement boat if the boat owner has to cancel.

Timing also matters. Companies may offer last-minute specials that are available only online. These special rates—usually for specific dates, destinations, and boats—are updated weekly or even daily.

PREPARING FOR YOUR CHARTER

British Virgin Islands—anchorage in a tropical sea with breakfast on board

PROVISIONING

Bareboaters must do their own provisioning. It's a good idea to arrange provisioning at least a week in advance.

Provisioning packages from the charter company are usually a bit more expensive, at $30 to $35 per person per day, but they save you the hassle of planning the details. You can also shop on arrival. Both St. Thomas and Tortola have markets, though larger grocery stores may require a taxi ride. If you shop carefully, this route can still save you money. Just be sure to allow yourself a few hours after arrival to get everything done.

PLANNING

For a crewed charter, your broker will send a preference sheet for both food and your wishes for the trip. Perhaps you'd like lazy days of sleeping late, sunning, and swimming. Or you might prefer active days of sailing with stops for snorkeling and exploring ashore. If there's a special spot you'd like to visit, list it so your captain can plan the itinerary accordingly.

PACKING TIPS

Pack light for any type of charter. Bring soft-sided luggage (preferably a duffle bag) since space is limited and storage spots are usually odd shapes. Shorts, T-shirts, and swimsuits are sufficient. Bring something a bit nicer if you plan to dine ashore. Shoes are seldom required except ashore, but you might want beach shoes to protect your feet in the water. Most boats provide snorkel equipment, but always ask. Bring sunscreen, but a type that will not stain cockpit cushions and decks.

WHAT YOU'LL SEE IN THE USBVI

Cruz Bay in St. John

MAIN CHARTER BASES

The U.S. and British Virgin Islands boast more than 100 stepping-stone islands and cays within a 50-nautical-mile radius. This means easy line-of-sight navigation and island-hopping in protected waters, and it's rare that you'll spend more than a few hours moving between islands.

Tortola, in the British Virgin Islands, is the crewed charter and bareboat mecca of the Caribbean. This fact is plainly apparent from the forest of masts rising out from any marina.

The U.S. Virgin Islands fleet is based in **St. Thomas**. Direct flights from the mainland, luxurious accommodations, and duty-free shopping are drawing cards for departures from the U.S. Virgin Islands, whereas the British Virgins are closer to the prime cruising grounds.

POPULAR ANCHORAGES

On a typical weeklong charter you could set sail from Red Hook, St. Thomas, then cross Pillsbury Sound to St. John, which offers popular north-shore anchorages in Honeymoon, Trunk, or Francis Bays.

But the best sailing and snorkeling always includes the British Virgin Islands (which require a valid passport or passport card). After clearing customs in West End, Tortola, many yachts hop along a series of smaller islands that run along the south side of the Sir Francis Drake Channel. But some yachts will also visit Guana Island, Great Camanoe, or Marina Cay off Tortola's more isolated east end.

The islands south of Tortola include **Norman Island**, the rumored site of Robert Lewis Stevenson's *Treasure Island*. The next island over is **Peter Island**, famous for it's posh resort and a popular anchorage for yachters. Farther east, off Salt Island, is the wreck of the **RMS *Rhone***—the most magnificent dive site in the eastern Caribbean. Giant boulders form caves and grottos called The Baths at the southern end of **Virgin Gorda**.

A downwind run along Tortola's north shore ends at **Jost Van Dyke**, where that famous guitar-strumming calypsonian Foxy Callwood sings personalized ditties that make for a memorable finale.

Loose Mongoose

$$$$ | ECLECTIC | The Balinese-style wooden design features and thatched roof give this restaurant—located on the beach at the far end of Trellis Bay—a sophisticated feel, especially with its Sunday brunch featuring colorful signature cocktails, lobster Benedict, pancakes, and omelets alongside Caribbean specialties like saltfish and coconut bread. The dinner menu features fresh seafood, steaks, and chops. **Known for:** weekend brunch; espresso; beachside dining. $ Average main: $32 ☒ Trellis Bay Rd. ☎ 284/340–5544 ⊕ www.loosemongoosebvi.com.

Marché at Trellis Bar and Grill

$$$ | ECLECTIC | This laid-back beachfront restaurant's eclectic around-the-world menu includes both sushi and street tacos, with a lively atmosphere that's busy most nights. Dine at a picnic table on the beach under fairy lights, or watch chefs make your roll indoors at the beautiful wooden custom-built sushi bar. **Known for:** sushi bar; beachfront dining; tacos. $ Average main: $30 ☒ East End ☎ 284/545–0259 ☉ Closed Mon.

Turtle Restaurant & Bar

$$$ | ECLECTIC | If you're touring the island, Turtle is a good place to stop for breakfast, lunch, or dinner with Caribbean-Mediterranean flair, including pizza and pasta dishes, West Indian roti, and lobster with lemon butter sauce. Sitting near the ocean at the Wyndham Lambert Beach Resort, this casually elegant restaurant provides a relaxing respite from the rigors of navigating mountain roads. **Known for:** beachfront location; fusion dining; relaxed elegance. $ Average main: $30 ☒ Wyndham Lambert Beach Resort, Lambert Bay, East End ☎ 284/495–2877 ⊕ lambertbeach.com.

 Hotels

Wyndham Lambert Beach Resort

$ | RESORT | Although this isolated location on the northeast coast puts you far from Road Town, Lambert Bay is one of the island's loveliest stretches of sand and the main reason to recommend this resort. **Pros:** lovely beach; beautiful setting; good restaurant. **Cons:** lacks local flavor; isolated location; need car to get around. $ Rooms from: $169 ☎ 284/495–1269 ⊕ www.lambertbeach.com ⇄ 67 rooms ⦿ No Meals.

 Activities

BOATING

Island Time Power Boat Rentals

BOATING | Island Time rents a small fleet of open sportfishing boats (23 to 30 feet), charging from $305 for an eight-passenger inflatable to $695 per day for a 28-foot Cobia. ☒ Nanny Cay Marina, Nanny Cay ☎ 284/340–0357, 284/346–0356 ⊕ www.islandtimebvi.com.

CRICKET

Fans of this sport are fiercely loyal and exuberant. Matches are held at Greenland Field at East End. Check the BVI Cricket Association's social media pages or ask at your hotel front desk for information on times and teams.

DIVING AND SNORKELING

Clear waters and numerous reefs afford some wonderful opportunities for underwater exploration. In some spots visibility reaches 100 feet, but colorful reefs teeming with fish are often just a few feet below the sea surface. The BVI's system of marine parks means the underwater life visible through your mask will stay protected.

There are several popular dive spots around the islands, including some new sites arising from the destruction of 2017's Hurricane Irma. The Willy T party boat, which sunk in Pirate's Bight off Norman Island, has reopened. Local nonprofit Beyond the Reef has turned it into an elaborate artificial reef, complete with skeletal pirates drinking "rum" at the bar. It's good fun for younger divers, and your dive shop will ask you for a small

Did You Know?

The wreck of the RMS *Rhone*, which sank in 75 feet of water near Salt Island in 1867, is one of the most famous wreck dives in the Caribbean.

donation if you go. Several small planes that wrecked at the BVI airport have been repurposed as the **Sharkplano** site near Great Dog Island. **Alice in Wonderland** is a deep dive south of Ginger Island, with a wall that slopes gently from 15 feet to 100 feet. It's an area overrun with huge mushroom-shaped coral, hence its name. Crabs, lobsters, and shimmering fan corals make their homes in the tunnels, ledges, and overhangs of **Blonde Rock,** a pinnacle that goes from 15 feet below the surface to 60 feet deep. It's between Dead Chest and Salt Island. When the currents aren't too strong, **Brewers Bay Pinnacle** (20 to 90 feet down) teems with sea life. Located on Tortola's Atlantic side, it's one of the only easily accessible walk-in sites, great for an experienced diver wanting to avoid the dive shops and go with a buddy. At the **Indians,** near Pelican Island, colorful corals decorate canyons and grottoes created by four large, jagged pinnacles that rise 50 feet from the ocean floor. The **Painted Walls** is a shallow dive site where corals and sponges create a kaleidoscope of colors on the walls of four long gullies. It's northeast of Dead Chest. **Carval Rock,** a stunning stony formation full of grottoes that look like they could host mermaids, is between Cooper and Ginger, goes down 90 feet, and is always teeming with life.

The *Chikuzen,* sunk northwest of Brewers Bay in 1981, is a 246-foot vessel in 75 feet of water; it's home to thousands of fish, colorful corals, and big rays. In 1867 the RMS *Rhone,* a 310-foot Royal Mail steamer, split in two when it sank in a devastating hurricane. It's so well preserved that it was used as an underwater prop in the movie *The Deep.* You can see the crow's nest and bowsprit, the cargo hold in the bow, and the engine and enormous propeller shaft in the stern. Its four parts are at various depths from 30 to 80 feet. Get yourself some snorkeling gear and hop aboard a dive boat to this wreck near Salt Island (across the channel from Road Town). Every dive outfit in the BVI

runs scuba and snorkel tours to this part of the BVI National Parks Trust; if you only have time for one trip, make it this one. Rates start at around $100 for a one-tank dive and around $130 for a two-tank dive.

Your hotel probably has a dive company right on the premises. If not, the staff can recommend one nearby. Using your hotel's dive company makes a trip to the offshore dive and snorkel sites a breeze. Just stroll down to the dock and hop aboard. All dive companies are certified by PADI, the Professional Association of Diving Instructors, which ensures that your instructors are qualified to safely take vacationers diving. The boats are also inspected to make sure they're seaworthy. If you've never dived, try a short introductory dive, often called a resort course, which teaches you enough to get you underwater. In the unlikely event you get a case of the bends, a condition that can happen when you rise to the surface too fast, your dive team will whisk you to the decompression chamber at Schneider Regional Medical Center in nearby St. Thomas.

RECOMMENDED DIVE OPERATORS
Blue Water Divers

SCUBA DIVING | Located in the Nanny Cay marina, this first-rate company teaches resort, open-water, rescue, and advanced diving courses, and also makes daily dive trips, including to the fabled RMS *Rhone* wreck. Rates include all equipment as well as instruction. Reserve two days in advance. ⊠ *Nanny Cay Marina* ☎ *284/494–2847, 284/340–4311* ⊕ *www. bluewaterdiversbvi.com.*

FISHING

Most of the boats that take you deep-sea fishing for bluefish, wahoo, swordfish, and shark leave from nearby St. Thomas, but there is at least one boat operating on Tortola. Rates start at $1,450 for a half-day trip for up to 6 people, and $1,850 for a full-day excursion. Local anglers also like to fish the shallower water for bonefish. Information on fishing regulations and charter operations can be found on the BVI Tourism website (⊕ www.bvitourism.com).

Jack Trout Fly Fishing

FISHING | Wade into the shallow waters of Tortola in pursuit of bonefish and tarpon. A half-day wading trip is $445 for up to two people; full-day is $575. Lunch, drinks, and gear are included. ⊠ Nanny Cay Marina ☎ 530/926–4540 ⊕ www. jacktrout.com.

HIKING

Sage Mountain National Park attracts hikers who enjoy the quiet trails that crisscross the island's loftiest peak. There are some lovely views and the chance to see rare plant species that grow only at higher elevations.

SAILING

The BVI is among the world's most popular sailing destinations. The islands are clustered together and surrounded by calm waters, so it's fairly easy to sail from one mooring or anchorage to the next. Most of the Caribbean's biggest sailboat charter companies have operations in Tortola. If you know how to sail, you can charter a bareboat (perhaps for your entire vacation); if you're unschooled, you can hire a boat with a captain. Prices vary depending on the type and size of the boat you wish to charter, as well as the included services. Don't feel like cooking all your own meals onboard? Fully-crewed charters, staffed with enthusiastic folks who do it all—from sailing to cooking to cleaning—are also an option, albeit for a hefty price tag. In season, a weekly charter runs from $5,500 to $35,000. Book early to make sure you get the boat that fits you best. Most of Tortola's marinas have hotels, which give you a convenient place to spend the nights before and after your charter.

If a day sail to some secluded anchorage is more your spot of tea, the BVI has numerous boats of various sizes

and styles that leave from many points around Tortola. Prices start at around $135 per person for a full-day sail, including lunch and snorkeling equipment.

Aristocat Charters

SAILING | This company's 45-foot catamarans, Sugar Rush and Sweet Escape, set off for sailing and snorkeling trips to Jost Van Dyke, Norman Island, Cooper Island, and other small islands, as well as The Baths. Day-sailing charters run from Hannah Bay, Soper's Hole (Frenchman's Cay), and West End. ☎ 284/499–1249 ⊕ www. aristocatcharters.com.

The Catamaran Company

SAILING | The catamarans available for charter come with or without a captain; sailing cats range in length from 35 to 54 feet, with three to six double cabins. ⊠ Hodges Creek Marina, East End ☎ 284/544–6661, 800/262–0308 ⊕ www. catamarans.com.

Horizon Yacht Charters BVI

SAILING | Horizon rents monohull and catamaran sailing vessels with bareboat, captain-only, or full-crew options. ⊠ Nanny Cay ☎ 284/494–8787, 877/494–8787 ⊕ www.horizonyachtcharters.com.

The Moorings

BOATING | One of the world's best bareboat operations, the Moorings has a large fleet of both monohull boats and catamarans (sail and power, or power only). Catamarans, the most popular option, range in size from 36 to 50 feet and have three to five cabins. Hire a captain or sail the boat yourself for a week or more of island hopping in the U.S. and British Virgin Islands. The Moorings base in Road Town has extensive facilities, including provisioning, a restaurant, and a hotel. ⊠ Wickham's Cay II, Road Town ☎ 888/416–0814 ⊕ www.moorings.com.

Regency Yacht Vacations

BOATING | If you prefer a powerboat, call Regency Yacht Vacations. It handles captain and full-crew sail and powerboat charters, as well as sail and powered catamarans and everything up to megayachts. The range of vessels is impressive: you can spend about $16,000 for a week on a catamaran with a crew of two or more than half a million bucks to take 12 guests along for a cruise on the three-mast megayacht *Maltese Falcon*. ✉ *Wickham's Cay I, Road Town* ☎ *800/524–7676, 284/495–1970* ⊕ *www. yachtfleet.com.*

Sunsail

SAILING | A full fleet of boats, including catamarans and monohull sailboats, can be chartered with or without a captain. Prices start at around $3,200 for a week's bareboat sail. ✉ *Wickham's Cay II, Road Town* ☎ *866/514–9778* ⊕ *www.sunsail. com.*

Voyage Charters

SAILING | Voyage has a variety of sailboats for charter, with or without a captain and crew. Their fleet includes electric-powered 48- and 59-foot sailing catamarans as well as conventional sailing and power cats. ✉ *Soper's Hole Marina* ☎ *443/569–7007, 888/869–2436* ⊕ *www.voyagecharters.com.*

SURFING AND WINDSURFING

Surfing is big on Tortola's North Shore, particularly when the winter swells come into Josiah's and Apple bays. Rent surfboards starting at $65 for a full day.

Steady trade winds make windsurfing a breeze. Three of the best spots for sailboarding are Nanny Cay, Slaney Point, and Trellis Bay on Beef Island. Rates for sailboards start at about $50 a day.

BVISUPCO

WINDSURFING | This water-sports company rents windsurfing equipment as well as stand-up paddleboards, kayaks, and other water toys. ✉ *Trellis Bay, Road Town* ☎ *284/346–1981* ⊕ *www.bvisupco.com.*

Island Surf and Sail

WATER SPORTS | Based in Soper's Hole, Island Surf and Sail rents kayaks, paddleboards, SUP boards, surfboards, fishing equipment, snorkeling equipment, various water toys, and—amusingly—guitars. The company also offers private sailing day trips and dive instruction. ✉ *Soper's Hole Marina, Soper's Hole* ☎ *284/345–0123* ⊕ *www.bviwatertoys. com.*

TENNIS

Tortola's tennis options range from simple, untended, concrete courts to professionally maintained facilities that host organized tournaments. Some hotels have one or two courts for guests.

Tortola Sports Club

TENNIS | The Tortola Sports Club in Road Town has four lighted hard-court tennis courts as well as indoor squash courts and other recreational facilities, including a gym. You must book ahead of time on the club's website. Members get priority for court time but visitors can play here on a day pass; courts are more available during the day than in the evenings. ✉ *Long Bay Rd., Road Town* ☎ *284/494–3457* ⊕ *tortolasportsclub.com.*

Chapter 7

VIRGIN GORDA

Updated by
Claire Shefchik

⊙ Sights	🍽 Restaurants	🛏 Hotels	🛍 Shopping	🍸 Nightlife
★★★★☆	★★★★☆	★★★★☆	★★★☆☆	★★★☆☆

WELCOME TO VIRGIN GORDA

TOP REASONS TO GO

★ **Beautiful beaches:** Virgin Gorda's stunning, white, sandy beaches are the number one reason to visit. Spring Bay Beach and The Baths are highly recommended.

★ **The Baths:** The ever-popular Baths, an area strewn with giant boulders—many as big as houses—draw many visitors during peak hours. Go early or late to enjoy some solitude.

★ **Vacation villas:** Virgin Gorda villas come in all sizes and price ranges. Or, stay at a stunning resort like Rosewood Little Dix Bay.

★ **North Sound:** Even if you aren't a guest at one of North Sound's handful of resorts, you still should visit. Stay for lunch, or just enjoy an afternoon drink.

★ **Solitude:** You don't go to Virgin Gorda for the nightlife (although there is some here and there) or endless activities (but you might want to rent a kayak). This is a spot for relaxation.

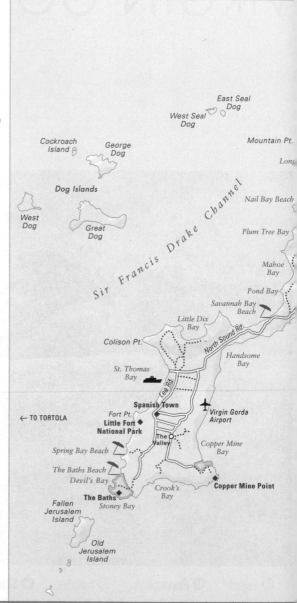

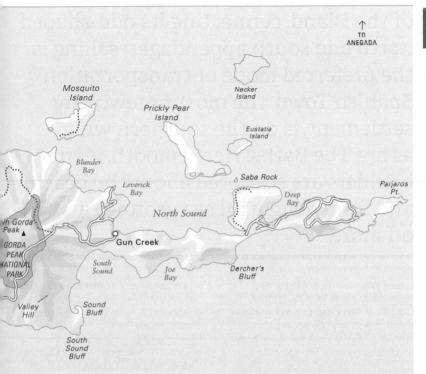

↑
TO
ANEGADA

Mosquito
Island

Prickly Pear
Island

Necker
Island

Eustatia
Island

Blunder
Bay

Saba Rock

Leverick
Bay

Deep
Bay

Pajaros
Pt.

in Gorda
Peak ▲

North Sound

GORDA
PEAK
NATIONAL
PARK

Gun Creek

South
Sound

Joe
Bay

Dercher's
Bluff

Valley
Hill

Sound
Bluff

South
Sound
Bluff

C a r i b b e a n   S e a

0   2 mi

0   2 km

Mountainous and arid Virgin Gorda runs the gamut from laid-back to more laid-back. Its main road sticks to the center of the island, connecting its odd-shaped north and south appendages; sailing is the preferred mode of transportation. Spanish Town, the most noteworthy settlement, is on the southern wing, as are The Baths. Here smooth, giant boulders are scattered about the beach and form delightful sea grottoes just offshore.

Lovely Virgin Gorda, or "Fat Virgin," received its name from Christopher Columbus. The explorer envisioned the island as a reclining pregnant woman, with Virgin Gorda Peak being her belly and the boulders of The Baths her toes.

Compared to other British Virgin Islands, Virgin Gorda runs at a slow pace, and goats still wander across the roads in places like North Sound. But that's changing. Virgin Gorda Yacht Harbour, the center of commerce and activity in Spanish Town, is expanding, and the Oil Nut Bay development has raised the bar on high-end stays on Virgin Gorda along with the return of the luxury Rosewood Little Dix Bay resort. That said, budget travelers can still find modest villas and guesthouses all over the island to while away a few days or more.

Virgin Gorda isn't all that easy to get to, but once you're here you can find enough diversions to make getting out of your chaise longue worthwhile. You can drive from one end of the island to the other in about 20 minutes, but make sure to take time to visit Copper Mine Point to learn about the island's history or to hike up Virgin Gorda Peak to survey the surroundings. At numerous spots with stellar views, the local government has thoughtfully built viewing platforms with adjacent parking. It's worth a stop to snap some photos.

The scenery on the northeastern side of the island is the most dramatic, with a steep road ending at Leverick Bay and Gun Creek in North Sound. Head to the other end of the island for views of the huge boulders that spill over from The Baths into the southwest section of Virgin Gorda. You can find several restaurants dotted around this end of the island.

In truth, though, it's the beaches that make Virgin Gorda special. Stretches of powdery sand fringe aquamarine waters. Popular places like The Baths see hordes of people, but just a quick walk down the road brings you to quieter beaches like Spring Bay. On the other side of Spanish Town you may be the only person at such sandy spots as Savannah Bay.

If shopping's on your agenda, you can find stores in Spanish Town selling items perfect for rounding out your tropical wardrobe or tucking into your suitcase to enjoy when you get home. Additional shops can be found at the Top of the Baths.

Virgin Gorda has very little crime and hardly any frosty attitudes among its more than 4,500 permanent residents. In short, the island provides a welcome respite in a region that's changing rapidly.

Planning

Getting Here and Around

AIR

There's no nonstop service from the continental United States to Virgin Gorda. Cape Air flies between Virgin Gorda and San Juan, Puerto Rico. Cape Air and Seaborne offer scheduled flights from St. Thomas to Beef Island, Tortola.

CAR

Virgin Gorda has a small road system, and a single, very steep road links the north and south ends of the island. You will probably need a car to get around for at least a few days of your stay unless you plan on staying put at your resort. If your resort is reachable only by boat, you should rent only for those days when you want to explore the island.

Remember that driving is on the *left*, British-style, even though almost all cars are American-made.

The main route sticks resolutely to the center of the island, linking The Baths on the southern tip with Gun Creek and Leverick Bay at North Sound. An alternate route, Nail Bay Road, goes through Nail Bay and connects to the scenic North Sound Road. Signage is erratic, so come prepared with a map.

CAR RENTAL

Alamo has a rental office in Spanish Town, and you can also rent a car from several local companies like Speedy's and Virgin Gorda Car Rental.

CONTACTS Andy's Car & Jeep Rental. ☎ *284/495–5253.* **L&S Jeep Rental.** ✉ *Spanish Town* ☎ *284/495–5297* ⊕ *www.landsjeeprental.com.* **Mahogany Rentals & Taxi Service.** ✉ *Spanish Town* ☎ *284/495–5469, 284/545–0058* ⊕ *www.mahoganycarrentalsbvi.com.* **Speedy's Car Rentals.** ✉ *Spanish Town* ☎ *284/495–5240, 284/495–5235, 284/341–7145 mobile* ⊕ *www.speedyscarrentals.com.*

FERRY

Ferries connect St. Thomas with Virgin Gorda; they leave daily from both Charlotte Amalie and less regularly from Red Hook. Ferries also link St. John and Tortola with Virgin Gorda. Ferries to Virgin Gorda land in Spanish Town. Ferry schedules vary by day, and not all companies make daily trips. The BVI Tourist Board website (⊕ *www.bvitourism.com*) has links for all the ferry companies, and their individual websites are the best up-to-date sources of information for specific routes and schedules.

■ TIP➜ **The ferry service from the public dock in Spanish Town can be a tad chaotic. Get there early and ask at the dock whether you're getting on the right boat.**

TAXI

Taxi rates are regulated by the government throughout the BVI, but it's always best to verify the cost of your trip with your driver. It's cheaper to travel in groups; fares are per trip, not per person. The taxi number is also the license plate number. Andy's Rentals & Tours offers service from one end of Virgin Gorda to the other. Mahogany Rentals & Taxi Service provides taxi service all over Virgin Gorda. The Valley Taxi Association, a group of independent taxi operators, also offers service from the ferry dock and around Virgin Gorda.

Beaches

Although some of the best beaches are reachable only by boat, don't worry if you're a landlubber, because you can find plenty of places to sun and swim. Anybody going to Virgin Gorda must experience swimming or snorkeling among its unique boulder formations, which can be visited at several sites along Lee Road. The most popular is The Baths, but there are several other similar places nearby that are easily reached.

Hotels

Virgin Gorda's charming hostelries appeal to a select, appreciative clientele; repeat business is extremely high. Those who prefer Sheratons, Marriotts, and the like may feel they get more for their money on other islands, but the peace and pampering offered on Virgin Gorda are priceless to the discriminating traveler. Villas are plentiful on the island and are widely distributed, but most of the resorts are concentrated in three places: The Valley (a catch-all geographic name that encompasses the southwestern part of the island), the Northwest Shore, and the North Sound, which is reachable only by ferry.

⇨ *Hotel prices are the lowest cost of a standard double room in high season.*

WHAT IT COSTS in U.S. Dollars			
$	$$	$$$	$$$$
HOTELS			
under $276	$276– $375	$376– $475	over $475

PRIVATE VILLAS

Visitors craving seclusion would do well at a villa. Most have full kitchens and maid service. Prices per week in winter run from around $2,000 for a one- or two-bedroom villa, up to $10,000 for a five-room beachfront villa. Rates in summer are substantially less. On Virgin Gorda a villa in the North Sound area means you can pretty much stay put at night unless you want to make the drive on narrow roads. If you opt for a spot near The Baths, it's an easier drive to town.

BOOKING AGENCIES

McLaughlin-Anderson Luxury Villas

TRAVEL AGENCIES | The St. Thomas–based McLaughlin–Anderson Luxury Villas represents more than two dozen properties on Virgin Gorda and Tortola. Villas range in size from one bedrooms to five bedrooms, and come with full kitchens, pools, stellar views, and other amenities. The company can hire a chef and stock your kitchen with groceries. Most villas have a seven-night minimum stay during the winter season and a five-night minimum in the off-season. ☎ *340/776–0635, 800/537–6246 ⊕ www.mclaughlinanderson.com.*

Villas Virgin Gorda

TRAVEL AGENCIES | This management company's dozen-plus properties stretch from The Baths to the Nail Bay area. Several budget properties are included among the pricier offerings. Most houses have private pools, and a few are right on the beach. ☎ *284/540–8002 ⊕ www.villasvirgingorda.com.*

Did You Know?

The Baths, at Virgin Gorda's western end, is one of the best snorkeling spots on the island, but you can also arrange a snorkeling trip by boat from your resort.

Virgin Gorda Villa Rentals

TRAVEL AGENCIES | This company's 20-plus properties are all near Leverick Bay Resort and Mahoe Bay, so they are perfect for those who want to be close to activities. Many of the accommodations—from one to six or more bedrooms—have private swimming pools and air-conditioning, at least in the bedrooms. All have full kitchens, are well maintained, and have spectacular views. ✉ *Mahoe Bay* ☎ *284/542–4014, 284/542–4011* ⊕ *www.vgvirgingordavilla-rentals.com.*

Restaurants

Dining out on Virgin Gorda is a mixed bag, with everything from hamburgers to lobster available; restaurants range from simple to elegant. Most folks opt to have dinner at or near their hotel to avoid driving on Virgin Gorda's twisting roads at night. Hotels that are accessible only by boat will arrange transport in advance upon request from nonguests who wish to dine at their restaurants. Most other independent restaurants are in The Valley or the vicinity. It's wise to make dinner reservations almost everywhere except at really casual spots.

⇨ *Restaurant prices are the average cost of a main course at dinner or, if dinner is not served, at lunch.*

WHAT IT COSTS in U.S. Dollars			
$	$$	$$$	$$$$
RESTAURANTS			
under $13	$13–$20	$21–$30	over $30

Safety

Although crime is rare, use common sense: don't leave your camera on the beach while you take a dip, or your wallet on a hotel dresser when you go for a walk.

Shopping

Most boutiques are within hotel complexes or in Spanish Town, but some resorts also have specialty shops.

Sights

Virgin Gorda's most popular attractions are those provided by Mother Nature. Beautiful beaches, crystal clear water, and stellar views are around nearly every bend in the road. That said, remember to get a taste of the island's past at Copper Mine Point.

Tours

Romney Associates/Travel Plan Tours, Virgin Gorda Tours Association, Speedy's, and Valley Taxi Association can arrange island tours, boat tours, snorkeling and scuba-diving trips, dolphin swims, and yacht charters.

CONTACTS Romney Associates/Travel Plan Tours. ☎ *284/494–4000* ⊕ *romascogroup.com.*

Visitor Information

CONTACTS Virgin Gorda BVI Tourist Board. ✉ *Spanish Town* ☎ *284/852–6020* ⊕ *www.bvitourism.com.*

BANKS
Banco Popular is in Virgin Gorda Yacht Harbour.

The Valley

◉ Sights

★ **The Baths National Park**
BEACH | FAMILY | At Virgin Gorda's most celebrated sight, giant boulders are scattered about the beach and in the water. Some are almost as large as houses

The Baths are filled with grottoes and hidden pools.

and form remarkable grottoes. Climb between these rocks to swim in the many placid pools. Snorkelers and divers will find even more tumbled boulders below the surface. Early morning and late afternoon are the best times to visit if you want to avoid crowds. If it's privacy you crave, follow the shore northward to quieter bays—Spring Bay, the Crawl, Little Trunk, and Valley Trunk—or head south to Devil's Bay. ⊠ *Off Tower Rd., Spanish Town* ☎ *284/494-2069* ⊕ *www. bvitourism.com* ✉ *$3*.

Copper Mine National Park

RUINS | A tall stone shaft silhouetted against the sky, a small stone structure that overlooks the sea, and a deep cistern are part of what was once a copper mine, now in ruins. Established 400 years ago, it was worked first by the Spanish, then by the English until the mid-19th century. There's not too much in the way of interpretive signs at the site, but the location is beautiful. ⊠ *Copper Mine Rd., Spanish Town* ✉ *Free*.

Spanish Town

TOWN | Virgin Gorda's peaceful main settlement, on the island's southern wing, is so tiny that it barely qualifies as a town at all. In the part of the island known as "The Valley," Spanish Town has a marina, some shops, a few restaurants and bars, and a couple of car-rental agencies. Just north of town is the ferry terminal.

Beaches

★ The Baths Beach

BEACH | FAMILY | The most popular tourist destination in the BVI, this stunning maze of huge granite boulders extending into the sea is usually crowded midday with day-trippers, especially when cruise ships are in port (come early in the morning or toward evening for more solitude). The snorkeling is good, and you're likely to see a wide variety of fish. Public bathrooms and a handful of bars and shops are close to the water and at the start of the path that leads to the beach. Visitors also come to The Baths from charter boats moored just offshore;

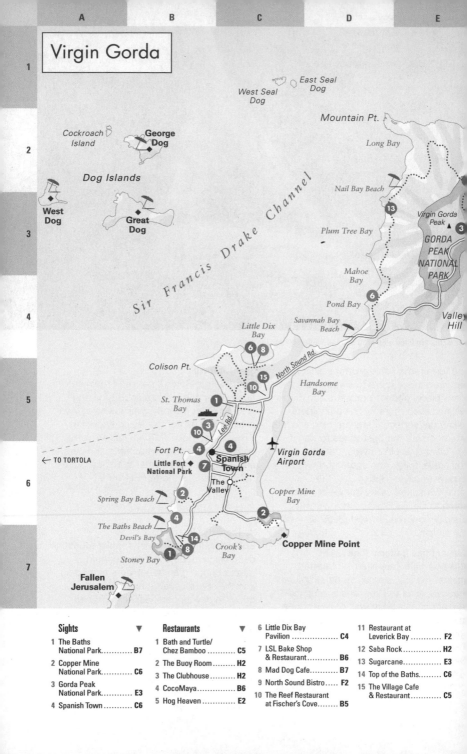

Virgin Gorda

	A	B	C	D	E

West Seal Dog

East Seal Dog

Mountain Pt.

Cockroach Island

George Dog

Dog Islands

Long Bay

Nail Bay Beach

13

Virgin Gorda Peak ▲

3

GORDA PEAK NATIONAL PARK

West Dog

Great Dog

Plum Tree Bay

Mahoe Bay

Sir Francis Drake Channel

Pond Bay

6

Savannah Bay Beach

Valley Hill

Little Dix Bay

6 **8**

North Sound Rd.

Handsome Bay

Colison Pt.

15

10

St. Thomas Bay

1

Lee Rd.

Virgin Gorda Airport

10 **3**

Fort Pt.

4

4

Spanish Town

← TO TORTOLA

7

Little Fort National Park

The Valley

Copper Mine Bay

Spring Bay Beach

2

2

The Baths Beach

4

Devil's Bay

14

Copper Mine Point

1

8

Crook's Bay

Stoney Bay

Fallen Jerusalem

Sights ▼

1 The Baths National Park............ **B7**

2 Copper Mine National Park............ **C6**

3 Gorda Peak National Park............ **E3**

4 Spanish Town **C6**

Restaurants ▼

1 Bath and Turtle/ Chez Bamboo **C5**

2 The Buoy Room.......... **H2**

3 The Clubhouse **H2**

4 CocoMaya.............. **B6**

5 Hog Heaven **E2**

6 Little Dix Bay Pavilion **C4**

7 LSL Bake Shop & Restaurant **B6**

8 Mad Dog Cafe........... **B7**

9 North Sound Bistro..... **F2**

10 The Reef Restaurant at Fischer's Cove........ **B5**

11 Restaurant at Leverick Bay **F2**

12 Saba Rock............... **H2**

13 Sugarcane................. **E3**

14 Top of the Baths......... **C6**

15 The Village Cafe & Restaurant............ **C5**

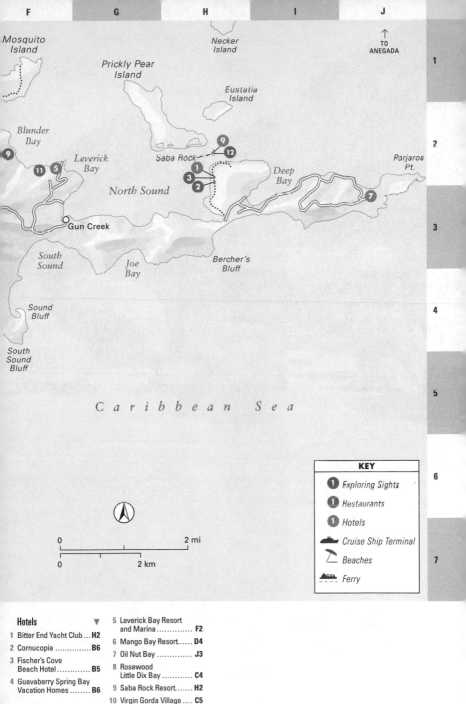

F   G   H   I   J

Mosquito
Island

Necker
Island

↑
TO
ANEGADA

1

Prickly Pear
Island

Eustatia
Island

Blunder
Bay

9

Leverick
Bay

11   5

North Sound

9
Saba Rock
12
1
3
2

Deep
Bay

Parjaros
Pt.

7

2

Gun Creek

3

South
Sound

Joe
Bay

Bercher's
Bluff

Sound
Bluff

4

South
Sound
Bluff

Caribbean Sea

5

KEY

1 Exploring Sights

1 Restaurants

1 Hotels

Cruise Ship Terminal

Beaches

Ferry

6

7

0   2 mi

0   2 km

Did You Know?

With large boulders, powdery sand, and turquoise waters, Spring Bay is considered a quieter version of The Baths.

You can luxuriate in many beachside lodgings across Virgin Gorda.

use the swim line to get to shore, since boats no longer launch dinghies to transport guests back and forth. Lockers are available to keep belongings safe. **Amenities:** food and drink; parking; toilets. **Best for:** snorkeling; swimming. ✉ *Tower Rd., about 1 mile (1½ km) west of Spanish Town ferry dock, Spanish Town* ☎ *284/494–2069* 🎟 *$3.*

Spring Bay Beach

BEACH | This national park beach gets much less traffic than the nearby Baths but has similarly large, imposing boulders that create interesting grottoes for swimming. Plus, there's the added benefit of no admission fee. The snorkeling is excellent, and the grounds include swings and picnic tables. Guavaberry Spring Bay Vacation Homes has villas and cottages right near the beach. **Amenities:** none. **Best for:** snorkeling; swimming. ☎ *284/494–2069* 🎟 *Free.*

🍴 Restaurants

Bath and Turtle/Chez Bamboo

$$$ | **ECLECTIC** | These two friendly restaurants share the same lovely hideaway and serve tasty meals all day between them, with informal Bath and Turtle your go-to for breakfast and lunch fare and candlelit Chez Bamboo turning out burgers, seafood, and other Caribbean-style dishes. Additionally, a coffeehouse called Chez B Grind attracts a morning crowd seeking stimulation with cappuccino and refreshment from tropical smoothies. **Known for:** bar scene with live music and popular happy hour; chic, gardenlike setting; sushi on Fridays. [$] *Average main: $26* ✉ *Lee Rd., Spanish Town* ☎ *284/545–1861* 🌐 *www.bathandturtle.com.*

★ CocoMaya

$$$$ | **ASIAN FUSION** | Tucked into a sleepy corner of Spanish Town, CocoMaya has a dreamy waterfront location, a buzzing, Balinese-inspired atmosphere, and delicious Asian fusion fare that makes it a jewel of the island's restaurant scene. Lounge near the crashing waves of Spring Bay with beach games and live music while you enjoy sushi rolls or small plates like shrimp lettuce wraps and spicy pork bao buns. **Known for:** Balinese-style décor; beach lounging and games; creative Asian fusion cuisine. [$] *Average main: $34* ✉ *Spanish Town* ☎ *284/495–6344* 🌐 *www.cocomayavg.com* 🕒 *No lunch.*

★ Little Dix Bay Pavilion

$$$$ | **CARIBBEAN** | For an elegant evening, you can't beat dining in this enchanting, candlelight, open-air pavilion, with its always-changing sophisticated contemporary fare and attentive service. The superbly prepared seafood, meat, and vegetarian entrées, most drawing upon Caribbean cooking traditions, including dishes like a Trinidad-style seafood pot, Montego Bay–marinated fish with Jamaican spices, and tandoori-marinated lamb chops. **Known for:** refined atmosphere; stellar Caribbean-influenced cuisine; excellent service. [$] *Average main: $45* ✉ *Little Dix Bay Resort, off Little Rd., Spanish Town* ☎ *284/495–5555* 🌐 *www.rosewoodhotels.com* 👔 *Daytime: Resort casual; cover-up and footwear required. Evening: Resort chic; T-shirts, jeans, tennis shoes, and beach sandals are not permitted.*

LSL Bake Shop & Restaurant

$$ | **ECLECTIC** | Along the road to The Baths, this small restaurant with pedestrian décor is a local favorite for fresh bread, cakes and pastries, and informal dining. You can always find fresh fish on the menu, accompanied by traditional local sides like peas and rice. **Known for:** Friday-night barbecues; local fish; fresh-baked cakes. [$] *Average main: $16* ✉ *Tower Rd., Spanish Town* ☎ *284/495–5151* 🌐 *www.lslbakeshop.com* 🕒 *Closed Sun.*

Mad Dog Cafe

$ | **AMERICAN** | **FAMILY** | Piña coladas are *the* thing at this breezy bar just outside the entrance to The Baths. The menu includes great triple-decker sandwiches, BLTs, and hot dogs. **Known for:** piña coladas; sandwiches; quick bites. [$] *Average main: $9* ✉ *The Baths, Tower Rd., Spanish Town* ☎ *284/495–5830* 🕒 *No dinner.*

The Reef Restaurant at Fischer's Cove

$$$ | **CARIBBEAN** | Dine seaside at this alfresco restaurant that's open to the breezes and features occasional live music. If pumpkin soup is on the menu, give it a try for a true taste of the Caribbean, although you can also get burgers, pizza, and salads at lunch, and local fish and conch fritters. **Known for:** friendly staff; great views; Saturday-night pig roasts. [$] *Average main: $26* ✉ *Lee Rd., Spanish Town* ☎ *284/495–5253* 🌐 *www.fischerscove.com.*

Top of the Baths

$$$ | **ECLECTIC** | **FAMILY** | At the entrance to The Baths, this popular restaurant has tables on an outdoor terrace or in an open-air pavilion; all have stunning views of the Sir Francis Drake Channel. The restaurant starts serving early for breakfast; for lunch, hamburgers, coconut chicken sandwiches, fish-and-chips, and sushi are among the offerings. **Known for:** great location with a swimming pool; stunning views; key lime pie. [$] *Average main: $23* ☎ *284/495–5497* 🌐 *www.topofthebaths.com* 🕒 *Closed Mon. No dinner.*

The Village Cafe & Restaurant

$$$ | **ECLECTIC** | Meals are served poolside under the shade of umbrellas at this casual eatery at the Virgin Gorda Village condo complex. The lunch menu includes salads, pizzas, rotis, and burgers, but the "lobster pocket" is a must-have. **Known for:** lobster pocket; casual lunch; poolside dining. [$] *Average main: $26* ✉ *Olde Yard Village, North Sound Rd., Spanish Town* ☎ *284/343–8092, 284/495–5350* 🌐 *www.villagecafebvi.com* 🕒 *Closed Mon. and Tues.*

Rosewood Little Dix Bay resort has two pools that overlook the beach.

Hotels

Cornucopia

$$$ | B&B/INN | Imported French linens, vibrant local art, and antique detailing give Cote d'Azur-meets-the-Caribbean vibes at this boutique adults-only establishment overlooking Little Trunk Bay. Five uniquely and elegantly decorated one-bedroom units can be rented out in multiples for larger groups. Your stay includes an honor bar when the staff is off, plus a white-tablecloth breakfast service on the veranda. An on-site chef cooks eggs your way, with freshly baked breads and fruit grown on the property. There's no pool, but you get easy beach access, with an outdoor shower and changing room, plus the chance to swap stories around the firepit after the sun goes down. **Pros:** beach access; gourmet breakfast included; unique vintage details in rooms. **Cons:** minimum three-night stay; no pool; lower level rooms are cave-like. [$] *Rooms from: $400* ✉ *Spanish Town* ☎ *284/542–4014, 284/541–6888* 🌐 *cornucopiabvi.com* 🛏 *5 rooms* 🍴 *Free Breakfast.*

Fischer's Cove Beach Hotel

$ | RESORT | This beachfront hotel has standard hotel rooms, beachside studios, and beach cottages to choose from. **Pros:** beachfront location; budget price; good restaurant. **Cons:** basic units; no meals included; no air-conditioning in some rooms. [$] *Rooms from: $165* ✉ *Lee Rd., Spanish Town* ☎ *284/495–5253* 🌐 *www.fischerscove.com* 🛏 *6 units* 🍴 *No Meals.*

Guavaberry Spring Bay Vacation Homes

$ | HOTEL | Rambling back from the beach, these hexagonal one-, two-, and three-bedroom villas give you all the comforts of home—and the resort's own stretch of striking, boulder-fringed beach is a short walk minutes away. **Pros:** short walk to The Baths (and excellent snorkeling); easy drive to town; scenic outdoor decks with ocean views. **Cons:** few amenities; extra charge for air-conditioning; basic décor. [$] *Rooms from: $200*

✉ *Tower Rd., Spanish Town* ☎ *284/544–7186* 🌐 *www.guavaberryspringbay.com* 🛏 *19 units* 🍴 *No Meals.*

★ **Rosewood Little Dix Bay**
$$$$ | **RESORT** | **FAMILY** | This swanky laid-back resort offers a gorgeous crescent of sand, plenty of activities, excellent restaurants, and sleek rooms, suites, and villas with bright, clean mid-century modern furniture and a casual feel that matches the resort's "barefoot luxury" ethos. **Pros:** relaxed sophistication; gorgeous grounds; outstanding amenities. **Cons:** expensive; very spread out; insular though not isolated. [$] *Rooms from: $850* ✉ *Off Little Rd., Spanish Town* ☎ *284/495–5555* 🌐 *www.rosewoodhotels.com* 🛏 *82 rooms* 🍴 *No Meals.*

Virgin Gorda Village
$ | **APARTMENT** | All the condos in this upscale complex a few minutes' drive from Spanish Town have at least partial ocean views. **Pros:** close to Spanish Town; lovely pool, recently built units. **Cons:** no beach; on a busy street; noisy roosters nearby. [$] *Rooms from: $189* ✉ *North Sound Rd., Spanish Town* ☎ *284/495–5544* 🌐 *www.virgingordavillage.com* 🛏 *31 condos* 🍴 *No Meals.*

Nightlife

Most nights during the high season, Chez Bamboo, CocoMaya, and The Rum Room at Rosewood Little Dix Bay will be your top destinations in The Valley for live music, DJs, and dancing. Check social media or call ahead for schedules and details.

Bath and Turtle/Chez Bamboo
BARS | During high season, the Bath and Turtle (and the adjacent Chez Bamboo) is one of the liveliest spots on Virgin Gorda, hosting DJs and live music several nights a week. ✉ *Lee Rd., Spanish Town* ☎ *284/545–1861* 🌐 *www.bathturtle.com.*

Festival on Virgin Gorda

Festival coincides with Easter on Virgin Gorda. The celebration is smaller than those you'll find on more heavily touristed islands, but people visiting family and friends do come from around the Caribbean. If you're heading to Virgin Gorda during the three-day annual event, make sure you've booked your room well in advance.

★ **CocoMaya**
COCKTAIL LOUNGES | CocoMaya features the mellow sounds of acoustic guitarist Oren Hodge every Wednesday, a rotating lineup of live music on weekends (along with karaoke on Sunday), and a DJ virtually every night of the week. Check social media or call for details. ✉ *Spanish Town* ☎ *284/495–6344* 🌐 *www.cocomayavg.com.*

The Rum Room
BARS | The Rum Room at Little Dix Bay presents live entertainment several nights a week in season. ✉ *Little Dix Bay Resort, Little Rd., Spanish Town* ☎ *284/495–5555* 🌐 *www.rosewoodhotels.com.*

Shopping

FOOD

RiteWay Virgin Gorda
FOOD | The store isn't much to look at, inside or out, but it has the best wine prices on Virgin Gorda, along with the usual basic supermarket items. ✉ *Long Rd., Spanish Town* ☎ *284/347–1205* 🌐 *www.riteway.vg.*

Rosy's Supermarket
SUPERMARKET | This store carries the basics plus an interesting selection of ready-to-cook meals, such as whole seasoned chickens. ✉ *Rhymer Rd., Spanish Town* ☎ *284/495–5245* 🌐 *www.rosysvg.com.*

GIFTS

The Beach House at Rosewood Little Dix Bay
GENERAL STORE | This tony hotel shop has the latest in resort wear for men and women, as well as jewelry, books, housewares, and expensive T-shirts. ✉ *Little Dix Bay Resort, Little Rd., Spanish Town* ☎ *284/495–5555* 🌐 *www.rosewoodhotels.com.*

Northwest Shore

👁 Sights

Gorda Peak National Park
NATIONAL PARK | There are two trails at this 260-acre park, which contains the island's highest point, at 1,359 feet. Signs on North Sound Road mark both entrances. It's a short but steep 30- to 50-minute hike (depending on which trail you take) through a rare Caribbean dry forest to a small clearing, where you can enjoy some high-level views. ✉ *North Sound Rd.* ☎ *284/393–9284* 🎟 *Free.*

⛱ Beaches

Fallen Jerusalem and the Dog Islands
BEACH | You can easily reach these quaintly named islands by boat, which you can rent in either Tortola or Virgin Gorda; they're also a popular destination for dive and snorkeling charter boats. Fallen Jerusalem and the Dogs are part of the National Parks Trust of the Virgin Islands, and their seductive beaches and unparalleled snorkeling display the BVI at their hedonistic best. Fallen Jerusalem has two small beaches for a Robinson Crusoe experience. **Amenities:** none. **Best for:** solitude; snorkeling. ☎ *284/393–9284* 🎟 *Free.*

Nail Bay Beach
BEACH | At the island's north tip, the three beaches on Nail Bay are ideal for snorkeling. Mountain Trunk Bay is perfect for beginners, and Nail Bay and Long Bay beaches have coral caverns just offshore. The Sugarcane Restaurant at the nearby Nail Bay Sports Club serves lunch and dinner. **Amenities:** food and drink. **Best for:** snorkeling; swimming. ✉ *Nail Bay Resort, off Plum Tree Bay Rd., Nail Bay* 🎟 *Free.*

Savannah Bay Beach
BEACH | This is a wonderfully private beach close to Spanish Town. It may not always be completely deserted, but you can find a spot to yourself on this long stretch of soft white sand in front of the tall dunes. Bring your own mask, fins, and snorkel, as there are no facilities. Nearby villas are available through rental property agencies. The view from atop the dunes is a photographer's delight. **Amenities:** none. **Best for:** solitude; snorkeling; swimming. ✉ *Off N. Sound Rd., ¾ mile (1¼ km) east of Spanish Town ferry dock, Savannah Bay* 🎟 *Free.*

🍴 Restaurants

Sugarcane
$$$$ | **CARIBBEAN** | Spectacular island views and gorgeous landscaping round out the romantic atmosphere at this intimate hillside hideaway, creating the perfect setting for an intimate dinner of fresh local fish prepared in a variety of ways. During the day, bring a group and have your food and cocktails brought to you in the pool or on one of the luxurious sofas or loungers, which are available for the diners' use. **Known for:** outdoor dining with stunning views; romantic ambience; poolside lounging. [$] *Average main: $34* ✉ *Nail Bay Sports Club, Off Plum Tree Bay Rd., Nail Bay* ☎ *284/495–5455* 🌐 *www.sugarcane.vg* 🕓 *Closed Tues.*

Getting Your Goat

Roaming livestock is a fact of life in the tropics, particularly in less-developed places like Virgin Gorda. Indeed, residents who leave their car windows open occasionally return to find a freshly laid egg on the front seat. If you have time to sit a spell at places like Virgin Gorda Yacht Harbour, you might see a mother hen followed by a string of little ones.

While crowing roosters can rouse annoyingly early, grazing goats pose traffic hazards. Some have owners, but many of them wander off to forage for food. Be particularly careful when you're driving around bends or over the top of hills. You might find a herd of goats, or maybe a sheep or two, camped out in the middle of the road. Sound your horn and be patient. They'll move in their own time.

And should you happen to see a vendor selling local dishes, the relatives of those goats and chickens are probably bubbling in the pot.

Hotels

Mango Bay Resort
$ | **RESORT** | Facing west to capture sunsets, this collection of whitewashed contemporary condos and villas will make you feel right at home. **Pros:** nice beach; lively location that's an easy drive from restaurants; homes come with floats, kayaks, and snorkeling equipment. **Cons:** drab décor; some units have lackluster views; no restaurant on-site. [$] *Rooms from: $250* ✉ *Plum Tree Bay Rd., Pond Bay* ☎ *284/340–8804* 🌐 *www.mangobayresort.com* 🛏 *17 units* 🍴 *No Meals.*

North Sound

Restaurants

The Buoy Room
$$$$ | **ECLECTIC** | Knots, art from regattas past, and signal flags from the hundreds of vessels decorate the newly revamped Buoy Room at the Bitter End Yacht Club, which serves as a buzzing way station for hungry salts from Virgin Gorda and parts beyond. Raft up—it's only accessible by boat—for all-day brick oven pizzas and shared plates like fresh-caught fish tacos, seared tuna, and shrimp mango lettuce cups. **Known for:** stone-fired pizzas and fish tacos; nautical atmosphere; social sailing crowd. [$] *Average main: $36* ✉ *North Sound* ☎ *284/393–2745* 🌐 *beyc.com/the-buoy-room.*

The Clubhouse
$$$$ | **ECLECTIC** | With a tropical-nautical flair, The Bitter End Yacht Club's open-air waterfront restaurant is a favorite rendezvous for sailors and their guests, so it's busy day and night. Dinner selections include green Thai curry, seared ahi tuna, local lobster, and rib-eye steak, as well as vegetarian dishes and a variety of housemade desserts, including key lime pie. **Known for:** yacht-club-like atmosphere; historical touches; surf and turf. [$] *Average main: $32* ✉ *Bitter End Yacht Club, North Sound* ☎ *284/393–2745* 🌐 *www.beyc.com.*

★ Hog Heaven
$$$ | **BARBECUE** | **FAMILY** | The million-dollar sunset view is the thing at this simple wooden restaurant perched on a hillside overlooking the North Sound. If the scenery alone isn't enough to make you feel as if you're ready to be singing with the angels, this barbecue joint's succulent pork, local fish, and conch in butter sauce

will help. **Known for:** spectacular views; barbecue; rum drinks. [$] *Average main: $22* ✉ *North Sound* ☎ *284/547–5964.*

North Sound Bistro

$$$$ | BISTRO | Dinghy up (or call the complementary launch) to North Sound's newest restaurant at Blunder Bay Marina, nestled in a massive holiday villa accessible only by boat. You can find a casual bistro-style lunch of crispy bang bang shrimp and lobster rolls, or dinner offerings like blackened swordfish or chicken Parmesan. **Known for:** plunge pool; bang bang shrimp; boat-only access. [$] *Average main: $35* ✉ *North Sound* ☎ *284/542–5400* ⊕ *www.blunderbaymarina.com.*

Restaurant at Leverick Bay

$$$ | ECLECTIC | Chef Stanley Ramotar's gourmet menu at this marina restaurant draws cruise ship passengers on tour as well as hotel guests, locals, and mariners. Anegada lobster is a perennial favorite along with rack of lamb and beef tenderloin. **Known for:** Friday-night beach barbecue party; happy hour with live music; Anegada lobster. [$] *Average main: $38* ✉ *Leverick Bay Resort & Marina, Leverick Bay Rd., Leverick Bay* ☎ *284/541–8879, 284/542–7241* ⊕ *www.leverickbayvg.com.*

Saba Rock

$$$$ | BRITISH | Accommodating staff and congenial patrons make this waterside restaurant, located on a miniscule 1½-acre island sitting in the middle of North Sound, a worthwhile trek by private boat or ferry. Fish tacos and burgers are among the lunch favorites, while seafood and steak lure dinner patrons. **Known for:** unique island setting; private beach for lounging; colorful atmosphere. [$] *Average main: $38* ✉ *North Sound* ☎ *284/393–9220* ⊕ *www.sabarock.com.*

Hotels

This area was particularly hard hit by the hurricane season of 2017 followed by closures from COVID-19 in 2020. The good news? Well-loved **Bitter End Yacht Club** and **Saba Rock Resort** have now reopened after renovations. There are also other worthy options to consider, including the villas at the new Oil Nut Bay.

★ Bitter End Yacht Club

$$$$ | RESORT | FAMILY | Sailing's the thing at this busy marina in the nautically inclined North Sound, where the long-popular hotel has been recently rebuilt with beautiful new overwater Marina Lofts packed with nautical touches, private swim-up decks, and outdoor showers. **Pros:** lots of water sports; good diving opportunities; beautiful newly designed rooms and restaurant. **Cons:** expensive; only two units as of this writing; limited activities unless you love the water. [$] *Rooms from: $750* ✉ *North Sound* ☎ *284/393–2745, 800/872–2392* ⊕ *beyc.com* ⇨ *2 rooms* ❢❍❘ *No Meals.*

Leverick Bay Resort and Marina

$ | RESORT | With its colorful buildings and bustling marina, Leverick Bay is a good choice for visitors who want easy access to water sports activities and who don't mind that the beach is quite small. **Pros:** fun location; good restaurant; small grocery store. **Cons:** basic rooms; no laundry in units; 15-minute drive to town. [$] *Rooms from: $160* ✉ *Off Leverick Bay Rd., Leverick Bay* ☎ *284/542–4011* ⊕ *www.leverickbayvg.com* ⇨ *18 units* ❢❍❘ *No Meals.*

Oil Nut Bay

$$$$ | RESORT | Part luxury resort and part villa community, Oil Nut Bay has rooms ranging from one-bedroom suites to six-bedroom villas, most with private swimming pools, artistic touches, and spectacular views of Virgin Gorda's east end and the Caribbean Sea. Most guests use electric golf carts to get around the vast, largely self-sufficient property and visit the private beach club to snorkel, lounge, and paddleboard. **Pros:** luxurious accommodations; ample amenities including spa and restaurants; fantastic views. **Cons:** expensive; far from other attractions; only accessible by boat or helicopter. *Rooms from: $650 284/393–1000, 284/346–0001, 800/761–0377 www.oilnutbay.com 29 villas and suites No Meals.*

Saba Rock Resort

$$$$ | RESORT | Reachable only by ferry or by private yacht, this resort on its own tiny cay is perfect for folks who enjoy seclusion and also mixing and mingling with the sailors who drop anchor for the night. **Pros:** convivial atmosphere; convenient transportation; good diving nearby. **Cons:** tiny beach; isolated location; on a very small island. *Rooms from: $550 North Sound 284/393–9220 www.sabarock.com 9 units Free Breakfast.*

Nightlife

Bitter End Yacht Club

LIVE MUSIC | Local bands play several nights a week at the Bitter End Yacht Club during the winter season. *North Sound 284/393–2745 beyc.com.*

Leverick Bay Resort

BARS | This marina resort's restaurant and Jumbie's Beach Bar has a nightly happy hour with a pirate-themed musical performance on Monday, Tuesday, and Wednesday, and hosts bands several other nights a week. Things really get going at the Friday night beach barbecue, which features moko jumbie stilt-walkers, fire dancers, and a DJ. *Leverick Bay Resort & Marina, Leverick Bay Rd., Leverick Bay 284/541–8879, 284/346–7241, 284/340–3005 www.leverickbayvg.com.*

Shopping

CLOTHING

Pusser's Company Store

MIXED CLOTHING | A trademark line of sportswear, rum products, and gift items is available here. *Leverick Bay Marina, Leverick Bay Rd., Leverick Bay 284/495–7369 www.pussers.com.*

FOOD

Bitter End Market

FOOD | This store at the Bitter End is the place for local fruits, cheeses, fresh baked goods, and gourmet prepared food. *Bitter End Yacht Club, North Sound 284/393–2745 beyc.com.*

Buck's Food Market

SUPERMARKET | Buck's is the closest to a full-service supermarket the island offers, and has everything from an in-store bakery and deli to fresh fish and produce departments. *North Sound Rd., Spanish Town 284/495–5423 www.bucksmarkets.com.*

Chef's Pantry

FOOD | This store in Leverick Bay has the fixings for an impromptu party in your villa or to provision your boat—fresh seafood, specialty meats, imported cheeses, daily baked breads and pastries, and an impressive wine and spirits selection. *Leverick Bay Marina, Leverick Bay Rd., Leverick Bay 284/541–2881 www.leverickbayvg.com.*

GIFTS

Reeftique

SOUVENIRS | This store carries island crafts and jewelry, clothing, and nautical odds and ends with the Bitter End logo. *Bitter End Yacht Club, North Sound 284/393–2745 beyc.com.*

Sailing is a popular pastime on Virgin Gorda.

🏃 Activities

CRICKET

You can catch a match at the Recreation Grounds in Spanish Town from February to April. The BVI Tourist Board at Virgin Gorda Yacht Harbour can give you information on game dates and times.

DIVING AND SNORKELING

Where you go snorkeling and what company you pick depends on where you're staying. Many hotels have on-site dive outfitters, but if yours doesn't, one won't be far away. If your hotel does have a dive operation, just stroll down to the dock and hop aboard—no need to drive anywhere. The dive companies are all certified by PADI. Costs vary, but count on paying about $100 for a one-tank dive and $150 for a two-tank dive with equipment. All dive operators offer introductory courses as well as certification and advanced courses. Should you get an attack of the bends, which can happen when you ascend too rapidly, the nearest decompression chamber is at Schneider Regional Medical Center in St. Thomas.

There are some terrific snorkel and dive sites off Virgin Gorda, including areas around The Baths, the North Sound, and the Dogs. The BVI Art Reef features a sculpture of a giant kraken engulfing the sunken hull of a historic U.S. Navy ship. The Chimney at Great Dog Island has a coral archway and canyon covered with a wide variety of sponges. At Joe's Cave, an underwater cavern on West Dog Island, huge groupers, eagle rays, and other colorful fish accompany divers as they swim. At some sites you can see 100 feet down, but snorkelers and divers who don't want to go that deep will find plenty to look at just below the surface.

Dive BVI

SCUBA DIVING | In addition to day trips, Dive BVI also offers expert scuba instruction and certification. The Yacht Harbour location is housed in a shipping container; there's a fancier location at the Scrub Island resort. Charter boats can also be met for rendezvous dives at various locations in the BVI. ⊠ *Virgin Gorda Yacht Harbour, Lee Rd., Spanish Town* 🕾 *284/541–9818 Yacht Harbour, 284/394–3440 Scrub Island* ⊕ *www. divebvi.com.*

Sunchaser Scuba

SCUBA DIVING | Resort, advanced, and rescue courses are all available here along with dive charters to northern BVI sites like the Dog Islands, the RMS *Rhone*, and other destinations—all 15 to 45 minutes away from their base at the Bitter End Yacht Club. ⊠ *Bitter End Yacht Club* 🕾 *284/344–2766* ⊕ *www.sunchaserscuba.com.*

SAILING AND BOATING

The BVI waters are calm and terrific places to learn to sail. You can also rent sea kayaks, water-skiing equipment, and powerboats.

Bitter End Watersports

SAILING | **FAMILY** | Bitter End offers classroom, dockside, and on-the-water lessons for sailors of all levels, as well as daily activities like Beer Can Regattas and Hobie Cat "out-of-bounds" races. Call the resort for the weekly schedule. ⊠ *Bitter End Yacht Club, North Sound* 🕾 *284/393–2745* ⊕ *beyc.com.*

Double D Charters

BOATING | If you just want to sit back, relax, and let the captain take the helm, choose a sailing or power yacht from Double D Charters. Rates start at $300 for a day trip to Cooper Island, Norman Island, Jost Van Dyke, or Anegada. Private full-day cruises or sails for up to eight people run from $750. ⊠ *Virgin Gorda Yacht Harbour, Lee Rd., Spanish Town* 🕾 *284/499–2479* ⊕ *www.doubledbvi.com.*

WATER SPORTS

Blue Rush Water Sports

WATER SPORTS | This company rents a variety of fun water toys, including flyboards, Jet Skis, clear-bottomed kayaks, Hobie Cats, and stand-up paddleboards. ⊠ *Leverick Bay Marina, North Sound* 🕾 *284/343–2002* ⊕ *www.bluerushwatersports.com.*

Chapter 8

OTHER BRITISH
VIRGIN ISLANDS

8

Updated by
Claire Shefchik

⊙ Sights	🍴 Restaurants	🏨 Hotels	💼 Shopping	🍸 Nightlife
★★★★★	★★★★☆	★★★★★	★★★☆☆	★★★★☆

WELCOME TO THE OTHER BRITISH VIRGIN ISLANDS

TOP REASONS TO GO

★ **Snorkeling and diving in Anegada:** The wrecks and reefs draw divers from all over the world to this beautiful, beach-fringed island.

★ **Barhopping in Jost Van Dyke:** The BVI's nightlife (and day drinking) capital is the place to go, especially for Foxy's Halloween and New Year's parties. The Soggy Dollar and Foxy's Tamarind are favorites.

★ **Communing with nature on Guana Island:** This private island resort has a world-famous conservation program and extensive hiking trails through rainforests and to secluded beaches.

★ **Turning back the clock at Cooper Island:** Although it's been updated in recent years with a rum bar and brewery, a stay here is like visiting the old Caribbean, and that's exactly how guests want it.

★ **Sailing the BVI:** Pick up a charter yacht in Tortola and enjoy a variety of experiences throughout the 50-some islands that make up the BVI.

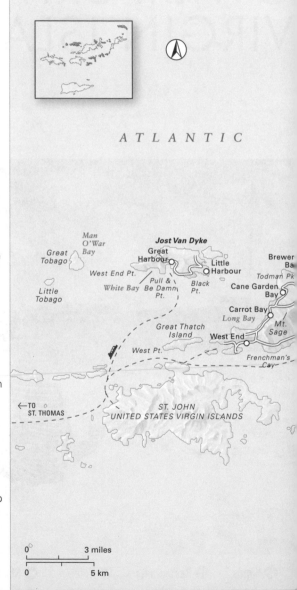

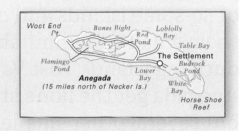

Anegada
(15 miles north of Necker Is.)

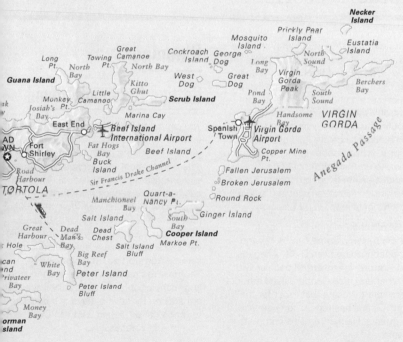

Tortola and Virgin Gorda are the largest—and most visited—of the British Virgin Islands, but the chain is made up of 50-some islands and cays, many of them small and uninhabited. Of these outlying islands, Jost Van Dyke and Anegada get the lion's share of visitors, but several other smaller islands have notable resorts.

Anegada is most popular with snorkelers, sailors, and those looking to escape the modest crowds of the BVI, while Jost Van Dyke attracts partiers to its lively beach bars, along with a smaller contingent of visitors who spend a few days. Among the other islands, Guana, Necker, and Scrub islands are luxe private-island resorts, while Cooper Island is a bit more down-to-earth in terms of price. Norman Island is uninhabited, but it does have a restaurant at Pirate's Bight and a floating bar on a ship moored off its coast.

Most of these islands are linked to Tortola by ferry. Some can be day-trip destinations (Jost Van Dyke, Anegada, and Norman Island are all popular with day-trippers), and Cooper Island attracts many charter boats that moor for the night. Guana has regular ferry service for guests; Necker remains completely private.

Planning

Getting Here and Around

You can fly to Anegada on a charter flight (affordable if you are traveling with a group), but all the other islands are reachable only by boat (or perhaps helicopter if you are visiting Necker Island). Anegada has daily ferry service from Tortola (three times a week from Road Town and four times a week from Trellis Bay). Both services make stops in Virgin Gorda. Jost Van Dyke has regularly scheduled ferry service from Tortola, St. John, and St. Thomas. You can rent a jeep on Anegada, and many people do, especially if they are staying for several days. It's possible to rent a car or jeep in Jost Van Dyke, but it's not really necessary.

CAR

You can rent a car or jeep on either Anegada or Jost Van Dyke. This may make sense in Anegada (which also offers Mini Moke rentals), where you might want to explore a variety of different beaches to maximize your snorkeling opportunities. However, in Jost Van Dyke, it's often just as easy to take a taxi or walk. On either island, both rentals and gas are expensive, so be sure to make room for those costs in your vacation budget.

ANEGADA

D.W. Jeep Rentals

FOUR-WHEELING | Dean Wheatley can rent you a jeep for $65 per day. ⊠ *The Settlement* ☎ 284/495–9677.

JOST VAN DYKE

Paradise Jeep Rentals

FOUR-WHEELING | This reliable company offers the ideal vehicles to tackle Jost Van Dyke's steep, winding roads. Even though Jost is a relatively small island, you really need to be in shape to walk from one bay to the next. This outfit rents two-door Suzuki Jimmys for $65 per day, four-door Grand Vitaras for $75, four-door Jeep Wranglers for $80, and eight-seat Kia Mojaves for $90. Discounts are available for rentals of six or more days. It's next to the fire station in Great Harbour. Reservations are a must. ⊠ *Great Harbour* ☎ 284/547–1040 ⊕ *www.paradisejeeprental.com.*

Hotels and Restaurants

Both Anegada and Jost Van Dyke offer a choice of resorts and independent restaurants and bars; however, true luxury is in short supply. Some of the other smaller islands in the BVI are private and have a single resort, including the luxe choices Necker Scrub, and Guana islands, as well as the more modest Cooper Island.

⇨ *Hotel and restaurant reviews have been shortened. For more information, visit Fodors.com. Hotel prices are the lowest cost of a standard double room in high season. Restaurant prices are the average cost of a main course at dinner or, if dinner is not served, at lunch.*

WHAT IT COSTS in U.S. Dollars			
$	$$	$$$	$$$$
HOTELS			
under $276	$276–$375	$376–$475	over $475
RESTAURANTS			
under $13	$13–$20	$21–$30	over $30

Visitor Information

BANKS AND ATMS

Be sure to take cash if you travel to the smaller islands in the BVI. None have an ATM or a bank, though most resorts and some stores take credit cards.

Jost Van Dyke

Named after an early Dutch settler, Jost Van Dyke is a small island northwest of Tortola and is *truly* a place to get away from it all. Mountainous and lush, the 4-mile-long (6½-km-long) island—with fewer than 300 full-time residents—has some tiny hotels, a few rental cottages and villas, a campground, a couple dozen cars, and a single main road, with a second rugged dirt road running along the top ridge. There are no banks or ATMs. Life definitely rolls along on "island time," especially during the off-season from August to November, when finding a restaurant open for dinner can be a challenge. Electricity came to Jost in the 1990s, and water conservation is encouraged, as the primary sources are rainwater collected in basementlike cisterns and desalinized seawater. Jost is one of the Caribbean's most popular anchorages, and there is a disproportionately large number of informal bars and restaurants, which have helped earn Jost its reputation as the "party island" of the BVI.

Boaters dock at Jost Van Dyke, known as the party island of the BVI.

GETTING HERE AND AROUND

The only way to get to Jost Van Dyke is by ferry or private boat. Day-sail operators, both in the USVI and the BVI, take guests here daily, and there are regularly scheduled ferries from West End, Tortola (25 minutes); St. John (30 minutes); and St. Thomas (60 minutes, via St. John). Ferries from Tortola run several times daily from West End; the St. Thomas/St. John ferry runs generally just once a day, six days per week. Always check the schedules, as they change. Once on the ground, you can walk most everywhere you might need to go, but you can also hire a taxi driver if you want to avoid some steep uphills on foot.

 Beaches

Great Harbour Beach

BEACH | FAMILY | Great Harbour has an authentic Caribbean feel that's not just for tourists. Small bars and restaurants line the sandy strip of beach that serves as the community's main street. While the island's main settlement may not

have the unspoiled natural beauty of some popular beaches, it holds a quaint charm. There are a few areas suited to swimming, with calm, shallow water perfect for children; however, the attraction here is more about the beach scene than the actual beach. Ali Baba's and Sea Crest Inn have rooms on the bay. Bring your bug spray for sand flies in the early evenings. **Amenities:** food and drink; toilets. **Best for:** walking; swimming. ⊠ Great Harbour.

Sandy Cay

BEACH | Just offshore, the 14-acre islet known as Sandy Cay is a gleaming sliver of white sand with marvelous snorkeling and an inland nature trail. Previously part of the private estate of the late philanthropist and conservationist Laurance Rockefeller, the Cay is now a protected area. You can hire any boatman on Jost Van Dyke to take you out; just be sure to agree on a price and a time to be picked up again. Jost Van Dyke Scuba also runs snorkel trips to the island. As this is a national park, visitors are asked to "take

only photos and leave only footprints."
Nevertheless, it's become an increasingly
popular location for weddings, which
require approval from the BVI National
Parks Trust. Experienced boaters can rent
a boat or dinghy to go here, but be aware
that winter swells can make beach land-
ings treacherous. **Amenities:** none. **Best
for:** snorkeling; swimming; walking.

★ White Bay Beach

BEACH | FAMILY | On the south shore of
Jost Van Dyke and the "next bay over"
from Great Harbour, this long stretch
of picturesque white sand is especially
popular with boaters who come ashore
for a libation at one of the many beach
bars that offer refuge from the sun.
Despite the sometimes rowdy bar scene,
the beach is large enough to find a quiet
spot, particularly late in the day when
most of the day trippers disappear and
the beach becomes serene. There are a
few small hotels with rooms just behind
the beach or a short walk uphill. Swim-
mers and snorkelers should be cautious
of boat traffic in the anchorage. **Amenities:**
food and drink; toilets. **Best for:** partiers;
swimming; walking. ⊠ White Bay.

🍴 Restaurants

Restaurants on Jost Van Dyke are informal (some serve meals family-style at
long tables), but charming. The island's
a favorite charter-boat stop, and you're
bound to hear people exchanging stories
about the previous night's anchoring
adventures. Reservations are not man-
datory, but it's a good idea to call ahead
in season for dinner. In all cases dress is
casual. Most of the restaurants are also
known for their nightlife, particularly during the weekends. Meal prices are fairly
consistent across the island, with dinner
entrées usually varying by a few dollars.

Abe's by the Sea

$$$$ | ECLECTIC | Many sailors who cruise
into this quiet bay come so they can dock
right at this open-air eatery to enjoy the
conch, lobster, and other fresh catches,
always with peas and rice and coleslaw
on the side. Chicken and ribs round
out the menu, and affable owners Abe
Coakley and his wife, Eunicy, add a pinch
of hospitality that makes a meal into a
memorable evening. **Known for:** fresh
seafood; outdoor dining; warm hospitality. $ *Average main: $40* ⊠ *Little Harbour*
☎ *284/496–8429.*

Ali Baba's

$$$ | SEAFOOD | Lobster is the main attrac-
tion at this beach bar with a sandy floor,
which is just some 20 feet from the sea.
Grilled local fish—including swordfish,
kingfish, and wahoo—are caught fresh
daily, and the BabaQ ribs are the house
specialty. **Known for:** chicken roti; barbecue ribs; potent rum punch. $ *Average
main: $30* ⊠ *Great Harbour* ☎ *284/495–
9280* ⊕ *www.alibabasrestaurantandbar-
bvi.com.*

B-Line Beach Bar

$$ | ECLECTIC | The simple, open-air B-Line
Beach Bar brings "getting away from it
all" to a new level—if you're on mainland
Jost Van Dyke you'll have to charter a
dinghy or boat, or wade (at low tide)
across the few hundred meters of water
between Little Jost Van Dyke and Jost
Van Dyke. Here you can have an ice-cold
beer, an assortment of rums, and great
grilled food like barbecued ribs and chick-
en on a beautiful, remote beach. **Known
for:** remote setting; beach bar atmosphere; good rum selection. $ *Average
main: $18* ☎ *284/343–3311.*

Cool Breeze Sports Bar & Restaurant

$$$ | ECLECTIC | This brightly colored eatery
with a pool table and big-screen TVs for
watching sports is frequented by locals
and visitors. Expect a range of dinner
options, including fresh grilled lobster,
barbecue chicken and ribs, and vegetarian dishes. **Known for:** local scene; Car-
ibbean-style barbecue; live sports on TV.
$ *Average main: $29* ⊠ *Great Harbour*
☎ *284/440–0302, 284/496–0855* ⊕ *www.
coolbreezejvd.com.*

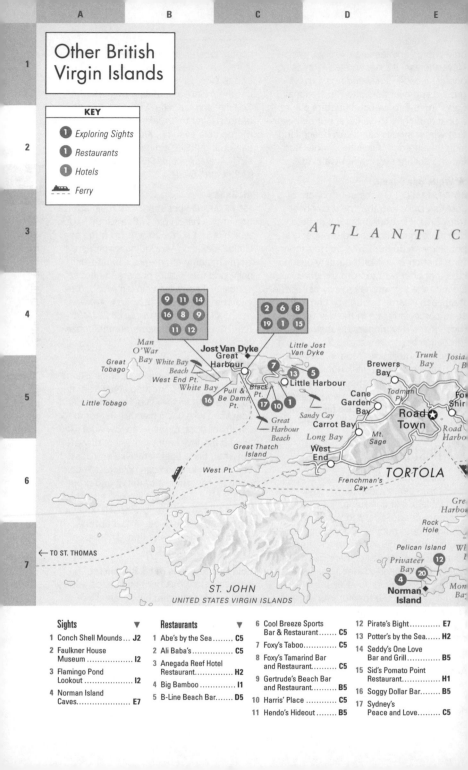

Other British Virgin Islands

KEY

- ① Exploring Sights
- ① Restaurants
- ① Hotels
- 🚢 Ferry

ATLANTIC

Man O'War Bay
Great Tobago
Little Tobago
White Bay Beach
West End Pt.
White Bay
Pull & Be Damn Pt.
Black Pt.
Jost Van Dyke
Great Harbour
Little Jost Van Dyke
Little Harbour
Great Harbour Beach
Great Thatch Island
Sandy Cay
Carrot Bay
Long Bay
West End
Great Harbour
West Pt.
Frenchman's Cay
Brewers Bay
Trunk Bay
Josia
Cane Garden Bay
Todman Pt.
Mt. Sage
Road Town
Road Harbo
For Shir
TORTOLA

Gre Harbou
Rock Hole
Pelican Island
Privateer Bay
Norman Island
Mon Ba

← TO ST. THOMAS

ST. JOHN
UNITED STATES VIRGIN ISLANDS

Sights ▼
1. Conch Shell Mounds ... **J2**
2. Faulkner House Museum **I2**
3. Flamingo Pond Lookout **I2**
4. Norman Island Caves.................... **E7**

Restaurants ▼
1. Abe's by the Sea **C5**
2. Ali Baba's **C5**
3. Anegada Reef Hotel Restaurant............... **H2**
4. Big Bamboo **I1**
5. B-Line Beach Bar....... **D5**
6. Cool Breeze Sports Bar & Restaurant........ **C5**
7. Foxy's Taboo............. **C5**
8. Foxy's Tamarind Bar and Restaurant.......... **C5**
9. Gertrude's Beach Bar and Restaurant.......... **B5**
10. Harris' Place **C5**
11. Hendo's Hideout **B5**
12. Pirate's Bight............ **E7**
13. Potter's by the Sea...... **H2**
14. Seddy's One Love Bar and Grill............. **B5**
15. Sid's Pomato Point Restaurant............... **H1**
16. Soggy Dollar Bar........ **B5**
17. Sydney's Peace and Love......... **C5**

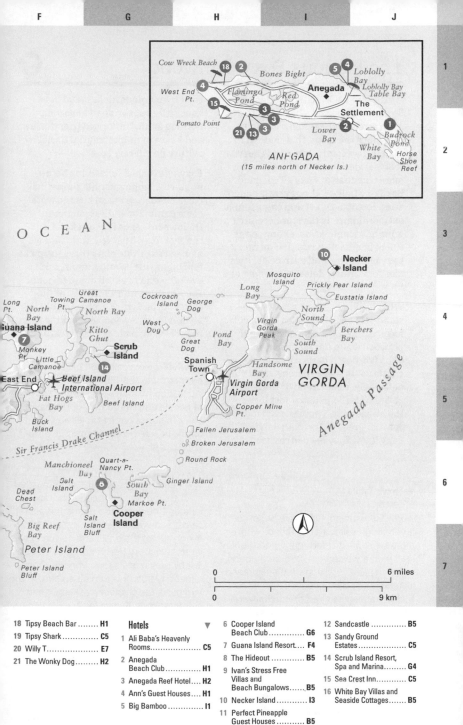

The Famous Foxy Callwood

It's the laid-back attitude of Jost Van Dyke, which boasts a beach as its main street and has had electricity only since the 1990s, that makes the famous feel comfortable and everyday folk feel glorious. At no locale is this more true than at Foxy's Tamarind Bar. Foxy Callwood, a seventh-generation Jost Van Dyker and calypsonian extraordinaire, is the star here, strumming and singing rib-tickling songs full of laughable lyrics that attract a bevy of boaters, and even celebrities like Tom Cruise, Kelsey Grammer, and Steven Spielberg.

What began in 1968 as a lemonade-stand-size bar, albeit with "modern" fixtures like a galvanized roof and plywood walls, has evolved into a bona fide beach bar with sandy floors, wattle walls, and a thatched roof that defines the eastern end of the beach at Great Harbour. Since Jost lacks the bustle of St. Thomas, cachet of St. John, or grace of Tortola, islanders like Foxy knew they needed to carve out their own unique niche—and have done so by appearing to have done nothing at all. Unhurried friendliness and a slice of quintessential Caribbean culture flow freely here.

Foxy, who fished for a living before he started singing for his supper, has traveled the world and has the world come to him for endless parties for Halloween, Labor Day weekend, and the New Year. The *New York Times* named Foxy's one of its three top picks for ringing in the millennium, and even Queen Elizabeth chose to honor Foxy, making him a Member of the Order of the British Empire (MBE) in 2009. A local newspaper headline from the occasion read: "Is Foxy Wearing Shoes?"

So what makes Foxy and his bar so popular, some 50-plus years on? He sums it up himself: "It's the quantity of people and the quality of the party. You can dance on the tables and sleep on the beach. No one is going to bother you."

★ Foxy's Taboo
$$ | **MEDITERRANEAN** | **FAMILY** | It's well worth the winding, hilly drive or sometimes rough sail to get to Taboo, where there's a sophisticated menu and friendly staff with a welcoming attitude. Kebabs, hummus, and veggie-stuffed pitas stand alongside eggplant cheesecake on the Mediterranean-inspired menu. **Known for:** Mediterranean fare with flair; scenic views; friendly staff. [$] *Average main: $15* ✉ *East End* ☎ *284/442–3074* 🌐 *www.foxysbvi.com.*

Foxy's Tamarind Bar and Restaurant
$$$$ | **ECLECTIC** | **FAMILY** | The big draw here is the owner, Foxy Callwood, a famed calypso singer who will serenade you with funny songs as you fork into grilled chicken, burgers, barbecue ribs, and lobster. Check out the pennants, postcards, and weathered T-shirts that adorn every inch of the walls and ceiling of this large, two-story beach bar; they've been left by previous visitors who are mostly either day-trippers from elsewhere in the Virgin Islands or those vacationing on charter yachts. **Known for:** Foxy, a Virgin Islands icon; live music and performances; late night scene. [$] *Average main: $35* ✉ *Great Harbour* ☎ *284/442–3074* 🌐 *foxysbar.com.*

Gertrude's Beach Bar and Restaurant
$$ | **ECLECTIC** | At this casual bar and West Indian restaurant right on White Bay Beach, owner Gertrude Callwood makes

guests feel at home with burgers, conch fritters, and rotis. Ask the bartender to mix you a drink, or you can pour your own. **Known for:** beachfront setting; giant Adirondack chair; conch fritters and burgers. $ *Average main: $20* ✉ *White Bay* 📞 *284/495–9104.*

Harris' Place

$$$$ | **ECLECTIC** | **FAMILY** | Owner Cynthia Jones is as famous for her friendliness as she is for her food. Lobster in a garlic butter sauce, and other freshly caught seafood, as well as pork, chicken, and ribs, are on the menu. **Known for:** fresh seafood; live music; house-made key lime pie. $ *Average main: $45* ✉ *Little Harbour* 📞 *284/344–8816* ⊕ *www.harris-placojvd.com* ⊗ *Closed Tues.*

★ Hendo's Hideout

$$$ | **ECLECTIC** | **FAMILY** | This upscale but family-friendly beach bar at White Bay beach features a handsome wood bar, lounge area, and hammocks nestled in among the palm trees. The pulled pork tacos are excellent, and bottomless mimosas are served with Sunday brunch. **Known for:** beachside dining; family-friendly atmosphere; lobster ravioli. $ *Average main: $30* ✉ *White Bay* 📞 *284/340–0074* ⊕ *www.hendoshideout.com* ⊗ *No dinner Mon.–Tues.*

Seddy's One Love Bar and Grill

$$$ | **ECLECTIC** | Freshly caught seafood is the star at this beachfront eatery. Local lobster finds its way into nachos and quesadillas, and the Food Network's Alton Brown once featured its stewed conch on a flavor-finding trip. **Known for:** beachy décor; Bushwacker cocktails; year-round Christmas tree out front. $ *Average main: $28* ✉ *White Bay* 📞 *937/470–8523* ⊕ *www.seddysonelovebarandgrill.com.*

★ Soggy Dollar Bar

$$ | **ECLECTIC** | Caribbean-style, casual beach fare rules at this must-stop destination for BVI boaters, whose habit of wading ashore for a drink gives the bar its distinctive name. Don't miss the Painkiller cocktail, the semi-official drink of the BVI, invented here. **Known for:** the Painkiller cocktail was invented here; lively beach party; wading ashore from your boat—that's where the name comes from. $ *Average main: $15* ✉ *White Bay* 📞 *284/495–9888* ⊕ *www.soggydollar.com* ⊗ *No dinner.*

Sydney's Peace and Love

$$$$ | **CARIBBEAN** | At this open-air terrace eatery on the water's edge, you can find great local lobster and fish, as well as barbecue chicken and ribs with all the fixings, including peas and rice, corn, coleslaw, and potato salad. Call ahead to find out the dates of their weekly pig roast. **Known for:** local flair; fresh lobster; jukebox. $ *Average main: $35* ✉ *Little Harbour* 📞 *284/541–4464.*

Tipsy Shark

$$$$ | **CARIBBEAN** | You might find a friendly dog lounging under a table at this welcome addition to the Great Harbour restaurant scene, where the Guyanese-born owner Renee Singh does it all, from chatting up customers to cooking fresh-out-of-the-net seafood, rotis, and quesadillas. Fruity and boozy cocktails—like the signature Shark Bite, with Cruzan raspberry rum, Mount Gay, club soda, pineapple, and guavaberry juices—are also served. **Known for:** friendly bar scene; signature cocktails; breakfast. $ *Average main: $36* ✉ *Great Harbour* 📞 *284/343–6866* ⊕ *www.tipsysharkjvd.com.*

Hotels

Ali Baba's Heavenly Rooms

$ | **B&B/INN** | Owner Wayson "Baba" Hatchett offers seven simple but attractive rooms—three renovated after the 2017 hurricane, the other four brand-new—steps from the beach, each equipped with queen beds, air-conditioning, a private bath, and a porch with water views, for one of the lowest rates on the island. **Pros:** convenient location; inexpensive; private bath. **Cons:** noisy

Did You Know?

In addition to some stellar beaches, Jost Van Dyke has some of the best beach bars in the Virgin Islands, including the famed Soggy Dollar Bar, home to the Painkiller rum cocktail.

Camping on Jost Van Dyke

Ivan's White Bay Campground. This bar, restaurant, and campground—hosted by the same Ivan of Ivan's Stress Free Villas and Beach Bungalows—is a popular destination on Jost Van Dyke for those who don't mind roughing it. You can pitch your tent 6 feet from the sea or farther back under the sea grape trees where there's an electric hookup and lamp. Or opt for a primitive cabin, where you can find just a bed, fan, light, and bucket of water to wash the sand off your feet. There's an outhouse, a sun shower (basically a plastic sack hung from a tree branch), and a communal kitchen stocked with pots and pans. Expect to pay $20 for a bare site, $40 for an equipped site, or $65–$75 for a cabin. Camping reservations are essential. ☎ *284/547–3375.*

area of Great Harbour; small; basic décor. [$] *Rooms from: $180* ✉ *Great Harbour* ☎ *284/495–9280* 🌐 *www.alibabasrestaurantandbarbvi.com* 🛏 *7 rooms* 🍴 *No Meals.*

The Hideout

$$$ | **RESORT** | The stunning hardwood, thatched-roof units of The Hideout, an offshoot of Hendo's restaurant next door, are about as close to the beach as it's possible to get. This means you'll be part of the bustle of White Bay but still get a quiet respite from the chaos on the resort's peaceful, landscaped grounds. Built on stilts Bali-style, the seven one- and two-bedroom units are stunning inside and out, with a modern, harmonious, driftwood-hued interior complete with matching customized furnishings. Not all of the units have ocean views, but no matter what, you'll still get to cool off in your own private plunge pool. All feature air-conditioning and come equipped with TVs, streaming services, and Bluetooth technology. The larger units include extensive patio areas underneath, ideal for entertaining. The two-bedroom villas include a full kitchen and the one-bedroom villas have a kitchenette, or you can order up some of JVD's best cuisine from right next door. **Pros:** plunge pools in every unit; prime location amid the White Bay beach bar scene; gorgeous and modern custom design. **Cons:** bustle of White Bay can intrude; expensive; not all units have beach views. [$] *Rooms from: $460* ✉ *White Bay* ☎ *284/393–9200* 🌐 *www.thehideoutbvi.com* 🛏 *7 units* 🍴 *No Meals.*

Ivan's Stress Free Villas and Beach Bungalows

$ | **APARTMENT** | Ivan's will give you a quintessential Caribbean experience in a comfortable setting. **Pros:** steps away from the best beach on the island; you can meet new friends at Ivan's convivial bar; air-conditioning. **Cons:** basic furnishings; not within walking distance to other restaurants and nightlife (except Ivan's); no pool or other outdoor amenities. [$] *Rooms from: $160* ✉ *White Bay* ☎ *284/547–3375* 🌐 *www.ivanswhitebay.net* 🛏 *6 units* 🍴 *No Meals.*

Perfect Pineapple Guest Houses

$ | **B&B/INN** | One-bedroom suites, as well as one- and two-bedroom guesthouses, all come equipped with private bath, air-conditioning, stove, satellite TV, and refrigerator. **Pros:** steps from popular White Bay beach; friendly owners; owner's taxi service can get you around the island. **Cons:** basic furnishings; in need of updating; no restaurant. [$] *Rooms from: $180* ✉ *White Bay* ☎ *284/543–2815* 🌐 *www.perfectpineapple.com* 🛏 *6 rooms* 🍴 *No Meals.*

Sandcastle

$$ | **HOTEL** | Sleep steps from beautiful White Bay beach at this tiny beachfront hideaway, an island favorite for more than 40 years. **Pros:** beachfront rooms; near restaurants and bars; comfy hammocks. **Cons:** some rooms lack air-conditioning; beach sometimes clogged with day-trippers; no children allowed. [$] *Rooms from: $310* ✉ *White Bay* ☎ *284/495–9888* 🌐 *www.soggydollar.com* 🛏 *2 rooms, 4 1-bedroom cottages* 🍴 *Free Breakfast.*

Sandy Ground Estates

$$ | **HOUSE** | Each of these seven privately owned one- and two-bedroom villas is distinct in décor, with interiors ranging from spartan to stylish. **Pros:** a place to get away from it all; secluded feel; each villa is unique. **Cons:** only reachable by boat; not accessible for people with disabilities; few convenient dining or nightlife options. [$] *Rooms from: $278* ✉ *Sandy Ground* ☎ *284/494–3391* 🌐 *www.sandygroundbvi.com* 🛏 *7 houses* 🍴 *No Meals.*

Sea Crest Inn

$$ | **B&B/INN** | Sea Crest is located smack-dab in the hub of Great Harbour. **Pros:** hospitable host; affordable rates; walking distance to restaurants and ferry. **Cons:** noise from nearby bar; basic rooms; taxi required to reach the beach bars of White Bay. [$] *Rooms from: $300* ✉ *Great Harbour* ☎ *284/443–5300* 🛏 *6 studio units* 🍴 *No Meals.*

★ **White Bay Villas and Seaside Cottages**

$$$ | **APARTMENT** | **FAMILY** | Beautiful views and friendly staff keep guests coming back to these hilltop one- to three-bedroom villas and cottages, the nicest accommodations on the island. **Pros:** incredible views; full kitchens; friendly staff. **Cons:** 10- to 15-minute walk to White Bay and Great Harbour's restaurants and beaches; rental car recommended; steep access roads. [$] *Rooms from: $389* ✉ *White Bay* ☎ *340/201–4976, 284/541–1900* 🌐 *www.jostvandyke.com* 🛏 *19 units* 🍴 *No Meals.*

Nightlife

Jost Van Dyke is the most happening place to go barhopping in the BVI, so much so that it is an all-day enterprise for some. In fact, yachties will sail over just to have a few drinks. All the spots are easy to find, clustered in three general locations: Great Harbour, White Bay, and Little Harbour. On the Great Harbour side you can find Foxy's, Corsairs, and Ali Baba's. They tend to stay open later in season, with Foxy's hosting monthly pig roasts and Full Moon parties, often with live music and/or dancing. On the White Bay side are the One Love Bar and Grill and the Soggy Dollar Bar, where legend has it the famous Painkiller was first concocted. These bars tend to shut down after sunset, when the boats leave to moor in Great Harbour. In Little Harbour are Harris' Place, Sydney's Peace and Love, and Abe's By The Sea. Foxy's Taboo is on Diamond Cay on the east end of the island, looking across shallow Long Bay at Little Jost Van Dyke, home of the B-Line beach bar. If you can't make it to Jost Van Dyke, you can have a Painkiller at almost any bar in the BVI.

Shopping

The FoxHole Boutique

SOUVENIRS | Australian-born Tessa, who is married to Foxy Callwood, first arrived here back in the 1970s, and her shop offers a surprisingly large selection for such an out-of-the-way island. As a complement to Foxy's Tamarind Bar Restaurant, the boutique offers a wide selection of "Foxy's-specific" merchandise both in store and online. The large store also offers Cuban cigars, gift items, Foxy's own Firewater rum, and women's and men's clothing (including hats, board shorts, and sandals). Tessa has a unique style that's evident in the interesting handbags, accessories, and jewelry that she's found around the Caribbean and the world. ✉ *Great Harbour* ☎ *284/442–3074* ⊕ *www.shopfoxysbvi.com.*

Laid-Back Boutique

MIXED CLOTHING | JVD Scuba has expanded its boutique from dive and snorkel gear—which you can still buy—to a large shop offering T-shirts, beach accessories, sandals from Flojos, Costa sunglasses, Corksicle drinkware, and souvenirs of all kinds. ✉ *Great Harbour* ☎ *284/443–2222* ⊕ *www.jostvandykescuba.com.*

 ## Activities

JVD Scuba and BVI Eco-Tours

SCUBA DIVING | Check out the undersea world around the island with dive master Colin Aldridge. One of the most impressive dives in the area is off the north coast of Little Jost Van Dyke. Here you can find the Twin Towers: a pair of rock formations rising an impressive 90 feet. Colin and crew also offer trips to Sandy Cay and Sandy Spit, Norman Island, Virgin Gorda (The Baths), and other dive sites in the northwest British Virgin Islands. You can also rent snorkel equipment, dive gear, stand-up paddleboards, and kayaks here. ✉ *Great Harbour* ☎ *284/443–2222* ⊕ *jostvandykescuba.com* ☾ *Closed Sat.*

Ocean Spa

SPAS | When life gives you hurricanes, turn the debris into a spa. That's what Jost Van Dyke resident Dale Mapp did following 2017's Hurricane Irma, salvaging various pieces of flotsam and jetsam and turning them into a floating spa, now permanently anchored in Great Harbour. The spa has two treatment rooms with sections of see-through flooring and windows open to allow in cooling breezes. Services include the signature Ocean Bliss massage package, featuring a hot seawater foot soak with healing Caribbean flowers and herbs, a reggae soundtrack, and a rum cocktail. ✉ *White Bay* ☎ *284/340–0772* ⊕ *www. theoceanspabvi.com.*

Paradise Jeep Rentals

FOUR-WHEELING | This reliable company offers the ideal vehicles to tackle Jost Van Dyke's steep, winding roads. Even though Jost is a relatively small island, you really need to be in shape to walk from one bay to the next. This outfit rents two-door Suzuki Jimmys for $65 per day, four-door Grand Vitaras for $75, four-door Jeep Wranglers for $80, and eight-seat Kia Mojaves for $90. Discounts are available for rentals of six or more days. It's next to the fire station in Great Harbour. Reservations are a must. ✉ *Great Harbour* ☎ *284/547–1040* ⊕ *www.paradise-jeeprental.com.*

Anegada

Anegada lies low on the horizon about 14 miles (22½ km) north of Virgin Gorda. Unlike the hilly volcanic islands in the chain, this is a flat coral-and-limestone atoll. Nine miles (14 km) long and 2 miles (3 km) wide, the island rises no more than 28 feet above sea level. In fact, by the time you're able to see it, you may have run your boat onto a reef. (More than 300 captains unfamiliar with the waters have done so since exploration days; note that bareboat charters don't allow their vessels to head here without a trained skipper.) Although the reefs are a sailor's nightmare, they are a primary attraction for many visitors. Snorkeling, especially in the waters around Loblolly Bay on the north shore, is a transcendent experience. You can float in shallow, calm water just a few feet from shore and see one coral formation after another, each shimmering with a rainbow of colorful fish. Many local captains are happy to take visitors out bonefishing or sport-fishing. These experiences are complemented by ever-so-fine, ever-so-white sand (the northern and western shores have long stretches of beach) and the occasional beach bar (stop in for burgers, local lobster, or a frosty beer). Several

Anegada has miles of beautiful white-sand beaches.

years ago, flamingos were reintroduced to the island. Seeking out the large, bright-pink birds in Anegada's salt ponds has become a popular diversion from the island's beaches when touring by vehicle.

For three days in late November, the island hosts the Anegada Lobster Festival, in which restaurants compete to come up with the most original sampler dish featuring the Caribbean spiny lobster. Past dishes have ranged from lobster ice cream to lobster-on-a-stick. Hotels and moorings fill up well in advance, so be sure to book early.

The island's population of about 300 lives primarily in a small south-side village called The Settlement, which has a handful of grocery stores, a bakery, and a general store. Mosquitoes and sand flies can be murderous around dusk and dawn on Anegada; never come here without bug repellent and long-sleeved clothing.

◀ TIP→ Note that the island has no banks or ATMs.

GETTING HERE AND AROUND
You can get to Anegada from Tortola by ferry or private boat. The Road Town Fast Ferry does two round-trips per day on Monday, Wednesday, and Friday. Anegada Express sails from Trellis Bay to Anegada, with stops on Virgin Gorda on both legs of the trip, on Tuesday, Thursday, Saturday, and Sunday. There are morning and afternoon departures, making it possible to visit the island for the day. VI Airlink has scheduled flights to Anegada three times a week. It's also possible to fly on a charter from Beef Island or St. Thomas; the flight from Beef Island takes only 10 minutes, and can be reasonably priced per person if you are traveling with a small group.

 Sights

Conch Shell Mounds
BEACH | The vanished indigenous residents of Anegada left their mark on the low-lying island by creating piles of thousands of conch shells that remain visible today. More modern fishermen

have also created large piles of pink, sun-bleached conch shells in the shallow emerald waters off the island's southeast tip, creating an artificial island that can be visited (in combination with snorkeling) on a tour with Kelly's Land and Sea Tours (☎ 284/496–0961) or Sherwin's Sea Adventures (☎ 284/440–3243). ⊠ East End.

Faulkner House Museum

HISTORIC HOME | Theodolph Halburn Faulkner, a native of tiny Anegada, played an outsized role in winning freedom and democracy for the people of the British Virgin Islands, leading a 1949 march of more than 1,500 people to Road Town to demand a constitution and legislative representation. Faulkner's modest home in The Settlement—the first built of concrete on the island—is preserved as a museum detailing this history and offering a window into life on Anegada as it was in the middle of the previous century. ⊠ The Settlement ☎ 284/468–2151 ⊠ Free ⊗ Closed weekends.

Flamingo Pond Lookout

VIEWPOINT | This raised viewing platform overlooking the Anegada Salt Ponds— which take up a large portion of the island's midsection—is generally as close as most visitors will get to the island's resident flock of flamingos, with boat traffic now discouraged in the ponds so as not to scare them off. Luckily, it's easily accessible from Anegada's one main road, via your tour operator, taxi, or rental vehicle. The help of the free "monocular" is usually enough to get a good gander at the spindly pink birds, along with various other avifauna calling the island home. ⊠ Setting Point.

Beaches

Cow Wreck Beach

BEACH | Named for the cow bones that once washed ashore, this stretch of soft white sand on the island's northwest coast has a casual beach bar and restaurant. Small crowds congregate near the bar, but there's also plenty of room for those looking for solitude. Look for the palm-thatched benches that provide some shade on the beach. **Amenities:** food and drink; toilets. **Best for:** snorkeling; walking. ⊠ Cow Wreck Bay.

Loblolly Bay

BEACH | A curve of shore on Anegada's northern coast, this bay is home to the best snorkeling on the island. This is a place for solitude, but with a dash of convenience thrown in. Loblolly has a popular beachfront restaurant, Big Bamboo, showers, a gift shop, and snorkel rentals. The cottages at Big Bamboo are steps from the beach. Some palm-thatched shelters on the beach offer shade. **Amenities:** food and drink; showers; toilets; water sports. **Best for:** swimming; snorkeling; walking. ⊠ Loblolly Bay.

Pomato Point

BEACH | A powder white-sand beach on Anegada's western shore, Pomato Point has the best sunset views. There is no easily accessible reef, but the water is calm (making it a good choice for children) and the views of Tortola and Jost Van Dyke are beautiful. Sid's Pomato Point Restaurant is on the beach, and nearby Setting Point offers several other restaurant options, along with lodging. **Amenities:** food and drink. **Best for:** swimming; walking. ⊠ Setting Point.

🍴 Restaurants

There are between 6 and 10 restaurants open at any one time, depending on the season and on a whim. Check when you're on the island. Fresh conch, fish, and lobster are the specialties here. The going rate for a lobster dinner is $50, and it's almost always the most expensive thing on any restaurant menu. Reservations are essential for dinner at all restaurants. Call ahead in the morning to ensure a table that night.

★ Anegada Reef Hotel Restaurant
$$$$ | **SEAFOOD** | Seasoned yachties gather here nightly to share tales of the high seas; the open-air bar is the busiest on the island. Dinner is by candlelight under the stars and always includes famous Anegada lobster, steaks, and succulent baby back ribs—all prepared on a large grill by a little open-air bar. **Known for:** grilled lobster; fun atmosphere; open-air bar. [$] *Average main: $38* ✉ *Setting Point* ☎ *284/495–8002* 🌐 *www.anegadareef.com.*

Big Bamboo
$$$ | **CARIBBEAN** | **FAMILY** | This beachfront bar and restaurant tucked among sea grape trees at famous Loblolly Bay is the island's most popular destination for lunch. After you've polished off a plate of succulent Anegada lobster, barbecue chicken, or fresh fish, you can spend the afternoon on the beach, where the snorkeling is excellent and the view close to perfection, or browsing through the gift shop. **Known for:** spectacular beach; free shuttle from ferry for dinner; frozen drinks. [$] *Average main: $30* ✉ *Loblolly Bay* ☎ *284/499–1680, 284/346–5850* 🌐 *www.bigbambooanegada.com.*

Potter's by the Sea
$$$ | **SEAFOOD** | Friendly staff and a lively atmosphere just a few steps from the dock complement freshly grilled lobster and other seafood selections such as snapper and grouper. Potter's also offers a beach shuttle, free Wi-Fi, moorings and a dingy dock, and live music (ask about the schedule when you call ahead for dinner reservations). **Known for:** local vibe; waterfront dining; local seafood. [$] *Average main: $30* ✉ *Setting Point* ☎ *284/341–9769* 🌐 *pottersanegada.com.*

Sid's Pomato Point Restaurant
$$$ | **ECLECTIC** | This relaxed restaurant and bar sits on one of the best beaches on the island and enjoys Anegada's most dramatic sunset views. Entrées include tacos, ribs, steaks, and freshly caught seafood, including local lobster and conch. **Known for:** fish tacos; sunset views; beautiful beach location. [$] *Average main: $30* ✉ *Pomato Point* ☎ *284/441–5565.*

Tipsy Beach Bar
$$$$ | **ECLECTIC** | Anegada Ann, the owner of the bright and cheery Ann's Guest Houses, runs this bar on the beach named for the cow bones that once washed up on shore. This wiggle-your-toes-in-the-sand eatery on the northern shore is a fun place to watch the antics of surfers and kiteboarders skidding across the bay, while tucking into stewed conch, curried lobster, lobster dip, or quesadillas and tacos. **Known for:** snorkeling on-site; beach vibes; bright and friendly atmosphere. [$] *Average main: $36* ✉ *Cow Wreck Bay* ☎ *284/440–4149, 954/516–8957* 🌐 *www.cowwreckbeachbvi.com.*

★ The Wonky Dog
$$$$ | **SEAFOOD** | The laid-back, low-key vibe of this Setting Point bar and restaurant is infectious. Lobster served on a seaside rooftop pairs with craft cocktails, but the menu is surprisingly diverse, offering everything from braised lamb shanks to cauliflower steak. **Known for:** friendly atmosphere; live music; lobster. [$] *Average main: $50* ✉ *Setting Point* ☎ *284/547–0539, 284/443–0539* 🌐 *www.thewonkydog.com.*

Hotels

Anegada Beach Club
$ | **RESORT** | This is a laid-back beach club setting with well-equipped hotel rooms and luxury "palapa retreats" overlooking the dunes. **Pros:** option to adjoin king and junior suites is handy for families; bar and restaurant on-site; plenty of outdoor activities. **Cons:** remote location; pricey; small pool. [$] *Rooms from: $235* ✉ *Keel Point* ☎ *284/346–4005* 🌐 *www.anegadabeachclub.com* 🛏 *23 units* 🍴 *No Meals.*

Anegada Reef Hotel

$ | **HOTEL** | Head here if you want to bunk in comfortable lodging near Anegada's most popular anchorage; this venerable hotel, a destination for more than 40 years, still feels like the nerve center for the island. **Pros:** everything you need is nearby; nice sunsets; rents cars and arranges tours. **Cons:** simple rooms; no beach; often a party atmosphere at the bar. $ *Rooms from: $225* ✉ *Setting Point* ☎ *284/495–8002* ⊕ *www.anegadareef. com* ⤢ *20 rooms* ⦿ *No Meals.*

Ann's Guest Houses

$ | **B&B/INN** | Brightly painted, furnished one- or two-bedroom villas with cheerful, beachy décor and full kitchens are within steps of Cow Wreck Beach and the Tipsy beach bar and restaurant, which has equally vivid sun shelters and picnic tables. **Pros:** secluded location; great snorkeling; fun restaurant. **Cons:** no breakfast; location too remote for some; need a car to get around, but vehicle-rental service is available. $ *Rooms from: $200* ✉ *Cow Wreck Bay* ☎ *284/440–4149, 954/516–8957* ⊕ *www. cowwreckbeachbvi.com* ⤢ *7 units* ⦿ *No Meals.*

Big Bamboo

$ | **HOTEL** | Location is this property's finest attribute: the four circular villas are just steps from beautiful Loblolly Bay. Painted in the Big Bamboo's signature green and blue, these one- and two-bedroom units offer full kitchens, spacious bedrooms, and the opportunity to wake up to one of the prettiest views on the island. **Pros:** beachfront location; near restaurant and snorkeling; nice views from balconies. **Cons:** some may feel isolated; beach popular during the day; simple furnishings in rooms. $ *Rooms from: $200* ✉ *Loblolly Bay* ☎ *284/346–5850, 284/344–6251, 284/499–1680* ⊕ *www. bigbambooanegada.com* ⤢ *4 villas* ⦿ *No Meals.*

Activities

Anegada Fly Fishing Guide Service

FISHING | Kevin and Garfield Faulkner take visitors fly-fishing for bonefish, tarpon, and other game fish in Anegada's flats and reefs. Trips range from four to eight hours and start at $400 for up to two anglers. Rates are subject to change. ✉ *The Settlement* ☎ *284/540–5100, 284/340–5100* ⊕ *www.anegadafly-fishing.com.*

Danny's Bonefishing

FISHING | Danny Vanterpool offers half-, three-quarter-, and full-day bonefishing excursions around Anegada. The cost is $400 for a half day (four hours) and $600 for a three-quarter-day (six hour) fishing trip for up to two people. Meet the boat at Setting Point. ✉ *Setting Point* ☎ *284/441–6334, 284/344–1226* ⊕ *www. dannysbonefishing.com.*

L and H Rentals

FISHING | Anegada's calm weather, compact size, and gentle terrain make it perfect for exploring by open-topped vehicles. This company based at the Anegada Reef Hotel will rent you a brightly colored Jeep-like Mini Moke that you can motor around in for the day in search of hidden beaches and friendly bars. ✉ *Anegada Reef Hotel, Setting Point* ☎ *284/441–0799* ⊕ *www. anegadareef.com.*

Other British Virgin Islands

Of the 50-odd islands in the British Virgin Islands chain only a little over a dozen are inhabited, and several of those are privately owned, having been turned into private-island resorts. Some of these—most notably Necker Island, which is owned by Sir Richard Branson and often visited by celebrities, are well-known among the jet-set crowd; others are not as well-known but equally beautiful.

Off the Beaten Path

Two small British Virgin Islands, Marina Cay and Peter Island, are worth a day trip for charter boaters and yacht sailors exploring the region. Although the hotels on these islands were destroyed by Hurricane Irma in 2017 and a stay is not currently possible, their beaches are open and blissfully uncrowded.

Marina Cay
Beautiful little Marina Cay is in Trellis Bay, not far from Beef Island. Sometimes you can see it and its large J-shape coral reefs—a most dramatic sight—from the air soon after takeoff from the airport on Beef Island.

Covering 8 acres, this islet is considered small even by BVI standards. A restaurant, Pusser's Store, a six-unit hotel, and the famous red English phone booth at the end of the dock all fell victim to Hurricane Irma in 2017, but its beaches still beckon.

Peter Island
Although Peter Island is home to the (currently closed) resort of the same name, it's also a popular destination for charter boaters and Tortola vacationers. The island is lush, with forested hillsides and white, sandy beaches. There are no roads other than those at the resort.

Cooper Island

This small, hilly island on the south side of the Sir Francis Drake Channel, about 8 miles (13 km) from Road Town, Tortola, is popular with the charter-boat crowd. There are no paved roads (which doesn't really matter, as there aren't any cars), but you can find a beach restaurant, rum bar, brewery, coffee shop, a casual hotel, a few houses (some are available for rent), and great snorkeling at the south end of Manchioneel Bay.

GETTING HERE AND AROUND
Unless you have your own sailboat, the only way to reach Cooper Island is on a private ferry from Road Harbour Marina. The 35-minute ride is included in the cost of your vacation at Cooper Island Beach Club if your schedule meshes with the hotel's boat service.

Hotels

★ Cooper Island Beach Club
$$ | RESORT | Relaxation is the focus at this small resort, but folks who want to simply swim, snorkel, or chill on the beach can also feel right at home in eight comfortable rooms with attractive recycled furniture, tile floors, and lovely sea views. **Pros:** laid-back vibe; easy access to diving, snorkeling, and other water sports; excellent brewery and rum bar. **Cons:** rooms have no air-conditioning; island beyond the resort is not accessible; minimal nightlife. $ *Rooms from: $325* ✉ *Manchioneel Bay* ☎ *284/543–2266, 800/542–4624* ⊕ *www.cooperislandbeachclub.com* ➷ *8 rooms* ⦿ *Free Breakfast.*

Take the ferry from Tortola to reach lush Guana Island, designated a wildlife sanctuary.

Guana Island

Guana Island sits off Tortola's northeast coast. Sailors often drop anchor at one of the island's bays for a day of snorkeling and sunning. The island is a designated wildlife sanctuary, and scientists often come here to study its flora and fauna. It's home to a back-to-nature resort that offers few activities other than relaxation. Unless you're a hotel guest or a sailor, there's no easy way to get onto the island.

GETTING HERE AND AROUND

Unless you have your own sailboat, the best way to reach Guana Island is by the resort's private ferry, which will pick you up at Beef Island, Tortola, if you are a guest. You can also take a water taxi from St. Thomas.

Hotels

★ Guana Island Resort

$$$$ | RESORT | This charming resort is perfect for those wanting to hike, snorkel, swim, and relax at the beach in comfort. **Pros:** secluded feel; lovely grounds; good for nature lovers. **Cons:** very expensive; no TVs or radios in rooms; minimal nightlife. [$] *Rooms from: $995* 🕾 *800/544–8262* ⊕ *www.guana.com* 🛏 *18 rooms* ⦿⦿ *All-Inclusive.*

Scrub Island

The main resort is located at the marina, while a hilly road leads to the spa, villas, and several secluded beaches. A narrow strip of land connects Big Scrub Island, where the resort is, to the mostly undeveloped Little Scrub Island. The island is close enough to Tortola to spend a day

exploring but there are enough activities that you might not want to leave.

GETTING HERE AND AROUND

Scrub Island is easily reachable from Beef Island by the resort's private ferry. The dock is just minutes from the airport.

Hotels

★ Scrub Island Resort, Spa and Marina
$$$$ | **RESORT** | This swanky resort is on a 230-acre island just off the east end of Tortola and provides a posh getaway for relaxing around the pool or beach, enjoying a water-sports excursion or two, and being pampered in the plush spa. **Pros:** full-service marina; lots of activities; very good spa. **Cons:** only reachable by boat; only a few dining options; expensive. *$ Rooms from: $749 ☎ 877/890–7444, 284/394–3440 🌐 www.scrubisland.com 🛏 65 units 🍴 No Meals.*

Necker Island

Necker Island sits off Virgin Gorda's northeast coast, reachable only by private ferry or helicopter. A mere speck in the British Virgin Islands, it's home to Sir Richard Branson's private estate. When he's not in residence, you and your friends are welcome to enjoy its gorgeous beaches and myriad amenities—for a hefty price tag.

GETTING HERE AND AROUND

Guests (and only guests) of Necker Island will be whisked away from Beef Island or Virgin Gorda on a private boat or helicopter.

Hotels

Necker Island
$$$$ | **RESORT** | You probably won't run into British magnate Sir Richard Branson, but you can live in his luxurious style when you rent his estate on Necker Island. **Pros:** gorgeous rooms; an island for you and a few dozen friends; spectacular views. **Cons:** very expensive; need boat to get here; limited availability for non-group stays. *$ Rooms from: $102,500 ☎ 877/577–8777 🌐 www.virginlimitededition.com/en/necker-island 🛏 24 rooms total: 11 in Great House, plus 13 in cottages and the Temple House 🍴 All-Inclusive ☞ Rate is per night for up to 48 people; individual rooms start at $5,400 nightly*

Norman Island

This uninhabited island is the supposed setting for Robert Louis Stevenson's *Treasure Island.* The famed caves at Treasure Point are popular with day sailors and powerboaters. There are nearly 12 miles (20 km) of hiking trails on the island. If you land ashore at the island's main anchorage in the Bight, you'll find a restaurant and behind it a trail that winds up the hillside and reaches a peak with a fantastic view of the Sir Francis Drake Channel to the north. Another trail (a dirt road, actually) leads to Turtle Cove. Call Pirate's Bight for information on ferry service to accommodate day-trippers.

GETTING HERE AND AROUND

The only way to reach this island is by private boat or on a charter boat that puts you aboard the *Willy T* for a meal and drinks. The Norman Island Ferry leaves from Hannah Bay, Tortola, and arrives at Pirates Bight.

Sights

★ Norman Island Caves

CAVE | A popular day trip for sailors, the caves at Treasure Point are a good place for snorkeling among tropical fish and coral formations. Although the caves inspired Robert Louis Stevenson's *Treasure Island*, you probably won't find any gold doubloons hidden inside. The only way to arrive is by boat; inquire about excursions at Pirate's Bight. ✉ *Treasure Point.*

Restaurants

Pirate's Bight

$$$$ | **SEAFOOD** | This breezy, open-air dining establishment boasts quirky beach-bar eccentricities (a cannon is fired at sunset and bar partrons play games like "giant" Jenga), all while maintaining a slightly refined feeling. The owners offer ferry service from Hannah Bay on Tortola, giving the restaurant the feel of a casual day resort, with resort prices for the food to match. **Known for:** beach club setting; fun atmosphere; live entertainment. [$] *Average main: $39* ✉ *The Bight* ☎ *284/443–1305* 🌐 *www.piratesbight.com.*

Willy T

$$ | **ECLECTIC** | *Willy T* is a floating bar and restaurant that's anchored in Pirate's Bight. The current boat is new; its predecessor, sunk in 2017's Hurricane Irma, lies nearby at the bottom of the Bight and is now a dive site, complete with skeleton crew. **Known for:** conch fritters; West Indian roti; party atmosphere. [$] *Average main: $18* ☎ *284/340-8603 for boaters, use VHF Channels 16/74* 🌐 *willy-t.com.*

Index

Photo Credits

Front cover: Danita Delimont/Alamy Stock Photo [**Description:** British Virgin Islands, Jost Van Dyke, White Bay]. Back cover, from left to right: Blue Orange Studio/Shutterstock. Napa74/iStockphoto. SeanPavonePhoto. **Spine:** Sasha Buzko/Shutterstock. **Interior, from left to right:** Eric Rubens/Shutterstock (1). Eric Rubens/Shutterstock (2-3). ESB Professional/Shutterstock (5). **Chapter 1: Experience the U.S. and British Virgin Islands:** BlueOrange Studio/Shutterstock (6-7). Jon Arnold Images Ltd/Alamy (8-9). Gary Felton (9). Gary Felton (9). TalbotImages/iStockphoto (10). Low Flite/iStockphoto (10). Emperorcosar/Shutterstock (10). Michael BVI/Shutterstock (11). USVI DoT (12). Michael Cisneros/Flickr (12). Emperorcosar/ Shutterstock (12). Ken Hayden Photography (13). C. Kurt Holter/Shutterstock (13). Carlos Villoch-MagicSea.com/Alamy (14). Vlad Ispas/Dreamstime (14). Shutterdo/Dreamstime (15). BlueOrange Studio/Shutterstock (18). Emperorcosar/Shutterstock (18). Malachi Jacobs/Shuttersotck (18). Luebeck.er/Shutterstock (18). Irishka777/Dreamstime (19). ESB Professional/Shutterstock (20). Bcampbell65/Shutterstock (20). Nicole R Young/Shutterstock (20). Emperorcosar/Shutterstock (21). Low Flite/iStockphoto (21). **Chapter 3: St. Thomas:** Vale_T/iStockphoto (47). MevZup/Shutterstock (50). Olga Lyubkina/Shutterstock (51). Melnikov Dmitriy/Shutterstock (51). Thomas USVI/Shutterstock (59). Gang Liu/Shutterstock (62-63). Eskystudio/Shutterstock (69). Jacob Boomsma/Shutterstock (71). World Pictures/Alamy (80). ShutterPrice/Shutterstock (83). Andrei Medvedev/Shutterstock (85). Solarisys/Shutterstock (87). Vlad Ispas/Shutterstock (88). **Chapter 4: St. John:** Terri Butler Photography/Shutterstock (91). Sherry Conklin/Shutterstock (96). Douglas Rissing/iStockphoto (99). LauraGilmore/Flickr (102). George Burba/Shutterstock (107). Ken Brown/iStockphoto (112-113). Nik Wheeler/Alamy (115). Ciaoarturo/Dreamstime (116). Carlos Villoch - MagicSea.com / Alamy (119). Kendra Nielsam/Shutterstock (121). Divemastorking2000/Flickr (123). Daniel Wilhelm Nilsson/Shutterstock (124). Julie de Leseleuc/iStockphoto (124). Marjorie McBride / Alamy (124). Brent Barnes/Shutterstock (125). David Coleman/iStockphoto (126). Steve Simonsen (126). **Chapter 5: St. Croix:** NAPA/Shutterstock (131). Brian Tanner/Shutterstock (139). Danita Delimont/Alamy (153). The Buccaneer (155). Napa735/Dreamstime (160). Marc Muench/Alamy (162). Ben Velazquez (166). EA Given/Shutterstock (170-171). KC Journeys/Shutterstock (173). **Chapter 6: Tortola:** Nicole R Young/Shutterstock (175). Gemma Fletcher/Shutterstock (183). Solarisys/Shutterstock (189). Irishka777/Dreamstime (194). Jason P Ross/Dreamstime (197). Jason Patrick Ross/Shutterstock (199). Leonard Zhukovsky/Shutterstock (201). Randy Lincks/Alamy (202). Steve Dangers/iStockphoto (202). Perris Tumbao/Shutterstock (203). Slavoljub Pantelic/iStockphoto (203). Kyle J Little/Shutterstock (204). Giovanni Rinaldi/iStockphoto (206). ESB Professional/Shutterstock (207). Fotograferen.net/Alamy (209). **Chapter 7: Virgin Gorda:** BlueOrange Studio/Shutterstock (213). Carlos Villoch-MagicSea.com/Alamy (219). BVI Tourist Board (221). idreamphoto/Shutterstock (224-225). Ken Hayden Photography (226). Ken Hayden Photography (228). Larwin/Shutterstock (234). **Chapter 8: Other British Virgin Islands:** Napa735/Dreamstime (237). Andre Jenny/Alamy (242). Napa/Shutterstock (248-249). Shalamov/iStockphoto (253). Mary Baratto/iStockphoto (255). Andrea Haase/Dreamstime (259). Anegada/iStockphoto (260). **About Our Writers:** All photos are courtesy of the writers except for the following. Carol Bareuther, courtesy of Dean Barnes; Anquanette Gaspard, courtesy of Nicole Canegata.

*Every effort has been made to trace the copyright holders, and we apologize in advance for any accidental errors. We would be happy to apply the corrections in the following edition of this publication.

Notes

Fodor's U.S. & BRITISH VIRGIN ISLANDS

Publisher: Stephen Horowitz, *General Manager*

Editorial: Douglas Stallings, *Editorial Director;* Jill Fergus, Amanda Sadlowski, *Senior Editors;* Brian Eschrich, Alexis Kelly, *Editors;* Angelique Kennedy-Chavannes, *Assistant Editor;* Yoojin Shin, *Associate Editor*

Design: Tina Malaney, *Director of Design and Production;* Jessica Gonzalez, *Senior Designer;* Jaimee Shaye, *Graphic Design Associate*

Production: Jennifer DePrima, *Editorial Production Manager;* Elyse Rozelle, *Senior Production Editor;* Monica White, *Production Editor*

Maps: Rebecca Baer, *Senior Map Editor;* David Lindroth, Mark Stroud (Moon Street Cartography), *Cartographers*

Photography: Viviane Teles, *Senior Photo Editor;* Namrata Aggarwal, Neha Gupta, Payal Gupta, Ashok Kumar, *Photo Editors;* Jade Rodgers, *Photo Production Intern*

Business and Operations: Chuck Hoover, *Chief Marketing Officer;* Robert Ames, *Group General Manager*

Public Relations and Marketing: Joe Ewaskiw, *Senior Director of Communications and Public Relations*

Fodors.com: Jeremy Tarr, *Editorial Director;* Rachael Levitt, *Managing Editor*

Technology: Jon Atkinson, *Director of Technology;* Rudresh Teotia, *Associate Director of Technology;* Alison Lieu, *Project Manager*

Writers: Carol Bareuther, Anquanette Gaspard, Claire Shefchik

Editor: Yoojin Shin

Production Editor: Monica White

28th Edition

ISBN 978-1-64097-645-0

ISSN 1070-6380

SPECIAL SALES

This book is available at special discounts for bulk purchases for sales promotions or premiums. For more information, e-mail SpecialMarkets@fodors.com.

PRINTED IN CANADA

0 9 8 7 6 5 4 3 2 1

About Our Writers

 Carol Bareuther, who lives in St. Thomas, works part-time for the government of the U.S. Virgin Islands. In her other life as a writer, she contributes to local, regional, and international publications on the topics of food, travel, and water sports. She's the author of two books, *Sports Fishing in the Virgin Islands* and *Virgin Islands Cooking*. She is the mother of Nikki and Rian, as well as the longtime partner of photographer Dean Barnes. She updated the Experience, Travel Smart, St. Thomas, and St. John chapters for this edition.

 Anquanette Gaspard, who was born and raised in St. Croix, is a food and travel entrepreneur, freelance writer, and social media influencer who shares the beauty of Caribbean food and culture in a way that is authentically Caribbean. Her blog, CruzanFoodie.com highlights the food, history, and culture in the USVI, Caribbean, and beyond. Her work has been featured in *Travel + Leisure, Discover USVI, Experience BVI, EBONY* Magazine, *Essence* Magazine, and *Marriott Destinations*. She updated the St. Croix chapter for this edition.

 Claire Shefchik is a writer and journalist based in Tortola, British Virgin Islands, her favorite place in the world. Her travel and lifestyle writing has also appeared in the *Washington Post, Travel & Leisure, Atlas Obscura, Business Insider, Cosmopolitan*, and more, and she is a member of the North American Travel Journalists Association. She has also published several novels under pseudonyms and is working on another. She updated the Tortola, Virgin Gorda, and Other British Virgin Islands chapters for this edition.